McCaulay's CFA Level I Practice Exams

Volume I of V

Philip Martin McCaulay

McCaulay's CFA Level I Practice Exams Volume I of V

McCaulay's CFA Level I Practice Exams
Volume I of V
Table of Contents

About the Book

McCaulay's CFA Level I Practice Exams are published in a five volume set, with each volume containing eight 120-question exams, for a total of 960 questions. The entire five volume set has forty exams and a total of 4,800 questions. Each exam has an answer key followed by the exam with the answers shown, including the formulas used to derive the numeric answers. The question formats and topic weights are similar to the actual CFA Level I exam. The questions were transformed from the study material in the CFA Institute Program Curriculum available from the CFA Institute. The practice exams are designed to complement the CFA Program curriculum and to facilitate the learning process, not to be used as a substitute for study of the prescribed curriculum.

About the Author

Philip Martin McCaulay has sold thousands of practice exam books and study guides for licensing and credentialing examinations in the fields of pensions, investments, finance, real estate, and massage therapy. He is an actuary with experience on the Society of Actuaries' Education & Examination Committee.

McCaulay's CFA Level I Practice Exams Topic Weights

CFA Level I Topic Area	Percent	Number of Questions	Question Numbers
Ethical and Professional Standards	**15%**	**18**	**1-18**
Quantitative Methods	12%	14	19-32
Economics	10%	12	33-44
Financial Reporting and Analysis	20%	24	45-68
Corporate Finance	8%	10	69-78
Investment Tools (total)	**50%**	**60**	**19-78**
Equity Investments	10%	12	79-90
Derivatives	5%	6	91-96
Fixed Income	12%	14	97-110
Alternative Investments	3%	4	111-114
Asset Classes (total)	**30%**	**36**	**79-114**
Portfolio Management and Wealth Planning	**5%**	**60**	**115-120**
Total	100%	120	1-120

1. CFA charterholder Shahperi's employer, an investment-banking firm, is the principal underwriter for an issue of convertible debentures by the Agusti Company. Shahperi discovers that Agusti Company has concealed severe third-quarter losses in its foreign operations. The preliminary prospectus has already been distributed. What is the most appropriate first step for Shahperi?

   A. Seek an independent legal opinion
   B. Report the situation to the appropriate supervisors
   C. Sever all connections with the underwriting

2. CFA charterholder Beltis, a mining analyst with Whitehurst Brothers, is invited by Optimus Mining to join a group of analysts at the Super Bowl. Optimus Mining pays for the airfare, hotel expenses, and tickets for the group, except CFA charterholder Zhang, who works for a large trust company and insists on following his company's policy and paying for one of the nights at the hotel himself. Were any Standards of Professional Conduct violated?

   A. No, the trip was strictly for business
   B. Yes, Beltis violated the standard on independence and objectivity
   C. Yes, Beltis and Zhang violated the standard on independence and objectivity

3. CFA charterholder Alami attends a seminar and hears a presentation by a quantitative analyst who discusses a new model in great detail. Alami returns to the office, tests the model, and is satisfied with the results. Alami makes slight modifications to the model. Alami tells his supervisor he discovered a new model. Did Alami violate any Standards of Professional Conduct?

   A. No
   B. Yes, relating to misrepresentation
   C. Yes, relating to duties to employers

4. CFA charterholder Koyama turns in false insurance claims to his employer's health plan administrator. Did Koyama violate any Standards of Professional Conduct?

   A. No
   B. Yes, relating to misconduct
   C. Yes, relating to misrepresentation

5. Executives at NBI serve as investment managers for pension funds. The executives use a broker with close ties to NBI to handle the trades, at a higher cost to the clients than other brokerage companies. Did the NBI executives violate any Standards of Professional Conduct?

    A. No
    B. Yes, relating to fair dealing
    C. Yes, relating to loyalty, prudence, and care

6. CFA charterholder Patel puts an earnings estimate in a research report and tells his larger clients that he expects the earnings to be higher than in the report. Which Standard of Professional Conduct did Patel most likely violate?

    A. Fair dealing
    B. Market manipulation
    C. Disclosure of conflicts

7. To meet the obligations under the Standard of Professional Conduct on performance presentation, the use of simulated results should

    A. Never be used
    B. Be accompanied by full disclosure of the source of the data
    C. Comply with the Global Investment Performance Standards (GIPS)

8. CFA charterholder McWillie is planning to leave his employer to join a competitor. He asks big accounts to leave his current employer and open accounts with his new employer. Did McWillie violate any Standards of Professional Conduct?

    A. No
    B. Yes, relating to loyalty
    C. Yes, relating to preservation of confidentiality

9. CFA charterholder Choi develops a stock selection model on his own before being employed by a firm, uses the model at the firm, then leaves the firm to work for a bank, and uses the same model at the bank. Did Choi violate any Standards of Professional Conduct?

    A. No
    B. Yes, relating to loyalty
    C. Yes, relating to disclosure of conflicts

10. CFA charterholder Heitman is given the responsibility to estimate IPO prices and due to time constraints and limited resources makes estimates after only categorizing the issues by size. Did Heitman violate any Standards of Professional Conduct?

    A. No
    B. Yes, relating to duties to employers
    C. Yes, relating to diligence and reasonable basis

11. Which is least likely to pose a conflict of interest for service as a director?

    A. Opportunity to act quickly on public information
    B. Conflict between duties to shareholders and duties to clients
    C. Trading actions that could increase the value of any securities or options received as compensation

12. CFA charterholder Morrison issued an RFP for an equity manager. CFA charterholder Madura is on Morrison's staff, and was one of several staff members who recommended Copeland Partners based on a review of all the firms' qualifications, suitability, and performance records. Morrison reviewed the recommendation and instead hired Tuttle Management. Two days later, Morrison went to work for Tuttle Management. Did Morrison violate any Standards of Professional Conduct?

    A. No
    B. Yes, related to conflicts of interest
    C. Yes, related to market manipulation

13. CFA charterholder Lambert concludes that a company's stock price will rise. Before revising his recommendation from hold to buy, Lambert tells his brother so that his brother can buy shares at the lower price. Did Lambert violate any Standards of Professional Conduct?

    A. No
    B. Yes, related to duty to clients, duty to employer, and priority of transactions
    C. Yes, related to duty to clients, duty to employer, priority of transactions, and diligence and reasonable basis

14. Which is an improper reference to the CFA Institute, the CFA designation, or the CFA program?

    A. John, a CFA-type portfolio manager
    B. Level I candidate in the CFA program
    C. John Ganesh, Chartered Financial Analyst

15. CFA charterholder Kolli is a research analyst for Company X. His research suggests the outlook is weak. However, at lunch he overhears an analyst from another firm offer different opinions. Upon returning to the office, Kolli issues a strong buy recommendation. Did Kolli violate any Standards of Professional Conduct?

    A. No
    B. Yes, he did not have a reasonable and adequate basis
    C. Yes, he did failed to distinguish between facts and opinions

16. CFA charterholder Chauhan is a portfolio manager. Chauhan uses the same broker exclusively for all portfolio transactions because the broker gives Chauhan lower prices for personal sales than to Chauhan's portfolio accounts and other investors. Did Chauhan violate any Standards of Professional Conduct?

    A. No
    B. Yes, related to misrepresentation
    C. Yes, related to loyalty, prudence, and care

17. Which is least likely to be required for firms claiming compliance with the GIPS?

    A. Undertake a verification process
    B. Make a composite list and description to any prospective client on request
    C. Document their policies and procedures used in establishing and maintaining compliance

18. The eight major sections of the GIPS include all of the following but

    A. Input data, disclosures, and venture capital
    B. Presentation and reporting, calculation methodology, and real estate
    C. Fundamentals of compliance, composite construction, and disclosures

19. Which is closest to the annual end-of-year retirement fund contribution for 40 years that will provide a 30-year annuity of $10,000 per year at retirement, if the fund earns 8% per year?

    A. $435
    B. $937
    C. $992

20. What is the net present value and internal rate of return for an investment costing $3.43 million that is expected to increase annual cash flows by $1 million for each of the next five years, using a cost of capital of 15%?

    A. NPV = -$0.08 million and IRR = 14%
    B. NPV = $0.00 million and IRR = 15%
    C. NPV = $0.08 million and IRR = 16%

21. What categorizes data but does not rank the data?

    A. Nominal scale
    B. Ordinal scale
    C. Ratio scale

22. What is the geometric mean return for a fund with ten years of annual returns of 2%, 6%, 9%, 9%, 10%, 11%, 16%, 14%, 5%, and 8%?

    A. 8.8%
    B. 8.9%
    C. 9.0%

23. Using Chebyshev's inequality, at least what proportion of observations must lie within 2 standard deviations of the mean?

    A. 36%
    B. 75%
    C. 89%

24. What is most likely the standard deviation of sales if 68.3% of the observations of sales are between 200,000 and 500,000?

    A. 50,000
    B. 75,000
    C. 150,000

25. If three independent screens are applied to 100 companies, 30 pass the first screen, 10 pass the second screen, and 40 pass the third screen, the probability of passing all three screens is closest to which percent?

    A. 1%
    B. 8%
    C. 10%

26. If there is a 25% probability of declining interest rates, a 60% probability of EPS of $10 and a 40% chance of an EPS of $8 if rates decline, and a 70% probability of an EPS of $6 and a 30% chance of an EPS of $4 if rates do not decline, what is the expected EPS?

    A. $6.35
    B. $7.30
    C. $10.95

27. If the prior probabilities are 1/3 that EPS exceeded expectations, 1/3 that EPS met expectations, and 1/3 that EPS fell short of expectations; the new probabilities of an expansion are 70% given that EPS exceeded expectations, 20% given that EPS met expectations, and 10% given that EPS fell short of expectations, what is the unconditional probability of an expansion?

    A. 33%
    B. 43%
    C. 81%

28. If a stock is selling for $50 and each year there is a 60% probability of an uptick in price of $1 and a 40% probability the price moves down $1, what is the probability that the price is $53 after 3 years?

    A. 0.216
    B. 0.288
    C. 0.432

29. Approximately what percent of normally distributed stock returns with a mean return of 10% and a standard deviation of 15% fall in the interval 0% to 20% return?

    A. 50%
    B. 68%
    C. 95%

30. Which is closest to the annualized volatility for a stock that closes for five consecutive days at $1.01, $0.98, $1.00, $1.02, and $1.03, based on 250 days in a year?

    A. 2%
    B. 15%
    C. 38%

31. If the mean income of companies on a stock index is $2 million with a standard deviation of $3 million, which is closest to the standard error of the sample mean for a sample size of 25?

    A. $0.4 million
    B. $0.5 million
    C. $0.6 million

32. What is the test statistic for 1: the variance of a single, normally distributed population and 2: the differences between variances of two normally distributed populations based on two random, independent samples?

    A. 1: t-test; 2: chi-square test
    B. 1: chi-square test; 2: F-test
    C. 1: F-test; 2: chi-square test

33. What is the demand elasticity when the percentage increase in quantity demanded is 5% when prices are reduced 10%?

    A. Unit elastic demand
    B. Inelastic demand
    C. Elastic demand

34. What is a consumer surplus?

    A. The price minus marginal cost, summed over the quantity sold
    B. The marginal benefit minus price, summed over the quantity bought
    C. The marginal cost minus price, summed over the quantity bought

35. Which method is technological efficient if method 1 uses 10 units of labor and 100 units of capital, method 2 uses 10 units of labor and 10 units of capital, and method 3 uses 50 units of labor and 10 units of capital to produce the same output?

    A. 1
    B. 2
    C. 3

36. What is closest to the Herfindahl-Hirschman Index (HHI) if the sales of the six firms in the industry are, in millions, $40, $20, $10, $10, $10, and $10?

    A. 2400
    B. 7000
    C. 8000

37. What is least likely to happen with a technological change that increases productivity?

    A. Shifts the total product curve upward
    B. Shifts marginal product curve and average product curve upward
    C. Shifts fixed cost curves downward

38. Which market structure is associated with the lowest possible average cost?

    A. Perfect competition
    B. Monopolistic competition
    C. Monopoly

39. What determines the demand for labor, and diminishes as the quantity of labor increases?

    A. Marginal revenue
    B. Marginal revenue product
    C. Derived demand

40. Who bears the burden of a tax if supply is perfectly elastic?

    A. The supplier bears the entire tax
    B. The buyer bears the entire tax
    C. It is shared by the buyer and supplier

41. What occurs when real GDP is less than potential GDP?

    A. Recessionary gap
    B. Inflationary gap
    C. Full employment

42. Which is closest to the money created from an initial increase in reserves of $100,000 if the desired currency holding is 20% of deposits and the desired reserves are 4% of deposits?

    A. $250,000
    B. $333,333
    C. $500,000

43. Which shows that relationship between inflation and unemployment?

    A. Ricardo-Barro equivalence
    B. Phillips curve
    C. Laffer curve

44. Which is least likely to be considered the Federal Reserve System's choice of monetary policy instrument?

    A. The required reserve ratio
    B. The federal funds rate
    C. A short term interest rate

45. Which step in analyzing financial statements uses communication with the client and supervisor, institutional guidelines, and sets timetables and budgets?

    A. Process data
    B. Collect input data
    C. Articulate the purpose and context of the analysis

46. Which is a residual claim?

    A. Asset
    B. Liability
    C. Owner's equity

47. Which is the most likely initial result receiving a $10,000 loan from a bank?

    A. There is no change in assets or liabilities
    B. Assets and liabilities increase by $10,000
    C. Liabilities increase by $10,000 and there is no change in assets

48. What are the qualitative characteristics of useful information under the IFRS framework?

    A. Understandability, relevance, reliability, and comparability
    B. Understandability, timeliness, reliability, and neutrality
    C. Accuracy, timeliness, relevance, and comparability

49. Which is least likely a conflicting approach under different financial reporting frameworks?

    A. Valuation
    B. Consistency
    C. Measurement

50. Which is closest to the revenue that will be reported in the first year under the completed contract method if the total revenue over four years is $4 million, the total costs over four years are $3 million, and the costs incurred in the first year are $0.3 million?

    A. $0.0 million
    B. $0.4 million
    C. $1.0 million

51. If a company sells $4,000 worth of products on consignment for a commission of $1,000, how much revenue should the company report?

    A. $1,000
    B. $3,000
    C. $4,000

52. What is closest to the cost of goods sold using the LIFO method if 2,000 units were purchased the prior year for $50 each; 3,000 units were purchased in the current year for $60 each; 4,000 units are sold in the current year for $70 each; and ending inventory was 1,000 units?

    A. $220,000
    B. $224,000
    C. $230,000

53. Which is closest to the weighted average number of shares outstanding for calculating EPS for a calendar year if a company had 360,000 shares outstanding on January 1st; issued 120,000 shares on February 1st; had a 2 for 1 stock split on December 1st; and had 960,000 shares outstanding on December 31st?

    A. 520,000
    B. 940,000
    C. 960,000

54. How are bonds issued two years ago for maturity in eight years measured on the balance sheet?

    A. Fair value
    B. Historical cost
    C. Amortized cost

55. Which is least likely to be included in the owners' equity section of the balance sheet?

    A. Minority interest
    B. Financial instruments
    C. Contributed capital

56. How much cash did a company receive from customers if the revenues were $90,000; beginning of year receivables were $10,000; and end of year receivables were $12,000?

    A. $78,000
    B. $88,000
    C. $92,000

57. How much cash did a company pay for interest and taxes if interest expense was $20 million; taxes were $8 million; interest payable decreased by $5 million; and taxes payable increased by $2 million?

    A. $15 million for interest and $6 million for taxes
    B. $25 million for interest and $6 million for taxes
    C. $25 million for interest and $10 million for taxes

58. If a company started in 2008; and in 2008 purchased 10,000 units of inventory at $12 each; and sold 5,000 units at $15 each; then in 2009 purchased 20,000 units of inventory at $18 each; and sold 22,000 units at $20 each; which is closest to the cost of goods sold for 2009 under the weighted average cost inventory method?

    A. $330,000
    B. $336,400
    C. $369,600

59. In a period of rising prices, how do profits for a company using LIFO most likely compare to FIFO if the company purchases more inventory then it sells?

    A. Greater under LIFO
    B. Lower under LIFO
    C. About the same under LIFO or FIFO

60. If a company reporting under U.S. GAAP purchased equipment for $100,000 with a five-year life and a salvage value of $10,000, which would make net income more volatile?

    A. Expensing the entire cost
    B. Capitalizing the entire cost
    C. Capitalizing and expensing result in the same volatility

61. What is least likely to increase as the retirement date of an asset retirement obligation approaches?

    A. Equity
    B. Liabilities
    C. Debt to equity ratio

62. Which are least likely to be based on the applicable tax rates on the balance sheet of an entity?

    A. Deferred taxes
    B. Current taxes payable
    C. Current taxes recoverable

63. If on January 1, 2009, a company issues $1 million worth of four-year bonds with interest payments of $50,000 at the end of each of the four years and the market rate is 6%, what will the company most likely record at the time of issue?

    A. $965,349 as a liability and a cash inflow from investing activities
    B. $965,349 as a liability and a cash inflow from financing activities
    C. $973,270 as a liability and a cash inflow from investing activities

64. After adjusting reported financials for a company that is a lessee with a large number of operating leases, which would most likely be higher?

    A. Debt-to-equity ratio but not interest coverage ratio
    B. Interest coverage ratio but not debt-to-equity ratio
    C. Both debt-to-equity ratio and interest coverage ratio

65. Which is the most appropriate conclusion if ROE increased, return on total assets decreased, and total asset turnover increased?

    A. Net profit margin and financial leverage decreased
    B. Net profit margin and financial leverage increased
    C. Net profit margin decreased but financial leverage increased

66. If ROE is 15%, what is true about company A compared to company B if company A has sales of $120 million, assets of $70 million, and liabilities of $25 million; and company B has sales of $300 million, assets of $140 million, and liabilities of $40 million?

    A. Greater profit margin
    B. Higher total assets turnover
    C. Lower financial leverage

67. Which is least likely a qualitative characteristic of financial statements to achieve the purpose of providing useful information?

    A. Relevance
    B. Predictive value
    C. Convergence

68. How are cash inflows for the receipt of interest treated under IASB standards?

    A. Operating cash flows
    B. Operating or investing cash flows
    C. Financing or investing cash flows

69. Which category of projects susceptible to the capital budgeting process is most likely to possibly not require careful analysis?

    A. Expansion
    B. Replacement
    C. New products and services

70. If a company has 50% long term debt with a marginal after-tax cost of 8%; 10% preferred stock with a marginal after-tax cost of 10%; and 40% long term debt with a marginal after-tax cost of 12.5%; which has an IRR greater than 10% if the warehouse project has an NPV of $100 million, the safety project has an NPV of $0, and the new product project has an NPV of negative $50 million?

    A. The warehouse project only
    B. The warehouse project and the safety project
    C. All three

71. Which is least likely to characterize a typical NPV profile for capital budgeting for a conventional project?

    A. The profile is convex from the origin
    B. The NPV declines at an increasing rate as the discount rate increases
    C. The profile goes through the vertical axis at the sum of the future cash flows where the discount rate is zero and through the horizontal axis where the discount rate is the IRR

72. Which is closest to the expected share price after new information about an investment with an NPV of $400 million if the share price before the new information was $10 and there are 200 million shares outstanding?

   A. $10
   B. $12
   C. $14

73. What is an estimate of the equity risk premium if the dividend yield is 5%, the dividend growth rate is 2%, and the risk-free rate is 4%?

   A. 3%
   B. 5%
   C. 7%

74. Which is closest to the beta of an asset using the pure-play method if the beta of equity is 1.5, equity is $10 million, debt is $4 million, and the marginal tax rate is 30%?

   A. 1.07
   B. 1.17
   C. 1.20

75. What is an estimate of the cost of equity adjusted for flotation costs if the current dividends are $5, the market price is $100, the dividend growth rate is 4%, flotation costs are $10, and the risk-free rate is 3%?

   A. 9.6%
   B. 9.8%
   C. 10.0%

76. What is the operating cycle if annual credit sales are $10 million, accounts receivable are $4 million, annual cost of goods sold is $12 million, inventory is $4 million, annual purchases are $10 million, and accounts payable are $2 million?

   A. 73.0
   B. 194.67
   C. 267.67

77. Which has the lowest effective cost of borrowing $1 million for one month: a line of credit at 6.5% with a 1/2 percent commitment fee; a banker's acceptance (BA) at 6.75%; or commercial paper (CP) at 6.15% with a commission of 1/8 percent and a backup line cost of 1/4 percent?

    A. BA
    B. CP
    C. Line of credit

78. If for 2008, in millions, sales were $9, cost of goods sold were $3, total assets were $4.5, current assets were $1.8, and current liabilities were $1.2; what is the estimate of the 2009 projected current assets if for 2009, the projected sales are $9.9, cost of goods sold are $3.45, and total assets are $4.45?

    A. $1.89
    B. $1.98
    C. $2.07

79. Which is most likely associated with primary capital markets?

    A. AMEX
    B. Nasdaq
    C. Shelf registration

80. Which is a market where security trades are executed at specific times at a single price after buy and sell orders have accumulated?

    A. Call market
    B. Stock exchange
    C. Continuous market

81. For a margin account with an initial deposit of $5,000 used to purchase 200 shares of stock at $50, what is the equity if the stock increases by 20%?

    A. $7,000
    B. $10,000
    C. $12,000

82. What type of security market index takes the average of the stock prices?

    A. Unweighted
    B. Price-weighted
    C. Value-weighted

83. What type of mean is used for an unweighted security market index?

   A. Geometric or harmonic
   B. Geometric or arithmetic
   C. Arithmetic or harmonic

84. Which form of the efficient market hypothesis (EMH) states that current stock prices fully reflect all security market information, and contends that investors should gain little from trading rules based on past rates of return or security market data?

   A. Weak form
   B. Strong form
   C. Semi-strong form

85. Which is closest to the value of preferred stock with a $100 par value and a dividend of $8 per year using a required rate of return of 9%?

   A. $89
   B. $91
   C. $100

86. Which is closest to the value of common stock with a current dividend of $1, a dividend growth rate of 20% for three years, a dividend growth rate of 8% from year 4 on, and a required rate of return of 11%?

   A. $46
   B. $49
   C. $51

87. The present value of operating free cash flows discounts the operating free cash flows

   A. After deducting payments to debt holders (interest and principal) as well as preferred stockholders
   B. Prior to the payment of interest to the bondholders but after deducting funds needed to maintain the firm's assets base (capital expenditures)
   C. After deducting the payment of interest to the bondholders and the funds needed to maintain the firm's assets base (capital expenditures)

88. Which is closest to the expected constant growth rate of dividends if sales per share are $40, EPS is $2.00, the asset turnover is 2, the financial leverage ratio is 3, and the most recent dividend was $0.80?

   A. 12%
   B. 18%
   C. 24%

89. What is the decision if expected earnings are $2 per share, the P/E ratio is expected to be in the 20 to 22 range, and the current price is $50?

    A. Buy
    B. Sell
    C. Hold

90. When stocks have negative earnings, a ranking by

    A. P/E is meaningful whereas a ranking by earnings yield is not
    B. Earnings yield is meaningful whereas a ranking by P/E is not
    C. P/E is not is meaningful and neither is a ranking by earnings yield

91. An investor short a put option has

    A. A right to sell at a specific price
    B. A potential obligation to buy at a certain price
    C. A potential obligation to sell at a certain price

92. Which statement is least accurate regarding equity forward contracts?

    A. Most equity forward contracts are based on LIBOR
    B. Equity forward contracts must take dividends into account
    C. Equity forward contracts can be written on individual stocks, specific stock portfolios, or stock indexes

93. What is the ending balance at the end of day 3 for a holder of a long position of 10 futures contracts if the initial futures price on day 0 is $100, the initial margin requirement is 5%, the maintenance margin requirement is 3%, the settlement price on day 1 is $103, the settlement price on day 2 is $96, and the settlement price on day 3 is $98?

    A. $70
    B. $80
    C. $100

94. A gold futures contract requires the long trader to buy 100 troy ounces of gold. The initial margin requirement is $2,000 and the maintenance requirement is $1,500. If an investor goes long one contract at $320 per ounce, at what price would the investor receive a margin call?

    A. Below $305
    B. Below $315
    C. Above $335

95. Which is closest to the lower bound on a European index call option expiring in 3 months with a strike price of $1,260, when the index is at $1,300 and the risk free rate is 5%?

    A. $24
    B. $40
    C. $55

96. What is the maximum loss to the buyer of a call option (long position), where the exercise price is X?

    A. Unlimited
    B. Option cost
    C. X - option cost

97. What would be most attractive to an investor who believes interest rates will decline?

    A. Inverse floater
    B. Floating-rate security
    C. Deferred coupon bond

98. Which is least accurate regarding noncallable and nonrefundable bonds?

    A. Refunding prevents redemption from all sources
    B. Call protection is more robust than refund protection
    C. Bonds are more likely to be called if interest rates decline

99. Which feature increases interest rate risk?

    A. High yield
    B. High coupon
    C. Long maturity

100. What does a 5-year rate duration of 2 mean?

    A. The approximate dollar price change is 2% for a 100 basis point change in the 5-year yield
    B. The approximate dollar price change is 5% for a 100 basis point change in the 2-year yield
    C. The portfolio's value will change by about 2% for a 100 basis point change in the 5-year yield

101. For amortizing bonds, the reinvestment risk for an investor holding bonds to maturity is greatest for bonds selling

   A. At par value
   B. Below par value
   C. Above par value

102. An increase in expected yield volatility will cause the value of

   A. Putable bonds to increase
   B. Callable bonds to increase
   C. Putable bonds to decrease

103. Mortgage passthrough securities

   A. Have more prepayment risk than individual mortgages
   B. Have more predictable prepayments than individual mortgages
   C. Are obligations of the U.S. Treasury and have no default risk

104. Under the liquidity preference theory, what is the most likely explanation for an upwardly sloping yield curve?

   A. Increasing yield premium required
   B. Expectations that short term rates will rise
   C. Different levels of supply and demand for short and long term funds

105. For an investor in the 40% tax bracket considering bond X, a taxable bond with a yield of 6.8%, and bond Y, a tax-exempt security with a yield of 4.8%, what is the after-tax yield of bond X and the taxable equivalent yield of bond Y?

   A. After-tax yield for bond X = 4.08%, taxable equivalent yield for bond Y = 8.00%
   B. After-tax yield for bond X = 4.08%, taxable equivalent yield for bond Y = 6.72%
   C. After-tax yield for bond X = 4.85%, taxable equivalent yield for bond Y = 8.00%

106. Which is closest to the change in present value of a 5-year security with a 7% annual coupon and a par value of $100, when the time to maturity changes from 5 years to 4 years, using a discount rate of 5%?

   A. Decrease of $1.56
   B. Decrease of $0.88
   C. Increase of $1.56

107. An investor buys a 6% coupon bond with 20 years to maturity at a price of $89.32, a par value of $100, and yield to maturity of 7%. Which is closest to the dollar return that must be generated from reinvestment income in order to generate a yield of 7%?

    A. $130.68
    B. $133.64
    C. $264.32

108. Which is a characteristic of an option free bond?

    A. The price moves in the same direction as the change in yield
    B. For large changes in the yield, the percentage price change for a given bond is roughly the same, whether the yield increases or decreases
    C. For a given large change in yield, the percentage price increase is greater than the percentage price decrease

109. If a 9% coupon 20-year option-free bond selling at 134.67 to yield 6% has a duration of 10.67, which is closest to the price if the yield increases to 6.2%?

    A. 131.8
    B. 133.2
    C. 137.6

110. Which is closest to percentage price change for a bond with modified duration of 6.5 and convexity of -42.4 if yields decrease by 100 basis points?

    A. -6.92%
    B. -0.42%
    C. 6.08%

111. An investor is considering 3 classes of mutual funds: class A has a 3% sales load on purchases, no deferred sales charge on redemptions, and 1.25% in annual expenses; class B has no sales load on purchases, a deferred sales charge on redemptions of 5% in the first year declining by 1 percentage point each year thereafter, and 1.50% in annual expenses for the first 6 years then 1.25% per year thereafter; and class C has no sales load on purchases, a deferred sales charge on redemptions of 1% per year for the initial two years, and 1.50% in annual expenses. What is the most appropriate class for an investor with a 6 year horizon if the expected gross return is 8% per year?

    A. Class B or C with terminal values of $1.4493 are most appropriate and class A with a terminal value of $1.4274 is least appropriate
    B. Class A or C with terminal values of $1.4493 are most appropriate and class B with a terminal value of $1.4274 is least appropriate
    C. Class A or B with terminal values of $1.4493 are most appropriate and class C with a terminal value of $1.4274 is least appropriate

112. An apartment investment has gross potential rental income of $120,000, a 6% estimated vacancy and collection losses, $29,000 in insurance, property taxes, utilities, repairs, and maintenance; $14,000 in depreciation; and $11,000 in interest on the proposed financing. Which is closest to the net operating income?

    A. $58,800
    B. $83,800
    C. $97,800

113. Which venture capital investments are least likely to be considered early stage financing?

    A. Start-up financing
    B. Seed state financing
    C. First stage financing

114. A commodity futures market is in contango if the futures prices are

    A. Less than the spot price, the market is most likely dominated by short hedgers, and the roll yield is most likely positive
    B. Less than the spot price, the market is most likely dominated by long hedgers, and the roll yield is most likely negative
    C. Greater than the spot price, the market is most likely dominated by long hedgers, and the roll yield is most likely negative

115. Which is least likely a reason for a policy statement?

    A. Security selection
    B. Evaluate performance
    C. Articulate investor goals

116. Which is least likely related to legal and regulatory factors?

    A. Liquidity
    B. Prudent investor rule
    C. Fiduciary responsibility

117. Which is least likely to be considered an assumption of Markowitz portfolio theory?

    A. Investors estimate the risk of the portfolio on the basis of the variability of expected returns
    B. Given a choice between two assets with equal rates of return, investors will select the asset with the higher level of risk
    C. Investors consider each investment alternative as being represented by a probability distribution of expected returns over some holding period

118. Which is closest to the standard deviation of a portfolio with a 20% weight in a security with an expected return of 10% and a standard deviation of 7%, and an 80% weight in a security with an expected return of 20% and a standard deviation of 10%, if the correlation coefficient is 0.0?

    A. 6%
    B. 7%
    C. 8%

119. Which is closest to the expected return on a portfolio with an 80% weight of a risky asset with an expected return of 8% and a standard deviation of 10%, and a 20% weight of the risk-free asset with an expected return of 3%?

    A. 6%
    B. 7%
    C. 8%

120. If the risk free rate is 5%, the return on the market portfolio is 9%, beta is 0.70, the current stock price is $25, and the expected price in one year is $26 after paying a $0.95 dividend, the stock is

    A. Overvalued
    B. Undervalued
    C. Properly valued

1. B	41. A	81. A
2. C	42. C	82. B
3. B	43. B	83. B
4. B	44. A	84. A
5. C	45. C	85. A
6. A	46. C	86. B
7. B	47. B	87. B
8. B	48. A	88. B
9. A	49. B	89. B
10. C	50. A	90. B
11. A	51. A	91. B
12. B	52. C	92. A
13. B	53. B	93. A
14. A	54. C	94. B
15. B	55. B	95. C
16. C	56. B	96. B
17. A	57. B	97. A
18. A	58. C	98. A
19. A	59. B	99. C
20. A	60. A	100. C
21. A	61. A	101. C
22. B	62. A	102. A
23. B	63. B	103. B
24. C	64. A	104. A
25. A	65. C	105. A
26. A	66. A	106. A
27. A	67. C	107. B
28. A	68. B	108. C
29. A	69. B	109. B
30. C	70. A	110. C
31. C	71. B	111. A
32. B	72. B	112. B
33. B	73. A	113. B
34. B	74. B	114. C
35. B	75. B	115. A
36. A	76. C	116. A
37. C	77. B	117. B
38. A	78. B	118. C
39. B	79. C	119. B
40. B	80. A	120. C

— start —

1. CFA charterholder Shahperi's employer, an investment-banking firm, is the principal underwriter for an issue of convertible debentures by the Agusti Company. Shahperi discovers that Agusti Company has concealed severe third-quarter losses in its foreign operations. The preliminary prospectus has already been distributed. What is the most appropriate first step for Shahperi?

    A. Seek an independent legal opinion
    *B. Report the situation to the appropriate supervisors (Standard I(A) - knowledge of the law)
    C. Sever all connections with the underwriting

2. CFA charterholder Beltis, a mining analyst with Whitehurst Brothers, is invited by Optimus Mining to join a group of analysts at the Super Bowl. Optimus Mining pays for the airfare, hotel expenses, and tickets for the group, except CFA charterholder Zhang, who works for a large trust company and insists on following his company's policy and paying for one of the nights at the hotel himself. Were any Standards of Professional Conduct violated?

    A. No, the trip was strictly for business
    B. Yes, Beltis violated the standard on independence and objectivity
    *C. Yes, Beltis and Zhang violated the standard on independence and objectivity (Standard I(B) - independence and objectivity)

3. CFA charterholder Alami attends a seminar and hears a presentation by a quantitative analyst who discusses a new model in great detail. Alami returns to the office, tests the model, and is satisfied with the results. Alami makes slight modifications to the model. Alami tells his supervisor he discovered a new model. Did Alami violate any Standards of Professional Conduct?

    A. No
    *B. Yes, relating to misrepresentation (Standard I(C) - misrepresentation)
    C. Yes, relating to duties to employers

4. CFA charterholder Koyama turns in false insurance claims to his employer's health plan administrator. Did Koyama violate any Standards of Professional Conduct?

    A. No
    *B. Yes, relating to misconduct (Standard I(D) - misconduct)
    C. Yes, relating to misrepresentation

5. Executives at NBI serve as investment managers for pension funds. The executives use a broker with close ties to NBI to handle the trades, at a higher cost to the clients than other brokerage companies. Did the NBI executives violate any Standards of Professional Conduct?

    A. No
    B. Yes, relating to fair dealing
    *C. Yes, relating to loyalty, prudence, and care (Standard III(A) - loyalty, prudence, and care)

6. CFA charterholder Patel puts an earnings estimate in a research report and tells his larger clients that he expects the earnings to be higher than in the report. Which Standard of Professional Conduct did Patel most likely violate?

    *A. Fair dealing (Standard III(B) - fair dealing)
    B. Market manipulation
    C. Disclosure of conflicts

7. To meet the obligations under the Standard of Professional Conduct on performance presentation, the use of simulated results should

    A. Never be used
    *B. Be accompanied by full disclosure of the source of the data (Standard III(D) - performance presentation)
    C. Comply with the Global Investment Performance Standards (GIPS)

8. CFA charterholder McWillie is planning to leave his employer to join a competitor. He asks big accounts to leave his current employer and open accounts with his new employer. Did McWillie violate any Standards of Professional Conduct?

    A. No
    *B. Yes, relating to loyalty (Standard IV(A) - loyalty)
    C. Yes, relating to preservation of confidentiality

9. CFA charterholder Choi develops a stock selection model on his own before being employed by a firm, uses the model at the firm, then leaves the firm to work for a bank, and uses the same model at the bank. Did Choi violate any Standards of Professional Conduct?

    *A. No (Standard IV(A) - loyalty)
    B. Yes, relating to loyalty
    C. Yes, relating to disclosure of conflicts

10. CFA charterholder Heitman is given the responsibility to estimate IPO prices and due to time constraints and limited resources makes estimates after only categorizing the issues by size. Did Heitman violate any Standards of Professional Conduct?

   A. No
   B. Yes, relating to duties to employers
   *C. Yes, relating to diligence and reasonable basis (Standard V(A) - diligence and reasonable basis)

11. Which is least likely to pose a conflict of interest for service as a director?

   *A. Opportunity to act quickly on public information (Standard VI(A) - disclosure of conflicts)
   B. Conflict between duties to shareholders and duties to clients
   C. Trading actions that could increase the value of any securities or options received as compensation

12. CFA charterholder Morrison issued an RFP for an equity manager. CFA charterholder Madura is on Morrison's staff, and was one of several staff members who recommended Copeland Partners based on a review of all the firms' qualifications, suitability, and performance records. Morrison reviewed the recommendation and instead hired Tuttle Management. Two days later, Morrison went to work for Tuttle Management. Did Morrison violate any Standards of Professional Conduct?

   A. No
   *B. Yes, related to conflicts of interest (Standard VI(A) - disclosure of conflicts)
   C. Yes, related to market manipulation

13. CFA charterholder Lambert concludes that a company's stock price will rise. Before revising his recommendation from hold to buy, Lambert tells his brother so that his brother can buy shares at the lower price. Did Lambert violate any Standards of Professional Conduct?

   A. No
   *B. Yes, related to duty to clients, duty to employer, and priority of transactions (Standard VI(B) - priority of transactions Standard III - duties to clients, and Standard IV - duties to employers)
   C. Yes, related to duty to clients, duty to employer, priority of transactions, and diligence and reasonable basis

14. Which is an improper reference to the CFA Institute, the CFA designation, or the CFA program?

    *A. John, a CFA-type portfolio manager (Standard VII(B) - reference to the CFA Institute, the CFA designation, and the CFA program)
    B. Level I candidate in the CFA program
    C. John Ganesh, Chartered Financial Analyst

15. CFA charterholder Kolli is a research analyst for Company X. His research suggests the outlook is weak. However, at lunch he overhears an analyst from another firm offer different opinions. Upon returning to the office, Kolli issues a strong buy recommendation. Did Kolli violate any Standards of Professional Conduct?

    A. No
    *B. Yes, he did not have a reasonable and adequate basis (Standard V(A) - diligence and reasonable basis)
    C. Yes, he did failed to distinguish between facts and opinions

16. CFA charterholder Chauhan is a portfolio manager. Chauhan uses the same broker exclusively for all portfolio transactions because the broker gives Chauhan lower prices for personal sales than to Chauhan's portfolio accounts and other investors. Did Chauhan violate any Standards of Professional Conduct?

    A. No
    B. Yes, related to misrepresentation
    *C. Yes, related to loyalty, prudence, and care (Standard III(A) - loyalty, prudence, and care)

17. Which is least likely to be required for firms claiming compliance with the GIPS?

    *A. Undertake a verification process
    B. Make a composite list and description to any prospective client on request
    C. Document their policies and procedures used in establishing and maintaining compliance

18. The eight major sections of the GIPS include all of the following but

    *A. Input data, disclosures, and venture capital
    B. Presentation and reporting, calculation methodology, and real estate
    C. Fundamentals of compliance, composite construction, and disclosures

19. Which is closest to the annual end-of-year retirement fund contribution for 40 years that will provide a 30-year annuity of $10,000 per year at retirement, if the fund earns 8% per year?

    *A. $435 ={$10,000 [1 - (1/1.08)^30)] / .08] / (1.08)^40} / [1 - (1/1.08)^40)] / .08];
      n = 30, i = 8, PMT = 10,000, FV = 0; PV = $112,578; n = 40, i = 8, PV = 0, FV =
      112,578; PMT = $435
    B. $937
    C. $992

20. What is the net present value and internal rate of return for an investment costing $3.43 million that is expected to increase annual cash flows by $1 million for each of the next five years, using a cost of capital of 15%?

    *A. NPV = -$0.08 million and IRR = 14% because 3.35 = [(1 - (1/1.15)^5] / .15;
      3.35 - 3.43 = -0.08; and 3.43 = [(1 - (1/1.14)^5] / .14; NPV: n = 5, i = 15%,
      PMT = 1,000,000, FV = 0; PV = $3,352,155; $3,352,155 - $3,430,000 = -
      $77,845 = -$0.08 million; IRR: n = 5, PV = -3,352,000, PMT = 1,000,000, FV =
      0; i = 14.04 percent = 14%
    B. NPV = $0.00 million and IRR = 15%
    C. NPV = $0.08 million and IRR = 16%

21. What categorizes data but does not rank the data?

    *A. Nominal scale
    B. Ordinal scale
    C. Ratio scale

22. What is the geometric mean return for a fund with ten years of annual returns of 2%, 6%, 9%, 9%, 10%, 11%, 16%, 14%, 5%, and 8%?

    A. 8.8%
    *B. 8.9% = 1.02(1.06)(1.09)(1.09)(1.10)(1.11)(1.16)(1.14)(1.05)(1.08)^.1
    C. 9.0%

23. Using Chebyshev's inequality, at least what proportion of observations must lie within 2 standard deviations of the mean?

    A. 36%
    *B. 75% = 1 - 1/(2)^2
    C. 89%

24. What is most likely the standard deviation of sales if 68.3% of the observations of sales are between 200,000 and 500,000?

   A. 50,000
   B. 75,000
   *C. 150,000 = (500,000 - 200,000)/2

25. If three independent screens are applied to 100 companies, 30 pass the first screen, 10 pass the second screen, and 40 pass the third screen, the probability of passing all three screens is closest to which percent?

   *A. 1% = 30% (10%) (40%)
   B. 8%
   C. 10%

26. If there is a 25% probability of declining interest rates, a 60% probability of EPS of $10 and a 40% chance of an EPS of $8 if rates decline, and a 70% probability of an EPS of $6 and a 30% chance of an EPS of $4 if rates do not decline, what is the expected EPS?

   *A. $6.35 = 25% [60% ($10) + 40% ($8)] + 75% [70% ($6) + 30% ($4)]
   B. $7.30
   C. $10.95

27. If the prior probabilities are 1/3 that EPS exceeded expectations, 1/3 that EPS met expectations, and 1/3 that EPS fell short of expectations; the new probabilities of an expansion are 70% given that EPS exceeded expectations, 20% given that EPS met expectations, and 10% given that EPS fell short of expectations, what is the unconditional probability of an expansion?

   *A. 33%
   B. 43% = 50%(70%) + 30%(20%) + 20%(10%)
   C. 81%

28. If a stock is selling for $50 and each year there is a 60% probability of an uptick in price of $1 and a 40% probability the price moves down $1, what is the probability that the price is $53 after 3 years?

   *A. 0.216 = .6^3
   B. 0.288
   C. 0.432

29. Approximately what percent of normally distributed stock returns with a mean return of 10% and a standard deviation of 15% fall in the interval 0% to 20% return?

   *A. 50%
   B. 68%
   C. 95%

30. Which is closest to the annualized volatility for a stock that closes for five consecutive days at $1.01, $0.98, $1.00, $1.02, and $1.03, based on 250 days in a year?

   A. 2%
   B. 15%
   *C.38% = 0.02386(250^.5) where .02386 is the SD of ln(.98/1.01), ln(1/.98), ln(1.02/1), and ln(1.03/1.02)

31. If the mean income of companies on a stock index is $2 million with a standard deviation of $3 million, which is closest to the standard error of the sample mean for a sample size of 25?

   A. $0.4 million
   B. $0.5 million
   *C.$0.6 million = $3 million / (25^.5)

32. What is the test statistic for 1: the variance of a single, normally distributed population and 2: the differences between variances of two normally distributed populations based on two random, independent samples?

   A. 1: t-test; 2: chi-square test
   *B.1: chi-square test; 2: F-test
   C. 1: F-test; 2: chi-square test

33. What is the demand elasticity when the percentage increase in quantity demanded is 5% when prices are reduced 10%?

   A. Unit elastic demand
   *B.Inelastic demand
   C. Elastic demand

34. What is a consumer surplus?

   A. The price minus marginal cost, summed over the quantity sold
   *B.The marginal benefit minus price, summed over the quantity bought
   C. The marginal cost minus price, summed over the quantity bought

35. Which method is technological efficient if method 1 uses 10 units of labor and 100 units of capital, method 2 uses 10 units of labor and 10 units of capital, and method 3 uses 50 units of labor and 10 units of capital to produce the same output?

   A. 1
   *B. 2
   C. 3

36. What is closest to the Herfindahl-Hirschman Index (HHI) if the sales of the six firms in the industry are, in millions, $40, $20, $10, $10, $10, and $10?

   *A. $2400 = 40^2 + 20^2 + 10^2 + 10^2 + 10^2 + 10^2$
   B. 7000
   C. 8000

37. What is least likely to happen with a technological change that increases productivity?

   A. Shifts the total product curve upward
   B. Shifts marginal product curve and average product curve upward
   *C. Shifts fixed cost curves downward

38. Which market structure is associated with the lowest possible average cost?

   *A. Perfect competition
   B. Monopolistic competition
   C. Monopoly

39. What determines the demand for labor, and diminishes as the quantity of labor increases?

   A. Marginal revenue
   *B. Marginal revenue product
   C. Derived demand

40. Who bears the burden of a tax if supply is perfectly elastic?

   A. The supplier bears the entire tax
   *B. The buyer bears the entire tax
   C. It is shared by the buyer and supplier

41. What occurs when real GDP is less than potential GDP?

    *A. Recessionary gap
    B. Inflationary gap
    C. Full employment

42. Which is closest to the money created from an initial increase in reserves of $100,000 if the desired currency holding is 20% of deposits and the desired reserves are 4% of deposits?

    A. $250,000
    B. $333,333
    *C.$500,000 = $100,000 (1 + 20%)/(20% + 4%)

43. Which shows that relationship between inflation and unemployment?

    A. Ricardo-Barro equivalence
    *B.Phillips curve
    C. Laffer curve

44. Which is least likely to be considered the Federal Reserve System's choice of monetary policy instrument?

    *A. The required reserve ratio
    B. The federal funds rate
    C. A short term interest rate

45. Which step in analyzing financial statements uses communication with the client and supervisor, institutional guidelines, and sets timetables and budgets?

    A. Process data
    B. Collect input data
    *C.Articulate the purpose and context of the analysis

46. Which is a residual claim?

    A. Asset
    B. Liability
    *C.Owner's equity

47. Which is the most likely initial result receiving a $10,000 loan from a bank?

    A. There is no change in assets or liabilities
    *B.Assets and liabilities increase by $10,000
    C. Liabilities increase by $10,000 and there is no change in assets

48. What are the qualitative characteristics of useful information under the IFRS framework?

    *A. Understandability, relevance, reliability, and comparability
    B. Understandability, timeliness, reliability, and neutrality
    C. Accuracy, timeliness, relevance, and comparability

49. Which is least likely a conflicting approach under different financial reporting frameworks?

    A. Valuation
    *B.Consistency
    C. Measurement

50. Which is closest to the revenue that will be reported in the first year under the completed contract method if the total revenue over four years is $4 million, the total costs over four years are $3 million, and the costs incurred in the first year are $0.3 million?

    *A. $0.0 million
    B. $0.4 million
    C. $1.0 million

51. If a company sells $4,000 worth of products on consignment for a commission of $1,000, how much revenue should the company report?

    *A. $1,000
    B. $3,000
    C. $4,000

52. What is closest to the cost of goods sold using the LIFO method if 2,000 units were purchased the prior year for $50 each; 3,000 units were purchased in the current year for $60 each; 4,000 units are sold in the current year for $70 each; and ending inventory was 1,000 units?

    A. $220,000
    B. $224,000
    *C.$230,000 = 1,000($50) + 3,000($60)

53. Which is closest to the weighted average number of shares outstanding for calculating EPS for a calendar year if a company had 360,000 shares outstanding on January 1st; issued 120,000 shares on February 1st; had a 2 for 1 stock split on December 1st; and had 960,000 shares outstanding on December 31st?

   A. 520,000
   *B.940,000 = [360,000(1/12) + 480,000 (11/12)] 2
   C. 960,000

54. How are bonds issued two years ago for maturity in eight years measured on the balance sheet?

   A. Fair value
   B. Historical cost
   *C.Amortized cost

55. Which is least likely to be included in the owners' equity section of the balance sheet?

   A. Minority interest
   *B.Financial instruments
   C. Contributed capital

56. How much cash did a company receive from customers if the revenues were $90,000; beginning of year receivables were $10,000; and end of year receivables were $12,000?

   A. $78,000
   *B.$88,000 = $90,000 - ($12,000 - $10,000)
   C. $92,000

57. How much cash did a company pay for interest and taxes if interest expense was $20 million; taxes were $8 million; interest payable decreased by $5 million; and taxes payable increased by $2 million?

   A. $15 million for interest and $6 million for taxes
   *B.$25 million for interest and $6 million for taxes; $20 + $5 = $25; $8 - $2 = $6
   C. $25 million for interest and $10 million for taxes

58. If a company started in 2008; and in 2008 purchased 10,000 units of inventory at $12 each; and sold 5,000 units at $15 each; then in 2009 purchased 20,000 units of inventory at $18 each; and sold 22,000 units at $20 each; which is closest to the cost of goods sold for 2009 under the weighted average cost inventory method?

    A. $330,000
    B. $336,400
    *C.$369,600 = 22,000 [5,000 ($12) + 20,000 ($18)] / (20,000 + 5,000)

59. In a period of rising prices, how do profits for a company using LIFO most likely compare to FIFO if the company purchases more inventory then it sells?

    A. Greater under LIFO
    *B.Lower under LIFO
    C. About the same under LIFO or FIFO

60. If a company reporting under U.S. GAAP purchased equipment for $100,000 with a five-year life and a salvage value of $10,000, which would make net income more volatile?

    *A. Expensing the entire cost
    B. Capitalizing the entire cost
    C. Capitalizing and expensing result in the same volatility

61. What is least likely to increase as the retirement date of an asset retirement obligation approaches?

    *A. Equity
    B. Liabilities
    C. Debt to equity ratio

62. Which are least likely to be based on the applicable tax rates on the balance sheet of an entity?

    *A. Deferred taxes
    B. Current taxes payable
    C. Current taxes recoverable

63. If on January 1, 2009, a company issues $1 million worth of four-year bonds with interest payments of $50,000 at the end of each of the four years and the market rate is 6%, what will the company most likely record at the time of issue?

   A. $965,349 as a liability and a cash inflow from investing activities
   *B.$965,349 as a liability and a cash inflow from financing activities = 50,000/1.06 + 50,000/1.06^2 + 50,000/1.06^3 + 1,050,000/1.06^4; n = 4, i = 6, PMT = 50,000, FV = 1,000,000; PV = 965,349
   C. $973,270 as a liability and a cash inflow from investing activities

64. After adjusting reported financials for a company that is a lessee with a large number of operating leases, which would most likely be higher?

   *A. Debt-to-equity ratio but not interest coverage ratio
   B. Interest coverage ratio but not debt-to-equity ratio
   C. Both debt-to-equity ratio and interest coverage ratio

65. Which is the most appropriate conclusion if ROE increased, return on total assets decreased, and total asset turnover increased?

   A. Net profit margin and financial leverage decreased
   B. Net profit margin and financial leverage increased
   *C.Net profit margin decreased but financial leverage increased

66. If ROE is 15%, what is true about company A compared to company B if company A has sales of $120 million, assets of $70 million, and liabilities of $25 million; and company B has sales of $300 million, assets of $140 million, and liabilities of $40 million?

   *A. Greater profit margin; 15%/[(120/70)(70/45)]>15%/[(300/140)(140/100)]; 5.625% > 5%
   B. Higher total assets turnover
   C. Lower financial leverage

67. Which is least likely a qualitative characteristic of financial statements to achieve the purpose of providing useful information?

   A. Relevance
   B. Predictive value
   *C.Convergence

68. How are cash inflows for the receipt of interest treated under IASB standards?

   A. Operating cash flows
   *B. Operating or investing cash flows
   C. Financing or investing cash flows

69. Which category of projects susceptible to the capital budgeting process is most likely to possibly not require careful analysis?

   A. Expansion
   *B. Replacement
   C. New products and services

70. If a company has 50% long term debt with a marginal after-tax cost of 8%; 10% preferred stock with a marginal after-tax cost of 10%; and 40% long term debt with a marginal after-tax cost of 12.5%; which has an IRR greater than 10% if the warehouse project has an NPV of $100 million, the safety project has an NPV of $0, and the new product project has an NPV of negative $50 million?

   *A. The warehouse project only; WACC = 50%(8%) + 10%(10%) + 40%(12.5%) = 10%; only the warehouse project has an NPV greater than $0 using 10%
   B. The warehouse project and the safety project
   C. All three

71. Which is least likely to characterize a typical NPV profile for capital budgeting for a conventional project?

   A. The profile is convex from the origin
   *B. The NPV declines at an increasing rate as the discount rate increases
   C. The profile goes through the vertical axis at the sum of the future cash flows where the discount rate is zero and through the horizontal axis where the discount rate is the IRR

72. Which is closest to the expected share price after new information about an investment with an NPV of $400 million if the share price before the new information was $10 and there are 200 million shares outstanding?

   A. $10
   *B. $12 = $10 + $400 / 200
   C. $14

73. What is an estimate of the equity risk premium if the dividend yield is 5%, the dividend growth rate is 2%, and the risk-free rate is 4%?

    *A. 3% = 5% + 2% - 4%
    B. 5%
    C. 7%

74. Which is closest to the beta of an asset using the pure-play method if the beta of equity is 1.5, equity is $10 million, debt is $4 million, and the marginal tax rate is 30%?

    A. 1.07
    *B.1.17 = 1.5 / [1 +(1-30%)($4/$10)]
    C. 1.20

75. What is an estimate of the cost of equity adjusted for flotation costs if the current dividends are $5, the market price is $100, the dividend growth rate is 4%, flotation costs are $10, and the risk-free rate is 3%?

    A. 9.6%
    *B.9.8% = ($5)(1.04)/($100 - $10) + 4%
    C. 10.0%

76. What is the operating cycle if annual credit sales are $10 million, accounts receivable are $4 million, annual cost of goods sold is $12 million, inventory is $4 million, annual purchases are $10 million, and accounts payable are $2 million?

    A. 73.0
    B. 194.67
    *C.267.67 = 121.67 + 146.0, 121.67 = $4 / ($12 / 365), 146.0 = $4 / ($10 / 365)

77. Which has the lowest effective cost of borrowing $1 million for one month: a line of credit at 6.5% with a 1/2 percent commitment fee; a banker's acceptance (BA) at 6.75%; or commercial paper (CP) at 6.15% with a commission of 1/8 percent and a backup line cost of 1/4 percent?

    A. BA
    *B.CP; CP: (6.15% + 0.125% + 0.25%)($1 million / 12) / [$1 million - (6.15%)($1 million / 12)](12) = 6.56%; BA: [6.75%($1 million / 12)] / [$1 million - 6.75%($1 million / 12)](12) = 6.79%; Line of credit: 6.5% + 0.5% = 7.0%
    C. Line of credit

78. If for 2008, in millions, sales were $9, cost of goods sold were $3, total assets were $4.5, current assets were $1.8, and current liabilities were $1.2; what is the estimate of the 2009 projected current assets if for 2009, the projected sales are $9.9, cost of goods sold are $3.45, and total assets are $4.45?

   A. $1.89
   *B.$1.98 = [1+($9.9 - $9) / $9] ($1.8) = ($9.9/$9)($1.8)
   C. $2.07

79. Which is most likely associated with primary capital markets?

   A. AMEX
   B. Nasdaq
   *C.Shelf registration

80. Which is a market where security trades are executed at specific times at a single price after buy and sell orders have accumulated?

   *A. Call market
   B. Stock exchange
   C. Continuous market

81. For a margin account with an initial deposit of $5,000 used to purchase 200 shares of stock at $50, what is the equity if the stock increases by 20%?

   *A. $7,000 = 1.2($50)(200) - $5,000
   B. $10,000
   C. $12,000

82. What type of security market index takes the average of the stock prices?

   A. Unweighted
   *B.Price-weighted
   C. Value-weighted

83. What type of mean is used for an unweighted security market index?

   A. Geometric or harmonic
   *B.Geometric or arithmetic
   C. Arithmetic or harmonic

84. Which form of the efficient market hypothesis (EMH) states that current stock prices fully reflect all security market information, and contends that investors should gain little from trading rules based on past rates of return or security market data?

 *A. Weak form
 B. Strong form
 C. Semi-strong form

85. Which is closest to the value of preferred stock with a $100 par value and a dividend of $8 per year using a required rate of return of 9%?

 *A. $89 = $8 / 9%
 B. $91
 C. $100

86. Which is closest to the value of common stock with a current dividend of $1, a dividend growth rate of 20% for three years, a dividend growth rate of 8% from year 4 on, and a required rate of return of 11%?

 A. $46
 *B.$49 = $1(1.2) / 1.11 + $1(1.2)^2 / 1.11^2 + $1(1.2)^3 / 1.11^3 +
    [$1[(1.2)^3](1.08) / (11% - 8%)] / 1.11^3
 C. $51

87. The present value of operating free cash flows discounts the operating free cash flows

 A. After deducting payments to debt holders (interest and principal) as well as preferred stockholders
 *B.Prior to the payment of interest to the bondholders but after deducting funds needed to maintain the firm's assets base (capital expenditures)
 C. After deducting the payment of interest to the bondholders and the funds needed to maintain the firm's assets base (capital expenditures)

88. Which is closest to the expected constant growth rate of dividends if sales per share are $40, EPS is $2.00, the asset turnover is 2, the financial leverage ratio is 3, and the most recent dividend was $0.80?

 A. 12%
 *B.18% =(1 - $0.80/$2.00))[($2/$40)(2)(3)]
 C. 24%

89. What is the decision if expected earnings are $2 per share, the P/E ratio is expected to be in the 20 to 22 range, and the current price is $50?

    A. Buy
    *B. Sell; $2 (20) < $2 (22) < $50
    C. Hold

90. When stocks have negative earnings, a ranking by

    A. P/E is meaningful whereas a ranking by earnings yield is not
    *B. Earnings yield is meaningful whereas a ranking by P/E is not
    C. P/E is not is meaningful and neither is a ranking by earnings yield

91. An investor short a put option has

    A. A right to sell at a specific price
    *B. A potential obligation to buy at a certain price
    C. A potential obligation to sell at a certain price

92. Which statement is least accurate regarding equity forward contracts?

    *A. Most equity forward contracts are based on LIBOR
    B. Equity forward contracts must take dividends into account
    C. Equity forward contracts can be written on individual stocks, specific stock portfolios, or stock indexes

93. What is the ending balance at the end of day 3 for a holder of a long position of 10 futures contracts if the initial futures price on day 0 is $100, the initial margin requirement is 5%, the maintenance margin requirement is 3%, the settlement price on day 1 is $103, the settlement price on day 2 is $96, and the settlement price on day 3 is $98?

    *A. $70 = $50 + $30 - $70 + $40 + $20; where $50 is the initial deposit, $30 is the gain on day 1, $70 is the loss on day 2, triggering a maintenance call, $40 is the deposit on day 3 to bring the balance to $50, and $20 is the gain on day 3; the ending balances days 0 through 3 are $50, $80, $10, and $70
    B. $80
    C. $100

94. A gold futures contract requires the long trader to buy 100 troy ounces of gold. The initial margin requirement is $2,000 and the maintenance requirement is $1,500. If an investor goes long one contract at $320 per ounce, at what price would the investor receive a margin call?

   A. Below $305
   *B. Below $315 = $320 - ($2,000 - $1,500) / 100
   C. Above $335

95. Which is closest to the lower bound on a European index call option expiring in 3 months with a strike price of $1,260, when the index is at $1,300 and the risk free rate is 5%?

   A. $24
   B. $40
   *C. $55 = $1,300 - $1,260/(1.05^.25)

96. What is the maximum loss to the buyer of a call option (long position), where the exercise price is X?

   A. Unlimited
   *B. Option cost
   C. X - option cost

97. What would be most attractive to an investor who believes interest rates will decline?

   *A. Inverse floater
   B. Floating-rate security
   C. Deferred coupon bond

98. Which is least accurate regarding noncallable and nonrefundable bonds?

   *A. Refunding prevents redemption from all sources
   B. Call protection is more robust than refund protection
   C. Bonds are more likely to be called if interest rates decline

99. Which feature increases interest rate risk?

   A. High yield
   B. High coupon
   *C. Long maturity

100. What does a 5-year rate duration of 2 mean?

    A. The approximate dollar price change is 2% for a 100 basis point change in the 5-year yield

    B. The approximate dollar price change is 5% for a 100 basis point change in the 2-year yield

    *C. The portfolio's value will change by about 2% for a 100 basis point change in the 5-year yield

101. For amortizing bonds, the reinvestment risk for an investor holding bonds to maturity is greatest for bonds selling

    A. At par value

    B. Below par value

    *C. Above par value

102. An increase in expected yield volatility will cause the value of

    *A. Putable bonds to increase

    B. Callable bonds to increase

    C. Putable bonds to decrease

103. Mortgage passthrough securities

    A. Have more prepayment risk than individual mortgages

    *B. Have more predictable prepayments than individual mortgages

    C. Are obligations of the U.S. Treasury and have no default risk

104. Under the liquidity preference theory, what is the most likely explanation for an upwardly sloping yield curve?

    *A. Increasing yield premium required

    B. Expectations that short term rates will rise

    C. Different levels of supply and demand for short and long term funds

105. For an investor in the 40% tax bracket considering bond X, a taxable bond with a yield of 6.8%, and bond Y, a tax-exempt security with a yield of 4.8%, what is the after-tax yield of bond X and the taxable equivalent yield of bond Y?

    *A. After-tax yield for bond X = 4.08%, taxable equivalent yield for bond Y = 8.00%; 6.8%(1 - 40%) = 4.08%; 4.8% / (1 - 40%) = 8.00%

    B. After-tax yield for bond X = 4.08%, taxable equivalent yield for bond Y = 6.72%

    C. After-tax yield for bond X = 4.85%, taxable equivalent yield for bond Y = 8.00%

106. Which is closest to the change in present value of a 5-year security with a 7% annual coupon and a par value of $100, when the time to maturity changes from 5 years to 4 years, using a discount rate of 5%?

   *A. Decrease of $1.56; where n = 5, i = 5, PMT = 7, FV = 100, resulting in PV = -108.65; n = 4, i = 5, PMT = 7, FV = 100, resulting in PV = -107.09, $107.09 - $108.65 = -$1.56
   B. Decrease of $0.88
   C. Increase of $1.56

107. An investor buys a 6% coupon bond with 20 years to maturity at a price of $89.32, a par value of $100, and yield to maturity of 7%. Which is closest to the dollar return that must be generated from reinvestment income in order to generate a yield of 7%?

   A. $130.68
   *B.$133.64 = [$89.32 (1.035)^40 - $89.32] - ($120 + $10.68)
   C. $264.32

108. Which is a characteristic of an option free bond?

   A. The price moves in the same direction as the change in yield
   B. For large changes in the yield, the percentage price change for a given bond is roughly the same, whether the yield increases or decreases
   *C.For a given large change in yield, the percentage price increase is greater than the percentage price decrease

109. If a 9% coupon 20-year option-free bond selling at 134.67 to yield 6% has a duration of 10.67, which is closest to the price if the yield increases to 6.2%?

   A. 131.8 = 134.67 - 10.67 (.002)(134.67)
   *B.133.2
   C. 137.6

110. Which is closest to percentage price change for a bond with modified duration of 6.5 and convexity of -42.4 if yields decrease by 100 basis points?

   A. -6.92%
   B. -0.42%
   *C.6.08% = 6.5 (.01) - 42.4 (.01)^2

111. An investor is considering 3 classes of mutual funds: class A has a 3% sales load on purchases, no deferred sales charge on redemptions, and 1.25% in annual expenses; class B has no sales load on purchases, a deferred sales charge on redemptions of 5% in the first year declining by 1 percentage point each year thereafter, and 1.50% in annual expenses for the first 6 years then 1.25% per year thereafter; and class C has no sales load on purchases, a deferred sales charge on redemptions of 1% per year for the initial two years, and 1.50% in annual expenses. What is the most appropriate class for an investor with a 6 year horizon if the expected gross return is 8% per year?

   *A. Class B or C with terminal values of $1.4493 are most appropriate and class A with a terminal value of $1.4274 is least appropriate; A: $0.97(1.08^6)(1-.0125)^6=$1.4274; B: $1(1.08^6)(1-0.015)^6=$1.4493; C: $1(1.08^6)(1-0.015)^6=$1.4493
   B. Class A or C with terminal values of $1.4493 are most appropriate and class B with a terminal value of $1.4274 is least appropriate
   C. Class A or B with terminal values of $1.4493 are most appropriate and class C with a terminal value of $1.4274 is least appropriate

112. An apartment investment has gross potential rental income of $120,000, a 6% estimated vacancy and collection losses, $29,000 in insurance, property taxes, utilities, repairs, and maintenance; $14,000 in depreciation; and $11,000 in interest on the proposed financing. Which is closest to the net operating income?

   A. $58,800
   *B. $83,800 = $120,000(1 - 6%) - $29,000
   C. $97,800

113. Which venture capital investments are least likely to be considered early stage financing?

   A. Start-up financing
   *B. Seed state financing
   C. First stage financing

114. A commodity futures market is in contango if the futures prices are

   A. Less than the spot price, the market is most likely dominated by short hedgers, and the roll yield is most likely positive
   B. Less than the spot price, the market is most likely dominated by long hedgers, and the roll yield is most likely negative
   *C. Greater than the spot price, the market is most likely dominated by long hedgers, and the roll yield is most likely negative

115. Which is least likely a reason for a policy statement?

   *A. Security selection
   B. Evaluate performance
   C. Articulate investor goals

116. Which is least likely related to legal and regulatory factors?

   *A. Liquidity
   B. Prudent investor rule
   C. Fiduciary responsibility

117. Which is least likely to be considered an assumption of Markowitz portfolio theory?

   A. Investors estimate the risk of the portfolio on the basis of the variability of expected returns
   *B.Given a choice between two assets with equal rates of return, investors will select the asset with the higher level of risk
   C. Investors consider each investment alternative as being represented by a probability distribution of expected returns over some holding period

118. Which is closest to the standard deviation of a portfolio with a 20% weight in a security with an expected return of 10% and a standard deviation of 7%, and an 80% weight in a security with an expected return of 20% and a standard deviation of 10%, if the correlation coefficient is 0.0?

   A. 6%
   B. 7%
   *C.8% = [(20%^2)(7%^2) + (80%^2)(10%^2) + 2(20%)(80%)(0.0)(7%)(10%)]^.5

119. Which is closest to the expected return on a portfolio with an 80% weight of a risky asset with an expected return of 8% and a standard deviation of 10%, and a 20% weight of the risk-free asset with an expected return of 3%?

   A. 6%
   *B.7% = 80%(8%) + 20%(3%)
   C. 8%

120. If the risk free rate is 5%, the return on the market portfolio is 9%, beta is 0.70, the current stock price is $25, and the expected price in one year is $26 after paying a $0.95 dividend, the stock is

   A. Overvalued
   B. Undervalued
   *C.Properly valued; 5% + 0.70(9% - 5%) = 7.80% = [($26 + $0.95) / $25] - 1 = 7.8%

1. If a member resides in a country with more strict securities laws than the CFA Institute's Code and Standards and does business in a country with less strict securities laws than the CFA Institute's Code and Standards, the member must adhere to the

   A. Code and Standards
   B. Law of the less strict country
   C. Law of the more strict county

2. CFA charterholder Sheth is the investment manager of the Rego County Employees Pension Plan. The plan requested proposals for a foreign equity manager, and after the board interviewed the most qualified firms, Sheth went against the staff recommendation and recommended Raman Advisors. A reporter called and asked if the recommendation was related to Raman Advisors being one of the sponsors of an investment fact-finding trip to Asia that Sheth made earlier in the year. The trip was arranged by the Pension Investment Academy. The Academy obtains support for trips from sponsors such as Raman Advisors, then the Academy pays for the expenses of pension fund managers like Sheth. Did Sheth violate any Standards of Professional Conduct?

   A. No
   B. Yes, relating to independence and objectivity
   C. Yes, relating to diligence and reasonable basis

3. CFA charterholder Ong creates and distributes marketing material for his firm. He creates and distributes a performance report showing the firm's Asian equity composite has 350 billion yen in assets. The correct number is 35 billion and the 50 billion was a typographical error. The material is distributed before Ong catches the mistake. Ong ceases distribution of the incorrect material, corrects it, and informs those who received the incorrect report of the error. Did Ong violate any Standards of Professional Conduct?

   A. No
   B. Yes, relating to misrepresentation
   C. Yes, relating to independence and objectivity

4. Which is an element of a firewall?

   A. Watch list
   B. Mosaic theory
   C. Selective disclosure

5. CFA charterholder Chakak has hedge fund clients who sold a security short, and Chakak releases a report to sensationalize negative results shortly before the company reports actual earnings. Chakak is least likely to have violated the Standards of Professional Conduct relating to

    A. Market manipulation
    B. Loyalty, prudence, and care
    C. Diligence and reasonable basis

6. CFA charterholder Sharmar is the CIO for an insurance company whose investment policy provides for liquid low-risk investments. Sharmar invests a portion of company assets in private equity. Which Standard of Professional Conduct did Sharmar least likely violate?

    A. Suitability
    B. Fair dealing
    C. Loyalty, prudence, and care

7. CFA charterholder Candela circulates marketing material showing 1, 2, and 3 year returns, plus a separate sheet with quarterly unaudited and unverified returns. Did Candela violate any Standards of Professional Conduct?

    A. No
    B. Yes, by using unaudited and unverified results
    C. Yes, by not complying with the Global Investment Performance Standards (GIPS)

8. CFA charterholder Gwyer is an asset manager for a pension fund and is advised that a client has probably violated tax and fiduciary regulations and laws related to a pension fund. What is Gwyer's least appropriate response after informing her supervisor, if her employer is not successful in taking steps to have the client remedy the situation, and after seeking the advice of legal counsel?

    A. Do nothing
    B. Resign as asset manager
    C. Disclose the evidence of the legal violations

9. CFA charterholder DeArmond signs an agreement with his employer to not solicit former clients for one year after termination. DeArmond terminates and consults an attorney, who advises him that the agreement is most likely not enforceable. DeArmond solicits former clients less than one year after termination. Did DeArmond violate any Standards of Professional Conduct?

    A. No
    B. Yes, relating to loyalty
    C. Yes, relating to disclosure of conflicts

10. CFA charterholder Yang supervises CFA charterholder Springer at a registered investment advisory and registered broker/dealer firm. Yang finds that Springer places a large number of trades of a thinly traded security at the end of each month and asks Springer about it, who replies that it was a client's request. Six months later, Springer is investigated for manipulating prices at month's end. Which Standard of Professional Conduct did Yang most likely violate?

   A. Misrepresentation
   B. Market manipulation
   C. Responsibilities of supervisors

11. CFA charterholder Bergman is an aggressive growth manager that has invested in small caps since inception. Bergman changed its maximum capitalization from $250 million to $500 million, and prepared literature to inform prospective clients and third-party consultants of the change. Did Bergman violate any Standards of Professional Conduct?

   A. No
   B. Yes, by misrepresenting the definition of small cap
   C. Yes, by not notifying all of the existing clients of the change

12. CFA charterholder Chim does not recommend purchase of a stock for his employer's account because he wants to purchase it for his personal account first. Did Chim violate any Standards of Professional Conduct?

   A. No
   B. Yes, relating to priority of transactions
   C. Yes, relating to disclosure of conflicts of interest

13. CFA charterholder Fossen manages accounts for high wealth investors and a family account. He only allocates IPO shares to the family account after the other clients. The best course of action for Fossen under the Standards of Professional Conduct is to

   A. Continue management of the family account and treat it like any other client
   B. Discontinue management of the family account and transfer it to another firm
   C. Discontinue management of the family account and transfer it to another broker at the same firm

14. Which is an improper reference to the CFA Institute, the CFA designation, or the CFA program?

   A. CFA, Expected 2012
   B. Passed CFA Level I
   C. CFA charterholders are committed to high ethical standards

15. CFA charterholder Shahperi works for an investment counseling firm. Sopko, a new client, meets Shahperi for the first time. After introducing themselves, before asking about investment objectives, Shahperi immediately explains to Sopko that she has found an undervalued stock and she recommends that Sopko buy it. Did Shahperi violate any Standards of Professional Conduct?

    A. No
    B. Yes, related to suitability
    C. Yes, related to diligence and reasonable basis

16. CFA charterholder Landrigan tells a prospective client that his clients have averaged 30% return per year. Landrigan does not mention that he has very few clients, and one client who ignored his advice has significant gains that brought the average up. Excluding the one client with the big gains, the average would have been 8%. Did Landrigan violate any Standards of Professional Conduct?

    A. No
    B. Yes, related to misrepresentation
    C. Yes, related to communication with clients and prospective clients

17. To comply with the GIPS, a firm must initially show GIPS-compliant history for a minimum of

    A. Two years, or since inception if the firm has been in existence less than two years
    B. Three years, or since inception if the firm has been in existence less than three years
    C. Five years, or since inception if the firm has been in existence less than five years

18. Which is an example of a GIPS composite?

    A. Large cap growth composite
    B. Mediterranean region composite
    C. Composite of portfolios over $100 million

19. What is the difference between a $100,000 lump sum and a 20-year annuity with $10,000 beginning-of-year payments using a discount rate of 8% per year?

    A. The lump sum is greater by $6,036
    B. The lump sum is greater by $1,819
    C. The annuity is greater by $6,036

20. What is the preferred performance measure for a portfolio?

    A. Internal rate of return (IRR)
    B. Time-weighted rate of return
    C. Money-weighted rate of return

21. What is the standard deviation of the deviation of a portfolio's return from the benchmark return?

    A. Tracking risk
    B. Coefficient of variation
    C. Cumulative relative frequency

22. What is the average squared deviation below the mean?

    A. Semivariance
    B. Semideviation
    C. Geometric mean

23. If stocks had a mean return of 12% with a standard deviation of 20%, bonds had a mean return of 6% with a standard deviation of 4%, and the risk-free rate is 4%, which had superior risk-adjusted performance as measured by the Sharpe Ratio?

    A. Stocks
    B. Bonds
    C. They are the same

24. What is a characteristic of a normal distribution?

    A. The mean is less than the median
    B. The mean is equal to the median
    C. The mean is greater than the median

25. If the probability of EPS increasing in a quarter is 60%, what is the probability that earnings will decrease or remain the same for two quarters in a row?

    A. 16%
    B. 36%
    C. 40%

26. What is the correlation between the S&P 500 and the EAFE for a portfolio with 40% in the S&P 500 with a variance of 2.25%, 35% in bonds with a variance of 0.25%, and 25% in the EAFE with a variance of 3.24%, given covariances between the S&P 500 and bonds of 0.60%, between the S&P 500 and the EAFE of 1.44%, and between bonds and the EAFE of 0.36%?

  A. -0.28
  B. 0.35
  C. 0.53

27. Given that P(X<=1)=0.10, P(X<=2)=0.50, P(X<=3)=0.70, and P(X<=4)=1.00, what is p(2)?

  A. 0.1
  B. 0.4
  C. 0.5

28. If 40% of pension funds have alternative investments, what describes the number of funds out of 100 that have alternative investments?

  A. Bernoulli trial
  B. Binomial random variable
  C. Continuous random variable

29. To estimate risks in extremely unfavorable combinations of events, a risk management technique that involves examination of the portfolio under specified situations is called

  A. Shortfall risk
  B. Value at risk
  C. Stress testing/scenario analysis

30. Which treats time as advancing in finite intervals?

  A. Continuous compounding
  B. Lognormal compounding
  C. Discrete compounding

31. If the mean income of companies on a stock index is $60 million with a standard deviation of $100 million, which is closest to the 95% confidence interval for the sample mean for a sample size of 100?

  A. $30 million to $90 million
  B. $40 million to $80 million
  C. $50 million to $70 million

32. Which is least accurate regarding the statistical decision in hypothesis testing?

    A. Reject the null hypothesis if the test statistic is at least as extreme as the value or values determined by the level of significance
    B. Reject the null hypothesis if the result is not statistically significant
    C. Do not reject the null hypothesis if the test statistic is less extreme than the value or values determined by the level of significance

33. What happens to total revenue after a price cut if demand is unit elastic?

    A. Increases
    B. Decreases
    C. Stays the same

34. What is the most likely long-run result from an increase in rents?

    A. Quantity of housing increases and rents fall
    B. Housing shortage, wasteful search, and a black market
    C. Quantity of housing decreases and rents increase

35. Which is the most likely result of a tax when demand is perfectly inelastic?

    A. Price increase and sellers pay the entire tax
    B. Price increase and buyers pay the entire tax
    C. No price increase and sellers pay the entire tax

36. What is the shape of the long-run cost curve with economies of scale?

    A. Upward sloping
    B. Downward sloping
    C. U-shaped

37. Which is least likely to apply to a single-price monopoly compared to a perfectly competitive market?

    A. The monopoly charges a higher price
    B. The monopoly has higher marginal cost
    C. The monopoly produces smaller output

38. Which is least likely to apply to an oligopoly with one firm that dominates?

    A. The dominant firm acts like a monopoly
    B. The prisoners' dilemma applies to the small firms
    C. The small firms act as price-takers

39. Which is least likely to cause movements along the demand curve for labor demand curve?

    A. The wage rate increases
    B. The wage rate increases
    C. The price of a firm's output changes

40. What type of unemployment arises from normal labor turnover?

    A. Frictional
    B. Structural
    C. Cyclical

41. The view that wage rates and prices of goods and services are sticky is most likely held by which school of thought?

    A. Classical
    B. New classical
    C. New Keynesian

42. Which is most likely to be considered a tool of the Federal Reserve System for influencing the quantity of money?

    A. Creating liquidity
    B. Making loans
    C. Conducting open market operations

43. Which is least likely to be an automatic stabilizer feature of fiscal policy?

    A. Induced taxes
    B. Needs-tested spending
    C. Increased exports

44. Which decision rule for monetary policy shoots for a target level of the monetary base and is based on the quantity theory of money?

    A. Instrument rule
    B. Taylor rule
    C. McCallum rule

45. How are business activities classified?

    A. Assets, liabilities, equity, revenue, and expense
    B. Operating activities, investing activities, and financing activities
    C. Balance sheet, income statement, statement of cash flows, and statement of owners' equity

46. Which category includes inventory?

    A. Assets
    B. Liabilities
    C. Owner's equity

47. What entry is made for cash movement in the same period as accounting recognition?

    A. Adjusting entry
    B. Originating entry
    C. No accrual entry needed

48. Under IAS No. 1, what component of a complete set of financial statements should include a summary of significant accounting policies and other explanatory information?

    A. Notes
    B. Management's letter
    C. Supplemental schedule

49. What is an income statement with a subtotal for gross profit?

    A. Multi-step format
    B. Single-step format
    C. Grouping by function

50. Which is least likely to be considered a special revenue recognition method?

    A. Accrual basis
    B. Cost recovery
    C. Completed contract

51. Which is closest to the profit that will be reported in the first year under the percentage-of-completion method if the costs incurred and paid are $0.6 million the first year, $3.0 million the second year, and $0.8 million the third year; and the amounts billed and received are $1.2 million the first year, $2.8 million the second year, and $1.3 million the third year?

    A. $0.0 million
    B. $0.1 million
    C. $0.2 million

52. Which would be least likely to require an estimate for depreciation expense recognition?

    A. Salvage value
    B. Assets' useful life
    C. Nonrecurring items

53. Which are closest to the basic and diluted EPS using the if-converted method if a company had $500,000 in net income; a weighted average of 400,000 shares outstanding, an outstanding 20,000 options with an exercise price of $30; and an average share price of $50?

    A. EPS = $1.22, diluted EPS = $1.25
    B. EPS = $1.25; diluted EPS = $1.23
    C. EPS = $1.25, diluted EPS = $1.21

54. What classification of unrealized gains and losses from financial instruments are recognized in shareholders' equity as a separate line item, as other comprehensive income?

    A. Held to maturity
    B. Available for sale
    C. Trading securities

55. If cash is $500; marketable securities are $200; receivables are $300; other current assets are $500; and current liabilities are $500, which is closest to the quick ratio?

    A. 1
    B. 2
    C. 3

56. What category on a cash flow statement includes buying and selling assets such as property?

  A. Operating
  B. Financing
  C. Investing

57. Which is the most likely effect if a company accrues wages of $1,000 and collects accounts receivable of $2,000?

  A. Current ratio will increase
  B. Net income will increase
  C. Cash from operations will increase

58. If a company wrote down inventory by $200,000 from $800,000 due to an oversupply, and the next year prices increased 15%, what will inventory most likely be reported at under IFRS?

  A. $600,000
  B. $800,000
  C. $920,000

59. In a period of declining prices, which is most likely greater for a company that uses FIFO compared to a company that uses LIFO?

  A. Net income
  B. Cost of sales
  C. Income taxes

60. Which would most likely be greater from capitalizing rather than expensing research and development costs?

  A. Cash flow from operations
  B. Financial leverage
  C. Total asset turnover

61. If company A has equipment that cost $6 million, accumulated depreciation of $4 million, and annual depreciation expense of $1 million; company B has equipment that cost $16 million, accumulated depreciation of $10 million, and annual depreciation expense of $2 million; and company C has equipment that cost $21 million, accumulated depreciation of $9 million, and annual depreciation expense of $3 million; which company's equipment has the lowest average age?

    A. Company A
    B. Company B
    C. Company C

62. If a U.S. company had U.S. EBIT of $100,000 and foreign EBIT of $100,000 for 2008 and the same for 2009; for 2009 had current federal income taxes of $28,000, current foreign income taxes of $20,000, deferred federal income taxes of negative $5,000, and deferred foreign income taxes of $1,000; and for 2008 had current federal income taxes of $20,000, current foreign income taxes of $22,000, deferred federal income taxes of $6,000, and deferred foreign income taxes of $2,000, in which year was the effective tax rate the highest?

    A. 2008
    B. 2009
    C. The same in 2008 and 2009

63. What would a company's cash tax payments be compared to the provision for taxes if the net deferred tax liability was smaller than the prior year?

    A. Higher
    B. Lower
    C. The same

64. If a company with $600 million in liabilities and $400 in shareholders' equity plans to make $200 in purchase commitments which an analyst will treat as debt, what is the new debt to total capital ratio?

    A. 50%
    B. 60%
    C. 67%

65. If for 2008 the average days sales outstanding is 15 and sales are $300 million, and for 2009 the average days sales outstanding is 12 and sales are $400 million, what is the change in accounts receivable from 2008 to 2009 closest to?

    A. Decrease of $2 million
    B. Decrease of $1 million
    C. Increase of $1 million

Exam 2

66. What is the most appropriate conclusion if company A had current assets of $4,000, current liabilities of $1,000, total debt of $6,000, and shareholders' equity of $3,000; and company B had current assets of $6,000, current liabilities of $5,000, total debt of $15,000, and shareholders' equity of $50,000?

   A. Company A is more liquid and solvent
   B. Company A is more liquid and company B is more solvent
   C. Company B is more liquid and company A is more solvent

67. What are the basic financial statements required to be presented under both IFRS and U.S. GAAP?

   A. Assets, liabilities, equity, income, and expenses
   B. Assets, liabilities, equity, statement of cash flows, and statement of changes in equity
   C. Balance sheet, income statement, statement of cash flows, and statement of changes in equity

68. How are inventory write-downs treated under U.S. GAAP?

   A. Not allowed
   B. Allowed but not reversible
   C. Allowed and subject to reversal

69. Which is least likely to be a basic principle of capital budgeting?

   A. Decisions are based on cash flows
   B. Timing of cash flows is crucial
   C. Cash flows are based on sunk costs

70. What is the investment decision using the profitability index (PI) method if the initial investment is $45 million, the cash flows are $15 million per year at the end of the each of 4 years, and the required rate of return is 10%?

   A. Do not invest because PI < 0
   B. Invest because PI > 1
   C. Do not invest because PI < 1

71. Which is least likely to apply to the NPV method of evaluating projects?

   A. Preferred to IRR method
   B. Sensitive to timing or pattern of cash flows
   C. Assumes cash flows reinvested at the IRR

72. What are the after-tax costs of debt and equity if the before-tax cost of debt is 8.0%, the before-tax cost of equity is 10.0%, and the tax rate is 20%?

    A. 6.4% for debt and 8.0% for equity
    B. 6.4% for debt and 10.0% for equity
    C. 10.0% for debt and 10.0% for equity

73. What is an estimate of the cost of equity for a company with a beta of 1.2 if the average T-bond rate for 100 years is 4% and the average market return for the same period is 9%?

    A. 9%
    B. 10%
    C. 11%

74. Which is closest to the cost of equity using CAPM if the unlevered beta for comparable companies is 1.6, the debt to equity ratio is 1.8, the marginal tax rate is 20%, the risk-free rate is 4%, and the equity risk premium is 5%?

    A. 23.5%
    B. 24.5%
    C. 25.5%

75. Which is closest to the weighted average cost of capital (WACC) if the average unlevered beta for comparable companies is 0.9, the tax rate is 30%, the target debt-to-equity ratio is 0.8, the risk-free rate is 3%, the equity risk premium is 5%, and the cost of debt is 150 basis points over the risk-free rate?

    A. 3%
    B. 4%
    C. 7%

76. Which is closest to the cost of trade credit if the terms are 2/10, net 30, and the account is paid on the 20th day?

    A. 9%
    B. 45%
    C. 109%

77. Which is closest to the net profit margin using DuPont analysis if, in millions, operating income is $530, revenues are $13,565, income before taxes is $461, taxes are $126, average total assets are $6,767, and average shareholders' equity is $3,223?

    A. 2.47%
    B. 4.95%
    C. 10.39%

78. Which is most likely to be considered good corporate governance?

    A. A company offering shares at discounted prices to management prior to a public offering but not to board members and insiders
    B. A company offering shares at discounted prices to board members and insiders prior to a public offering but not to management
    C. A company prohibiting itself from offering shares at discounted prices to management, board members, and insiders prior to a public offering

79. What attribute refers to rapid and unbiased adjustments to new information?

    A. Liquidity
    B. Internal efficiency
    C. External efficiency

80. The total market value of stock listed on the NYSE at the end of 2004 was closest to $12.5

    A. Billion
    B. Trillion
    C. Quadrillion

81. Who is least likely to execute a public order?

    A. Floor brokers
    B. Registered traders
    C. Commission brokers

82. For a margin account with an initial deposit of $50,000, a stock selling at $35, and a prevailing margin rate of 40%, which is closest to the profit if the price rises to $45?

    A. $24,000
    B. $36,000
    C. $48,000

83. Which is closest to the return on the unweighted index using the arithmetic mean for three stocks with prices at the beginning of the year for stocks A, B, and C of $60, $20, and $18, respectively, prices at the end of the year for stocks A, B, and C of $80, $35, and $25, respectively, and a market value of $1 million in each stock at the beginning of the year?

    A. 47.5%
    B. 48.0%
    C. 49.1%

84. Which is least likely to be considered an anomaly with respect to the semi-strong from of the EMH?

    A. Abnormal returns from low P/E stocks
    B. No abnormal returns following earnings surprises
    C. Abnormal returns in January compared to December

85. If markets are efficient, how can portfolio managers add value?

    A. Mismatching portfolios
    B. Providing diversification
    C. Maximizing transaction costs

86. Which is least likely to explain why valid anomalies may not be profitable?

    A. Conditions governing anomalies may change
    B. Documented anomalies are based on variances
    C. Positive abnormal returns do not mean positive returns

87. Which is least likely to decrease the growth rate of equity earnings without any external financing?

    A. Decreased payout ratio
    B. Decreased retention rate
    C. Decreased return on equity

88. Which is closest to value of a share with current dividends of $3 per share, return on equity (ROE) of 17.5%, a required rate of return of 15%, and current earnings per share of $5?

    A. $26.75
    B. $30.57
    C. $40.13

89. What are examples of structural economic changes that may influence industries?

    A. Demographics, technology, politics, and regulation
    B. Population growth, industry, politics, and regulation
    C. Population growth, industry, exchange rates, and oversight

90. Which is least likely to be considered a drawback of using price to earnings (P /E) ratios?

    A. EPS cannot be negative
    B. Management can distort EPS
    C. Earnings often have volatile, transient components

91. An investor long a forward contract has

    A. A right to buy at a specific price
    B. An obligation to deliver at a certain price
    C. An obligation to take delivery at a certain price

92. If short-term rates increase after an investor enters into a forward contract on 90-day Treasury bills, the short will have

    A. A gain on the contract because when short-term rates rise, Treasury bill prices fall
    B. A loss on the contract because when short-term rates rise, Treasury bill prices fall
    C. A loss on the contract because when short-term rates rise, Treasury bill prices rise

93. What options can be exercised at any time prior to expiration?

    A. American options
    B. European options
    C. European and American options

94. The party making the fixed-rate payment under a swap contract could also be required to make the variable under

    A. An equity swap
    B. A plain vanilla swap
    C. An interest rate swap

95. For a $50 million plain vanilla interest rate swap, the end user makes semi-annual fixed rate payments at the rate of 5.75%, and the dealer makes semiannual floating payments at LIBOR, which was 5.15% on the last settlement period. Payments are made on the basis of 180 days in a settlement period, floating payments are made on the basis of 360 days in a year, and fixed payments on the basis of 365 days in a year. Which party pays what amount after the payments are netted?

    A. The party paying fixed will pay the party paying floating $130,308
    B. The party paying fixed will pay the party paying floating $150,000
    C. The party paying floating will pay the party paying fixed$130,308

96. What is the profit on a covered call option, where the exercise price is X and the price of the underlying security is S?

    A. $S_t - S_0 - Max\ (0, S_t - X)$ - option cost
    B. $S_t - S_0 - Max\ (0, X - S_t)$ + option cost
    C. $S_t - S_0 - Max\ (0, S_t - X)$ + option cost

97. What is a contract between a company and its bondholders that could be positive, setting forth activities the borrower promises to do, or could be negative, setting forth limitations and restrictions on the borrower's activities?

    A. Covenant
    B. Indenture
    C. Embedded option

98. An investor who plans to hold a security one year is considering purchasing a Treasury security that matures in one year, or, alternatively, purchasing a Treasury security that matures in 30 years. Which best describes the difference in the major risk associated with the investment alternatives?

    A. The 1-year Treasury exposes the investor to interest rate risk
    B. The 30-year Treasury exposes the investor to interest rate risk
    C. The 1-year Treasury exposes the investor to liquidity risk

99. Which issue has the greatest interest rate risk: issue 1 with a 5% coupon and 15 year maturity, issue 2 with a 4% coupon and 20 year maturity, or issue 3 with a 6% coupon and 10 year maturity,

    A. Issue 1
    B. Issue 2
    C. Issue 3

100. Which is closest to the dollar price change of a bond, with a market value of $5 million and a duration of 10.44, for a 100 basis point change in yield?

    A. $130,500
    B. $261,000
    C. $522,000

101. Which feature is least likely to increase reinvestment risk?

    A. Callable
    B. Zero-coupon
    C. Pre-payment option

102. If interest rate volatility increases, which bond will have an decrease in price?

    A. Putable bond
    B. Callable bond
    C. Option-free bond

103. The accrued interest on Treasury strips

    A. Is tax free
    B. Is taxed in the year received
    C. Is taxed each year even though interest is not received

104. What is the absolute yield spread between a 5-year bond with a 5.11% yield and a 5-year on-the-run Treasury with a 4.18% yield?

    A. 93 basis points
    B. 22.2%
    C. 1.222

105. Which is closest to the present value of a 5-year amortizing security with end-of-year payments of $2,309.75 that include all interest and principal, using a discount rate of 6%?

    A. $9,729.51
    B. $10,012.89
    C. $10,313.28

106. What approach values a bond as a package of cash flows, with each cash flow viewed as a zero-coupon bond and each cash flow discounted at its own unique discount rate?

    A. Arbitrage-free approach
    B. Monte Carlo simulation model
    C. Traditional valuation methodology

107. Which is closest to the value of a $100 par, 2-year, 6% coupon Treasury bond if the forward rates for the periods 1, 2, 3 and 4 are 3.00%, 3.60%, 3.92%, and 5.15%, respectively?

    A. $96
    B. $102
    C. $104

108. For an 8% option-free bond, the price changes by 3% if the rates fall 50 basis points. What is the change if rates increase by 50 basis points?

    A. Less than 3%
    B. Exactly 3%
    C. More than 3%

109. If bond A has a price of 90 and modified duration of 6, and bond B has a price of 50 and modified duration of 4, then bond A will have a greater price volatility in terms of

    A. Dollar price change and percentage price change
    B. Dollar price change but not percentage price change
    C. Percentage price change but not dollar price change

110. Which is closest to percentage price change if yields change from 6% to 4% based on duration and the convexity adjustment of a 9% coupon 20-year option-free bond selling at 134.67 to yield 6%, if the price increases to 137.59 at a yield of 5.8%, and the price decreases to 131.84 at a yield of 6.2%?

    A. -24.6%
    B. -21.3%
    C. -18.0%

111. Which is least accurate regarding real estate investments?

    A. Liquid
    B. Bought and sold intermittently in a generally local marketplace
    C. Not directly comparable to other properties, only approximately comparable

112. An office building investment has gross potential rental income of $350,000; a 4% estimated vacancy and collection losses; $26,000 in insurance and property taxes; $18,000 in utilities; $23,000 in repairs and maintenance; $40,000 in depreciation; and $18,000 in interest on the proposed financing. A similar office building with $500,000 in operating income was sold for $4 million. Another similar office building with $225,000 in operating income was sold for $1.6 million. Which is closest to the appraised value of the office building investment using the income approach?

   A. $1,721,805
   B. $2,022,556
   C. $2,077,793

113. Which is most accurate regarding real estate indexes?

   A. Appraisal-based indexes are more volatile than REIT indexes
   B. Appraisal-based indexes have low correlation with REIT indexes
   C. Appraisal-based indexes are strongly correlated with the stock market

114. Which is closest to the NPV of a project with a $1 million investment and an expected $16 million payoff at the end of 7 years if it succeeds, with a failure probability in year 1 of 0.25, in year 2 of 0.22, and in each of years 3 through 7 of 0.20, and a cost of equity of 18%?

   A. -$37,165
   B. $37,165
   C. $154,527

115. Which investment strategy seeks growth in the portfolio through both capital gains and reinvesting income?

   A. Total return
   B. Current income
   C. Capital appreciation

116. Which is the most liquid?

   A. Real estate
   B. Treasury bills
   C. Venture capital

117. Which is closest to the standard deviation of a portfolio with a 50% weight in each of two securities, both of which have an expected return of 20% and a standard deviation of 10%, if the correlation coefficient is -1.0?

    A. 0%
    B. 5%
    C. 10%

118. How many correlation coefficients are needed for a two-asset portfolio?

    A. 1
    B. 2
    C. 3

119. How much of an investor's wealth is invested in the market portfolio if the investor's portfolio is to the right of the market portfolio on the capital market line (CML)?

    A. 100%
    B. Less than 100%
    C. Greater than 100%

120. If the risk free rate is 4%, the market risk premium is 8%, stocks A, B, C, and D have betas of 0.9, 1.0, 1.1, and 1.2, respectively, how many stocks are overvalued and undervalued if all four stocks have an estimated annual return of 12.8%?

    A. 1 overvalued and 2 undervalued
    B. 2 overvalued and 2 undervalued
    C. 2 overvalued and 2 undervalued

1. C	41. C	81. B
2. B	42. C	82. B
3. A	43. C	83. C
4. A	44. C	84. B
5. B	45. B	85. B
6. B	46. A	86. B
7. A	47. C	87. A
8. A	48. A	88. C
9. B	49. A	89. A
10. C	50. A	90. A
11. C	51. B	91. C
12. B	52. C	92. A
13. A	53. B	93. A
14. A	54. B	94. A
15. B	55. B	95. A
16. B	56. C	96. C
17. C	57. C	97. A
18. A	58. B	98. B
19. C	59. B	99. B
20. B	60. A	100. C
21. A	61. C	101. B
22. A	62. A	102. B
23. B	63. A	103. C
24. B	64. C	104. A
25. A	65. C	105. A
26. C	66. B	106. A
27. B	67. C	107. C
28. B	68. B	108. A
29. C	69. C	109. A
30. C	70. B	110. C
31. B	71. C	111. A
32. B	72. B	112. B
33. C	73. B	113. B
34. A	74. A	114. A
35. B	75. C	115. A
36. B	76. C	116. B
37. B	77. A	117. A
38. B	78. C	118. A
39. C	79. C	119. C
40. A	80. B	120. A

1. If a member resides in a country with more strict securities laws than the CFA Institute's Code and Standards and does business in a country with less strict securities laws than the CFA Institute's Code and Standards, the member must adhere to the

    A. Code and Standards
    B. Law of the less strict country
    *C.Law of the more strict county (Standard I(A) - knowledge of the law)

2. CFA charterholder Sheth is the investment manager of the Rego County Employees Pension Plan. The plan requested proposals for a foreign equity manager, and after the board interviewed the most qualified firms, Sheth went against the staff recommendation and recommended Raman Advisors. A reporter called and asked if the recommendation was related to Raman Advisors being one of the sponsors of an investment fact-finding trip to Asia that Sheth made earlier in the year. The trip was arranged by the Pension Investment Academy. The Academy obtains support for trips from sponsors such as Raman Advisors, then the Academy pays for the expenses of pension fund managers like Sheth. Did Sheth violate any Standards of Professional Conduct?

    A. No
    *B.Yes, relating to independence and objectivity (Standard I(B) - independence and objectivity)
    C. Yes, relating to diligence and reasonable basis

3. CFA charterholder Ong creates and distributes marketing material for his firm. He creates and distributes a performance report showing the firm's Asian equity composite has 350 billion yen in assets. The correct number is 35 billion and the 50 billion was a typographical error. The material is distributed before Ong catches the mistake. Ong ceases distribution of the incorrect material, corrects it, and informs those who received the incorrect report of the error. Did Ong violate any Standards of Professional Conduct?

    *A. No (Standard I(C) - misrepresentation)
    B. Yes, relating to misrepresentation
    C. Yes, relating to independence and objectivity

4. Which is an element of a firewall?

    *A. Watch list (Standard II(A) - material nonpublic information)
    B. Mosaic theory
    C. Selective disclosure

5. CFA charterholder Chakak has hedge fund clients who sold a security short, and Chakak releases a report to sensationalize negative results shortly before the company reports actual earnings. Chakak is least likely to have violated the Standards of Professional Conduct relating to

    A. Market manipulation
    *B.Loyalty, prudence, and care (Standard II(B) - market manipulation and Standard V(A) - diligence and reasonable basis)
    C. Diligence and reasonable basis

6. CFA charterholder Sharmar is the CIO for an insurance company whose investment policy provides for liquid low-risk investments. Sharmar invests a portion of company assets in private equity. Which Standard of Professional Conduct did Sharmar least likely violate?

    A. Suitability
    *B.Fair dealing (Standard III(C) - suitability and Standard III(A) - loyalty, prudence, and care)
    C. Loyalty, prudence, and care

7. CFA charterholder Candela circulates marketing material showing 1, 2, and 3 year returns, plus a separate sheet with quarterly unaudited and unverified returns. Did Candela violate any Standards of Professional Conduct?

    *A. No (Standard III(D) - performance presentation)
    B. Yes, by using unaudited and unverified results
    C. Yes, by not complying with the Global Investment Performance Standards (GIPS)

8. CFA charterholder Gwyer is an asset manager for a pension fund and is advised that a client has probably violated tax and fiduciary regulations and laws related to a pension fund. What is Gwyer's least appropriate response after informing her supervisor, if her employer is not successful in taking steps to have the client remedy the situation, and after seeking the advice of legal counsel?

    *A. Do nothing (Standard III(E) - preservation of confidentiality)
    B. Resign as asset manager
    C. Disclose the evidence of the legal violations

9. CFA charterholder DeArmond signs an agreement with his employer to not solicit former clients for one year after termination. DeArmond terminates and consults an attorney, who advises him that the agreement is most likely not enforceable. DeArmond solicits former clients less than one year after termination. Did DeArmond violate any Standards of Professional Conduct?

 A. No
 *B. Yes, relating to loyalty (Standard IV(A) - loyalty)
 C. Yes, relating to disclosure of conflicts

10. CFA charterholder Yang supervises CFA charterholder Springer at a registered investment advisory and registered broker/dealer firm. Yang finds that Springer places a large number of trades of a thinly traded security at the end of each month and asks Springer about it, who replies that it was a client's request. Six months later, Springer is investigated for manipulating prices at month's end. Which Standard of Professional Conduct did Yang most likely violate?

 A. Misrepresentation
 B. Market manipulation
 *C. Responsibilities of supervisors (Standard IV(C) - responsibilities of supervisors)

11. CFA charterholder Bergman is an aggressive growth manager that has invested in small caps since inception. Bergman changed its maximum capitalization from $250 million to $500 million, and prepared literature to inform prospective clients and third-party consultants of the change. Did Bergman violate any Standards of Professional Conduct?

 A. No
 B. Yes, by misrepresenting the definition of small cap
 *C. Yes, by not notifying all of the existing clients of the change (Standard V(B) - communications with clients and prospective clients)

12. CFA charterholder Chim does not recommend purchase of a stock for his employer's account because he wants to purchase it for his personal account first. Did Chim violate any Standards of Professional Conduct?

 A. No
 *B. Yes, relating to priority of transactions (Standard VI(B) - priority of transactions)
 C. Yes, relating to disclosure of conflicts of interest

13. CFA charterholder Fossen manages accounts for high wealth investors and a family account. He only allocates IPO shares to the family account after the other clients. The best course of action for Fossen under the Standards of Professional Conduct is to

    *A. Continue management of the family account and treat it like any other client (Standard VI(B) - priority of transactions and Standard III(B) - fair dealing)
    B. Discontinue management of the family account and transfer it to another firm
    C. Discontinue management of the family account and transfer it to another broker at the same firm

14. Which is an improper reference to the CFA Institute, the CFA designation, or the CFA program?

    *A. CFA, Expected 2012 (Standard VII(B) - reference to the CFA Institute, the CFA designation, and the CFA program)
    B. Passed CFA Level I
    C. CFA charterholders are committed to high ethical standards

15. CFA charterholder Shahperi works for an investment counseling firm. Sopko, a new client, meets Shahperi for the first time. After introducing themselves, before asking about investment objectives, Shahperi immediately explains to Sopko that she has found an undervalued stock and she recommends that Sopko buy it. Did Shahperi violate any Standards of Professional Conduct?

    A. No
    *B.Yes, related to suitability (Standard III(C) - suitability)
    C. Yes, related to diligence and reasonable basis

16. CFA charterholder Landrigan tells a prospective client that his clients have averaged 30% return per year. Landrigan does not mention that he has very few clients, and one client who ignored his advice has significant gains that brought the average up. Excluding the one client with the big gains, the average would have been 8%. Did Landrigan violate any Standards of Professional Conduct?

    A. No
    *B.Yes, related to misrepresentation (Standard I(C) - misrepresentation)
    C. Yes, related to communication with clients and prospective clients

17. To comply with the GIPS, a firm must initially show GIPS-compliant history for a minimum of

    A. Two years, or since inception if the firm has been in existence less than two years
    B. Three years, or since inception if the firm has been in existence less than three years
    *C.Five years, or since inception if the firm has been in existence less than five years

18. Which is an example of a GIPS composite?

    *A. Large cap growth composite
    B.   Mediterranean region composite
    C.   Composite of portfolios over $100 million

19. What is the difference between a $100,000 lump sum and a 20-year annuity with $10,000 beginning-of-year payments using a discount rate of 8% per year?

    A. The lump sum is greater by $6,036
    B. The lump sum is greater by $1,819
    *C. The annuity is greater by $6,036 = $10,000[(1 - 1/1.08^20) / (.08/1.08)] - $100,000; n = 20, i = 8, PMT = 10,000, FV = 0; PV (BEGIN) = $106,036; $106,036 - $100,000 = $6,036

20. What is the preferred performance measure for a portfolio?

    A. Internal rate of return (IRR)
    *B. Time-weighted rate of return
    C. Money-weighted rate of return

21. What is the standard deviation of the deviation of a portfolio's return from the benchmark return?

    *A. Tracking risk
    B. Coefficient of variation
    C. Cumulative relative frequency

22. What is the average squared deviation below the mean?

    *A. Semivariance
    B. Semideviation
    C. Geometric mean

23. If stocks had a mean return of 12% with a standard deviation of 20%, bonds had a mean return of 6% with a standard deviation of 4%, and the risk-free rate is 4%, which had superior risk-adjusted performance as measured by the Sharpe Ratio?

    A. Stocks
    *B. Bonds, (12% - 4%)/20% < (6% - 4%)/4%
    C. They are the same

24. What is a characteristic of a normal distribution?

    A. The mean is less than the median
    *B.The mean is equal to the median
    C. The mean is greater than the median

25. If the probability of EPS increasing in a quarter is 60%, what is the probability that earnings will decrease or remain the same for two quarters in a row?

    *A. 16% = (100% - 60%) (100% - 60%)
    B. 36%
    C. 40%

26. What is the correlation between the S&P 500 and the EAFE for a portfolio with 40% in the S&P 500 with a variance of 2.25%, 35% in bonds with a variance of 0.25%, and 25% in the EAFE with a variance of 3.24%, given covariances between the S&P 500 and bonds of 0.60%, between the S&P 500 and the EAFE of 1.44%, and between bonds and the EAFE of 0.36%?

    A. -0.28
    B. 0.35
    *C.0.53 = 1.44% / [(2.25%^.5)(3.24%^.5)

27. Given that P(X<=1)=0.10, P(X<=2)=0.50, P(X<=3)=0.70, and P(X<=4)=1.00, what is p(2)?

    A. 0.1
    *B.0.4
    C. 0.5

28. If 40% of pension funds have alternative investments, what describes the number of funds out of 100 that have alternative investments?

    A. Bernoulli trial
    *B.Binomial random variable
    C. Continuous random variable

29. To estimate risks in extremely unfavorable combinations of events, a risk management technique that involves examination of the portfolio under specified situations is called

    A. Shortfall risk
    B. Value at risk
    *C.Stress testing/scenario analysis

30. Which treats time as advancing in finite intervals?

    A. Continuous compounding
    B. Lognormal compounding
    *C.Discrete compounding

31. If the mean income of companies on a stock index is $60 million with a standard deviation of $100 million, which is closest to the 95% confidence interval for the sample mean for a sample size of 100?

    A. $30 million to $90 million
    *B.$40 million to $80 million = $60 million +/- 2[$100 million / (100^.5)]
    C. $50 million to $70 million

32. Which is least accurate regarding the statistical decision in hypothesis testing?

    A. Reject the null hypothesis if the test statistic is at least as extreme as the value or values determined by the level of significance
    *B.Reject the null hypothesis if the result is not statistically significant
    C. Do not reject the null hypothesis if the test statistic is less extreme than the value or values determined by the level of significance

33. What happens to total revenue after a price cut if demand is unit elastic?

    A. Increases
    B. Decreases
    *C.Stays the same

34. What is the most likely long-run result from an increase in rents?

    *A. Quantity of housing increases and rents fall
    B. Housing shortage, wasteful search, and a black market
    C. Quantity of housing decreases and rents increase

35. Which is the most likely result of a tax when demand is perfectly inelastic?

    A. Price increase and sellers pay the entire tax
    *B.Price increase and buyers pay the entire tax
    C. No price increase and sellers pay the entire tax

36. What is the shape of the long-run cost curve with economies of scale?

    A. Upward sloping
    *B.Downward sloping
    C. U-shaped

37. Which is least likely to apply to a single-price monopoly compared to a perfectly competitive market?

    A. The monopoly charges a higher price
    *B.The monopoly has higher marginal cost
    C. The monopoly produces smaller output

38. Which is least likely to apply to an oligopoly with one firm that dominates?

    A. The dominant firm acts like a monopoly
    *B.The prisoners' dilemma applies to the small firms
    C. The small firms act as price-takers

39. Which is least likely to cause movements along the demand curve for labor demand curve?

    A. The wage rate increases
    B. The wage rate increases
    *C.The price of a firm's output changes

40. What type of unemployment arises from normal labor turnover?

    *A. Frictional
    B. Structural
    C. Cyclical

41. The view that wage rates and prices of goods and services are sticky is most likely held by which school of thought?

    A. Classical
    B. New classical
    *C.New Keynesian

42. Which is most likely to be considered a tool of the Federal Reserve System for influencing the quantity of money?

    A. Creating liquidity
    B. Making loans
    *C.Conducting open market operations

43. Which is least likely to be an automatic stabilizer feature of fiscal policy?

    A. Induced taxes
    B. Needs-tested spending
    *C.Increased exports

44. Which decision rule for monetary policy shoots for a target level of the monetary base and is based on the quantity theory of money?

    A. Instrument rule
    B. Taylor rule
    *C.McCallum rule

45. How are business activities classified?

    A. Assets, liabilities, equity, revenue, and expense
    *B.Operating activities, investing activities, and financing activities
    C. Balance sheet, income statement, statement of cash flows, and statement of owners' equity

46. Which category includes inventory?

    *A. Assets
    B. Liabilities
    C. Owner's equity

47. What entry is made for cash movement in the same period as accounting recognition?

    A. Adjusting entry
    B. Originating entry
    *C.No accrual entry needed

48. Under IAS No. 1, what component of a complete set of financial statements should include a summary of significant accounting policies and other explanatory information?

    *A. Notes
    B. Management's letter
    C. Supplemental schedule

49. What is an income statement with a subtotal for gross profit?

    *A. Multi-step format
    B. Single-step format
    C. Grouping by function

50. Which is least likely to be considered a special revenue recognition method?

    *A. Accrual basis
    B. Cost recovery
    C. Completed contract

51. Which is closest to the profit that will be reported in the first year under the percentage-of-completion method if the costs incurred and paid are $0.6 million the first year, $3.0 million the second year, and $0.8 million the third year; and the amounts billed and received are $1.2 million the first year, $2.8 million the second year, and $1.3 million the third year?

    A. $0.0 million
    *B.$0.1 million = ($0.6/$4.4) $5.3 million - $0.6 million
    C. $0.2 million

52. Which would be least likely to require an estimate for depreciation expense recognition?

    A. Salvage value
    B. Assets' useful life
    *C.Nonrecurring items

53. Which are closest to the basic and diluted EPS using the if-converted method if a company had $500,000 in net income; a weighted average of 400,000 shares outstanding, an outstanding 20,000 options with an exercise price of $30; and an average share price of $50?

    A. EPS = $1.22, diluted EPS = $1.25
    *B.EPS = $1.25; diluted EPS = $1.23; $1.25 = $500,000 / 400,000; $1.23 = $500,000 / [400,000 + 20,000 - 20,000 ($30/$50)]
    C. EPS = $1.25, diluted EPS = $1.21

54. What classification of unrealized gains and losses from financial instruments are recognized in shareholders' equity as a separate line item, as other comprehensive income?

    A. Held to maturity
    *B.Available for sale
    C. Trading securities

55. If cash is $500; marketable securities are $200; receivables are $300; other current assets are $500; and current liabilities are $500, which is closest to the quick ratio?

    A. 1
    *B.2 = ($500 + $200 + $300) / $500
    C. 3

56. What category on a cash flow statement includes buying and selling assets such as property?

    A. Operating
    B. Financing
    *C.Investing

57. Which is the most likely effect if a company accrues wages of $1,000 and collects accounts receivable of $2,000?

    A. Current ratio will increase
    B. Net income will increase
    *C.Cash from operations will increase

58. If a company wrote down inventory by $200,000 from $800,000 due to an oversupply, and the next year prices increased 15%, what will inventory most likely be reported at under IFRS?

    A. $600,000
    *B.$800,000
    C. $920,000

59. In a period of declining prices, which is most likely greater for a company that uses FIFO compared to a company that uses LIFO?

    A. Net income
    *B.Cost of sales
    C. Income taxes

60. Which would most likely be greater from capitalizing rather than expensing research and development costs?

    *A. Cash flow from operations
    B. Financial leverage
    C. Total asset turnover

61. If company A has equipment that cost $6 million, accumulated depreciation of $4 million, and annual depreciation expense of $1 million; company B has equipment that cost $16 million, accumulated depreciation of $10 million, and annual depreciation expense of $2 million; and company C has equipment that cost $21 million, accumulated depreciation of $9 million, and annual depreciation expense of $3 million; which company's equipment has the lowest average age?

    A. Company A
    B. Company B
    *C.Company C; $9/$3 < $4/$1 < $10/$2

62. If a U.S. company had U.S. EBIT of $100,000 and foreign EBIT of $100,000 for 2008 and the same for 2009; for 2009 had current federal income taxes of $28,000, current foreign income taxes of $20,000, deferred federal income taxes of negative $5,000, and deferred foreign income taxes of $1,000; and for 2008 had current federal income taxes of $20,000, current foreign income taxes of $22,000, deferred federal income taxes of $6,000, and deferred foreign income taxes of $2,000, in which year was the effective tax rate the highest?

    *A. 2008; ($20,000 + $22,000 + $6,000 + $2,000) / ($100,000 + $100,000) >
         ($28,000 + $20,000 - $5,000 + $1,000) / ($100,000 + $100,000)
    B. 2009
    C. The same in 2008 and 2009

63. What would a company's cash tax payments be compared to the provision for taxes if the net deferred tax liability was smaller than the prior year?

    *A. Higher
    B. Lower
    C. The same

64. If a company with $600 million in liabilities and $400 in shareholders' equity plans to make $200 in purchase commitments which an analyst will treat as debt, what is the new debt to total capital ratio?

    A. 50%
    B. 60%
    *C.67% = ($600 + $200) / ($600 + $200 + $400)

65. If for 2008 the average days sales outstanding is 15 and sales are $300 million, and for 2009 the average days sales outstanding is 12 and sales are $400 million, what is the change in accounts receivable from 2008 to 2009 closest to?

    A. Decrease of $2 million
    B. Decrease of $1 million
    *C.Increase of $1 million = $400 million / (365/12) - $300 million / (365/15)

66. What is the most appropriate conclusion if company A had current assets of $4,000, current liabilities of $1,000, total debt of $6,000, and shareholders' equity of $3,000; and company B had current assets of $6,000, current liabilities of $5,000, total debt of $15,000, and shareholders' equity of $50,000?

    A. Company A is more liquid and solvent
    *B.Company A is more liquid and company B is more solvent; company A's current ratio is greater: $4,000/$1,000>$6,000/$5,000 and company B's debt-to-equity ratio is lower: $15,000/$50,000 < $6,000/$3,000
    C. Company B is more liquid and company A is more solvent

67. What are the basic financial statements required to be presented under both IFRS and U.S. GAAP?

    A. Assets, liabilities, equity, income, and expenses
    B. Assets, liabilities, equity, statement of cash flows, and statement of changes in equity
    *C.Balance sheet, income statement, statement of cash flows, and statement of changes in equity

68. How are inventory write-downs treated under U.S. GAAP?

    A. Not allowed
    *B.Allowed but not reversible
    C. Allowed and subject to reversal

69. Which is least likely to be a basic principle of capital budgeting?

    A. Decisions are based on cash flows
    B. Timing of cash flows is crucial
    *C.Cash flows are based on sunk costs

70. What is the investment decision using the profitability index (PI) method if the initial investment is $45 million, the cash flows are $15 million per year at the end of the each of 4 years, and the required rate of return is 10%?

    A. Do not invest because PI < 0
    *B.Invest because PI > 1; $47.55 / $45 > 1; n = 4, i = 10, PMT = 15, FV = 0; PV = 47.55
    C. Do not invest because PI < 1

71. Which is least likely to apply to the NPV method of evaluating projects?

    A. Preferred to IRR method
    B. Sensitive to timing or pattern of cash flows
    *C.Assumes cash flows reinvested at the IRR

72. What are the after-tax costs of debt and equity if the before-tax cost of debt is 8.0%, the before-tax cost of equity is 10.0%, and the tax rate is 20%?

    A. 6.4% for debt and 8.0% for equity
    *B.6.4% for debt and 10.0% for equity
    C. 10.0% for debt and 10.0% for equity

73. What is an estimate of the cost of equity for a company with a beta of 1.2 if the average T-bond rate for 100 years is 4% and the average market return for the same period is 9%?

    A. 9%
    *B.10% = 4% + 1.2(9% - 4%)
    C. 11%

74. Which is closest to the cost of equity using CAPM if the unlevered beta for comparable companies is 1.6, the debt to equity ratio is 1.8, the marginal tax rate is 20%, the risk-free rate is 4%, and the equity risk premium is 5%?

    *A. 23.5% = 4% + 3.90(5%); 3.90 = 1.6[1 + ((1-20%)(1.8))]
    B. 24.5%
    C. 25.5%

75. Which is closest to the weighted average cost of capital (WACC) if the average unlevered beta for comparable companies is 0.9, the tax rate is 30%, the target debt-to-equity ratio is 0.8, the risk-free rate is 3%, the equity risk premium is 5%, and the cost of debt is 150 basis points over the risk-free rate?

    A. 3%
    B. 4%
    *C.7% = [(.8/1.8)(3%+1.5%)(1-30%)] + [(1-.8/1.8){ 3% + (0.9)[1+(1-30%)0.8] 5%}]

76. Which is closest to the cost of trade credit if the terms are 2/10, net 30, and the account is paid on the 20th day?

    A. 9%
    B. 45%
    *C.109% = [1 + .02/(1-.02)]^(365/10) - 1

77. Which is closest to the net profit margin using DuPont analysis if, in millions, operating income is $530, revenues are $13,565, income before taxes is $461, taxes are $126, average total assets are $6,767, and average shareholders' equity is $3,223?

    *A. 2.47% = ($461 - $126) / $13,565
    B. 4.95%
    C. 10.39%

78. Which is most likely to be considered good corporate governance?

    A. A company offering shares at discounted prices to management prior to a public offering but not to board members and insiders
    B. A company offering shares at discounted prices to board members and insiders prior to a public offering but not to management
    *C.A company prohibiting itself from offering shares at discounted prices to management, board members, and insiders prior to a public offering

79. What attribute refers to rapid and unbiased adjustments to new information?

    A. Liquidity
    B. Internal efficiency
    *C.External efficiency

80. The total market value of stock listed on the NYSE at the end of 2004 was closest to $12.5

    A. Billion
    *B.Trillion
    C. Quadrillion

81. Who is least likely to execute a public order?

    A. Floor brokers
    *B.Registered traders
    C. Commission brokers

82. For a margin account with an initial deposit of $50,000, a stock selling at $35, and a prevailing margin rate of 40%, which is closest to the profit if the price rises to $45?

    A. $24,000
    *B.$36,000 = $45($50,000 / 40%) / $35 - ($50,000/40%)
    C. $48,000

83. Which is closest to the return on the unweighted index using the arithmetic mean for three stocks with prices at the beginning of the year for stocks A, B, and C of $60, $20, and $18, respectively, prices at the end of the year for stocks A, B, and C of $80, $35, and $25, respectively, and a market value of $1 million in each stock at the beginning of the year?

    A. 47.5%
    B. 48.0%
    *C.49.1% = {[($80 / $60) + ($35 / $20) + ($25 / $18)] / 3} - 1

84. Which is least likely to be considered an anomaly with respect to the semi-strong from of the EMH?

    A. Abnormal returns from low P/E stocks
    *B.No abnormal returns following earnings surprises
    C. Abnormal returns in January compared to December

85. If markets are efficient, how can portfolio managers add value?

    A. Mismatching portfolios
    *B.Providing diversification
    C. Maximizing transaction costs

86. Which is least likely to explain why valid anomalies may not be profitable?

    A. Conditions governing anomalies may change
    *B.Documented anomalies are based on variances
    C. Positive abnormal returns do not mean positive returns

87. Which is least likely to decrease the growth rate of equity earnings without any external financing?

    *A. Decreased payout ratio
    B. Decreased retention rate
    C. Decreased return on equity

88. Which is closest to value of a share with current dividends of $3 per share, return on equity (ROE) of 17.5%, a required rate of return of 15%, and current earnings per share of $5?

    A. $26.75
    B. $30.57
    *C.$40.13 = [$3 (1.07) / (15% - 7%)] where 7% = (1 - $3 / $5)(17.5%)

89. What are examples of structural economic changes that may influence industries?

    *A. Demographics, technology, politics, and regulation
    B. Population growth, industry, politics, and regulation
    C. Population growth, industry, exchange rates, and oversight

90. Which is least likely to be considered a drawback of using price to earnings (P /E) ratios?

    *A. EPS cannot be negative
    B. Management can distort EPS
    C. Earnings often have volatile, transient components

91. An investor long a forward contract has

    A. A right to buy at a specific price
    B. An obligation to deliver at a certain price
    *C.An obligation to take delivery at a certain price

92. If short-term rates increase after an investor enters into a forward contract on 90-day Treasury bills, the short will have

    *A. A gain on the contract because when short-term rates rise, Treasury bill prices fall
    B. A loss on the contract because when short-term rates rise, Treasury bill prices fall
    C. A loss on the contract because when short-term rates rise, Treasury bill prices rise

93. What options can be exercised at any time prior to expiration?

    *A. American options
    B. European options
    C. European and American options

94. The party making the fixed-rate payment under a swap contract could also be required to make the variable under

    *A. An equity swap
    B. A plain vanilla swap
    C. An interest rate swap

95. For a $50 million plain vanilla interest rate swap, the end user makes semi-annual fixed rate payments at the rate of 5.75%, and the dealer makes semiannual floating payments at LIBOR, which was 5.15% on the last settlement period. Payments are made on the basis of 180 days in a settlement period, floating payments are made on the basis of 360 days in a year, and fixed payments on the basis of 365 days in a year. Which party pays what amount after the payments are netted?

    *A. The party paying fixed will pay the party paying floating $130,308 = $50,000,000(5.75%)(180/365) - $50,000,000(5.15%)(180/360)
    B. The party paying fixed will pay the party paying floating $150,000
    C. The party paying floating will pay the party paying fixed$130,308

96. What is the profit on a covered call option, where the exercise price is X and the price of the underlying security is S?

    A. $S_t - S_0 - \text{Max}(0, S_t - X)$ - option cost
    B. $S_t - S_0 - \text{Max}(0, X - S_t)$ + option cost
    *C. $S_t - S_0 - \text{Max}(0, S_t - X)$ + option cost

97. What is a contract between a company and its bondholders that could be positive, setting forth activities the borrower promises to do, or could be negative, setting forth limitations and restrictions on the borrower's activities?

    *A. Covenant
    B. Indenture
    C. Embedded option

98. An investor who plans to hold a security one year is considering purchasing a Treasury security that matures in one year, or, alternatively, purchasing a Treasury security that matures in 30 years. Which best describes the difference in the major risk associated with the investment alternatives?

   A. The 1-year Treasury exposes the investor to interest rate risk
   *B.The 30-year Treasury exposes the investor to interest rate risk
   C. The 1-year Treasury exposes the investor to liquidity risk

99. Which issue has the greatest interest rate risk: issue 1 with a 5% coupon and 15 year maturity, issue 2 with a 4% coupon and 20 year maturity, or issue 3 with a 6% coupon and 10 year maturity,

   A. Issue 1
   *B.Issue 2
   C. Issue 3

100. Which is closest to the dollar price change of a bond, with a market value of $5 million and a duration of 10.44, for a 100 basis point change in yield?

   A. $130,500
   B. $261,000
   *C.$522,000 = 10.44% ($5 million)

101. Which feature is least likely to increase reinvestment risk?

   A. Callable
   *B.Zero-coupon
   C. Pre-payment option

102. If interest rate volatility increases, which bond will have an decrease in price?

   A. Putable bond
   *B.Callable bond
   C. Option-free bond

103. The accrued interest on Treasury strips

   A. Is tax free
   B. Is taxed in the year received
   *C.Is taxed each year even though interest is not received

104. What is the absolute yield spread between a 5-year bond with a 5.11% yield and a 5-year on-the-run Treasury with a 4.18% yield?

  *A. 93 basis points = 5.11% - 4.18%
  B. 22.2%
  C. 1.222

105. Which is closest to the present value of a 5-year amortizing security with end-of-year payments of $2,309.75 that include all interest and principal, using a discount rate of 6%?

  *A. $9,729.51; where n = 5, i = 6, PMT = 2309.75, FV = 0, resulting in PV = -- 9,729.51
  B. $10,012.89
  C. $10,313.28

106. What approach values a bond as a package of cash flows, with each cash flow viewed as a zero-coupon bond and each cash flow discounted at its own unique discount rate?

  *A. Arbitrage-free approach
  B. Monte Carlo simulation model
  C. Traditional valuation methodology

107. Which is closest to the value of a $100 par, 2-year, 6% coupon Treasury bond if the forward rates for the periods 1, 2, 3 and 4 are 3.00%, 3.60%, 3.92%, and 5.15%, respectively?

  A. $96
  B. $102
  *C.$104 = [$3 / 1.015] + [$3 / (1.015)(1.018)] + [$3 / (1.015)(1.018)(1.0196)] + [$103 / (1.015)(1.018)(1.0196)(1.02575)]

108. For an 8% option-free bond, the price changes by 3% if the rates fall 50 basis points. What is the change if rates increase by 50 basis points?

  *A. Less than 3%
  B. Exactly 3%
  C. More than 3%

109. If bond A has a price of 90 and modified duration of 6, and bond B has a price of 50 and modified duration of 4, then bond A will have a greater price volatility in terms of

　*A. Dollar price change and percentage price change
　B.　Dollar price change but not percentage price change
　C.　Percentage price change but not dollar price change

110. Which is closest to percentage price change if yields change from 6% to 4% based on duration and the convexity adjustment of a 9% coupon 20-year option-free bond selling at 134.67 to yield 6%, if the price increases to 137.59 at a yield of 5.8%, and the price decreases to 131.84 at a yield of 6.2%?

　A.　-24.6%
　B.　-21.3%
　*C.-18.0% = -2 / 100 {(137.59 - 131.84) / [2 (134.67) (0.002)]} + (2)(2) / 10000 {(137.59 + 131.84 - 2(134.67)) / [2 (134.67) (0.002)^2]}

111. Which is least accurate regarding real estate investments?

　*A. Liquid
　B.　Bought and sold intermittently in a generally local marketplace
　C.　Not directly comparable to other properties, only approximately comparable

112. An office building investment has gross potential rental income of $350,000; a 4% estimated vacancy and collection losses; $26,000 in insurance and property taxes; $18,000 in utilities; $23,000 in repairs and maintenance; $40,000 in depreciation; and $18,000 in interest on the proposed financing. A similar office building with $500,000 in operating income was sold for $4 million. Another similar office building with $225,000 in operating income was sold for $1.6 million. Which is closest to the appraised value of the office building investment using the income approach?

　A.　$1,721,805
　*B.$2,022,556 = [$350,000(1 - 4%) - $26,000 - $18,000 - $23,000] / {[($500,000 / $4,000,000) + ($225,000 / $1,600,000)] / 2}
　C.　$2,077,793

113. Which is most accurate regarding real estate indexes?

　A.　Appraisal-based indexes are more volatile than REIT indexes
　*B.Appraisal-based indexes have low correlation with REIT indexes
　C.　Appraisal-based indexes are strongly correlated with the stock market

114. Which is closest to the NPV of a project with a $1 million investment and an expected $16 million payoff at the end of 7 years if it succeeds, with a failure probability in year 1 of 0.25, in year 2 of 0.22, and in each of years 3 through 7 of 0.20, and a cost of equity of 18%?

  *A. -$37,165 = [-$1,000,000 + $16,000,000/1.18^7][(1 - 25%)(1 - 22%)(1 - 20%)^5]
     + (-$1,000,000){ 1 - [(1 - 25%)(1 - 22%)(1 - 20%)^5]}
  B. $37,165
  C. $154,527

115. Which investment strategy seeks growth in the portfolio through both capital gains and reinvesting income?

  *A. Total return
  B. Current income
  C. Capital appreciation

116. Which is the most liquid?

  A. Real estate
  *B. Treasury bills
  C. Venture capital

117. Which is closest to the standard deviation of a portfolio with a 50% weight in each of two securities, both of which have an expected return of 20% and a standard deviation of 10%, if the correlation coefficient is -1.0?

  *A. 0% = [(50%^2)(10%^2) + (50%^2)(10%^2) + 2(50%)(50%)(-1.0)(10%)(10%)]^.5
  B. 5%
  C. 10%

118. How many correlation coefficients are needed for a two-asset portfolio?

  *A. 1
  B. 2
  C. 3

119. How much of an investor's wealth is invested in the market portfolio if the investor's portfolio is to the right of the market portfolio on the capital market line (CML)?

  A. 100%
  B. Less than 100%
  *C. Greater than 100%

120. If the risk free rate is 4%, the market risk premium is 8%, stocks A, B, C, and D have betas of 0.9, 1.0, 1.1, and 1.2, respectively, how many stocks are overvalued and undervalued if all four stocks have an estimated annual return of 12.8%?

    *A. 1 overvalued and 2 undervalued; 13.6% > 12.8% > 12.0% > 11.2%
    B. 2 overvalued and 2 undervalued
    C. 2 overvalued and 2 undervalued

1. CFA charterholder Amonov's firm advertises its past performance record by showing the 10-year return of a composite of its client accounts. Amonov discovers that former clients have been left off and the result is the performance is overstated. Amonov is asked to use the erroneous promotional material when soliciting new business. What is the most appropriate action for Amonov?

    A. Use the promotional material because she did not calculate the performance
    B. Consider whether her obligation to dissociate from the activity would require her to seek other employment
    C. Bring the misleading number to the attention of the person responsible for calculating performance, her supervisor, or the compliance department at her firm

2. CFA charterholder Wang is an equity analyst with Tong Brokerage who covers the mining industry. He has concluded that the stock of Tapani Mining is overpriced, but is concerned that a negative report will hurt the relationship between Tapani Mining and the investment banking division of his firm, a division that has an outstanding proposal to underwrite a debt offering. Wang needs to issue a report right away and issues a favorable rating. Were any Standards of Professional Conduct violated?

    A. No, the analysis was objective
    B. Yes, Wang violated the standard on duties to employer
    C. Yes, Wang violated the standard on independence and objectivity

3. CFA charterholder Nikitin recommends that risk-averse clients with short investment horizons move their assets from equities to CDs and money market accounts with U.S. banks so the principal will be guaranteed up to a certain amount within the government-insured limit. The interest is not guaranteed. Did Nikitin violate any Standards of Professional Conduct?

    A. No
    B. Yes, relating to misrepresentation
    C. Yes, relating to independence and objectivity

4. What occurs when companies discriminate in making material nonpublic information public?

    A. Firewall
    B. Watch list
    C. Selective disclosure

5. CFA charterholder Brenza enters Internet chat rooms to start rumors to try to deflate the price of a stock. Brenza is most likely to have violated the Standards of Professional Conduct relating to

    A. Market manipulation
    B. Performance presentation
    C. Independence and objectivity

6. Which is least likely a recommended procedure for compliance with the Standard of Professional Conduct relating to fair dealing?

    A. Simultaneous dissemination
    B. Limit the number of people involved
    C. Lengthen the time frame between decision and dissemination

7. CFA charterholder Gupta distributes a performance sheet claiming compliance with GIPS when not all the requirements of GIPS were met. Did Gupta violate any Standards of Professional Conduct?

    A. No
    B. Yes, relating to records retention
    C. Yes, relating to performance presentation

8. After departing his former firm, CFA charterholder Volkmann uses public information to contact former clients. Did Volkmann violate any Standards of Professional Conduct?

    A. No
    B. Yes, relating to loyalty
    C. Yes, relating to preservation of confidentiality

9. CFA charterholder Ganesh sits on a board of directors. Ganesh does not receive monetary compensation but does receive paid club memberships. Ganesh does not disclose the arrangement with his employer. Did Ganesh violate any Standards of Professional Conduct?

    A. No
    B. Yes, relating to independence and objectivity
    C. Yes, relating to additional compensation arrangements

10. CFA charterholder Doyon produces a report that describes an investment strategy for bond trading that will benefit from declines in interest rates. The report states that the strategy is proprietary information and does not describe the characteristics of the strategy. The report does not discuss how the portfolio would perform in periods of rising interest rates. Did Doyon violate any Standards of Professional Conduct?

    A. No
    B. Yes, relating to misrepresentation
    C. Yes, relating to communications with clients and prospective clients

11. CFA charterholder Potvin accepts additional compensation from a stock promoter for sales of a certain stock without telling his clients or his employer. Potvin is least likely to have violated the Standard of Professional Conduct on

    A. Disclosure of conflicts
    B. Professional misconduct
    C. Additional compensation arrangements

12. CFA charterholder Laksana attends a closed-circuit broadcast to her firm's branches in which CFA charterholder Khalid makes negative comments about a company. Khalid's comments will be in a report to be published the next day for distribution to clients. Laksana closes out long positions in the stock and buys put options immediately after the broadcast. Which Standard of Professional Conduct did Laksana most likely violate?

    A. Market manipulation
    B. Priority of transactions
    C. Communication with clients and prospective clients

13. CFA charterholder Delo receives compensation and benefits for the recommendation of products or services, and does not mention the arrangement. Did Delo violate any Standards of Professional Conduct?

    A. No
    B. Yes, related to conflicts of interest
    C. Yes, related to diligence and reasonable basis

14. Kyle Prible, who earned the right to use the CFA designation in 1974, retires. Prible stops paying his CFA Institute dues and does not file a completed Professional Conduct Statement with CFA Institute. According to the Standards of Professional Conduct, how should Prible refer to his affiliation with the CFA program?

    A. Kyle Prible, CFA
    B. Kyle Prible, CFA retired
    C. I was awarded the CFA charter in 1974

15. The mosaic theory holds that an analyst

    A. Should use all available and relevant information in support of an investment recommendation
    B. Can use material public information or nonmaterial nonpublic information in the analyst's analysis
    C. Violates the Code and Standards if the analyst fails to have knowledge of and comply with applicable laws

16. CFA charterholder Freeman discovers that CFA charterholder Gosselin has been altering trade order records in violation of firm policies, and notifies the firm's compliance officer. Weeks later, Freeman observes that Gosselin is still altering records. Freeman dissociates herself from the unethical activity, but does not report Gosselin to the CFA Institute Professional Conduct Program. Did Freeman violate any Standards of Professional Conduct?

    A. No
    B. Yes, related to duties to clients
    C. Yes, related to duties to employers

17. CFA charterholder Neyar attends a luncheon with executives of a company and analysts from other firms. The executives reveal material nonpublic information. Neyar's best course of action is to

    A. Refrain from discussing the information with anyone
    B. Encourage the company to make the information public
    C. Disclose the information to the firm's compliance personnel

18. A firm has met the GIPS requirements if prospective clients receive a compliant presentation within the previous

    A. 3 months
    B. 12 months
    C. 24 months

19. What is the value a perpetual annuity with $10,000 beginning-of-year payments using a discount rate of 8% per year?

    A. $112,578
    B. $125,000
    C. $135,000

20. What is the annual time-weighted rate of return when one share is purchased for $200 in year 0, a second share is purchased for $300 in year 1, and both are sold for $610 in year 2?

    A. 15%
    B. 23%
    C. 53%

21. What is a bar chart of data from a frequency distribution?

    A. Histogram
    B. Frequency polygon
    C. Cumulative relative frequency

22. What uses the harmonic mean?

    A. Cost averaging
    B. Chebyshev's inequality
    C. Volatility measurements

23. Investors should be attracted to a return distribution with which type of skew because the mean falls above the median?

    A. Zero skewness
    B. Positive skewness
    C. Negative skewness

24. What is the sum of the probabilities of mutually exclusive and exhaustive events?

    A. 0.0
    B. 0.5
    C. 1.0

25. If stocks have positive returns 75% of the time, bonds have positive returns 80% of the time, and both have positive returns 65% of the time, what is the probability that at least one of the two asset classes is positive?

    A. 60%
    B. 75%
    C. 90%

26. If the probability that the change in EPS in the next quarter is 60%, the probability that the change in EPS in the prior quarter is 60%, and the probability that the change is positive in the next quarter given positive change in the prior quarter is 80%, what is the probability of a negative or zero change for the next quarter, given a positive change for the prior quarter?

    A. 30%
    B. 47%
    C. 48%

27. How many ways can five analysts be assigned to each monitor one of five different investment managers?

    A. 25
    B. 32
    C. 120

28. If the price for a stock in one year is predicted to be in the $50 to $100 range, what is the probability the stock will be under $70 in one year, assuming a continuous uniform distribution?

    A. 10%
    B. 20%
    C. 40%

29. Which allocation is optimal when the minimum acceptable return is 5%: allocation 1 with an expected return of 10% and a standard deviation of 20%, allocation 2 with an expected return of 8% and a standard deviation of 10%, or allocation 3 with an expected return of 11% and a standard deviation of 30%?

    A. 1
    B. 2
    C. 3

30. When is Monte Carlo simulation least helpful?

    A. Financial risk management
    B. Valuing complex securities
    C. Providing exact results

31. How many degrees of freedom does a t-distribution for a sample of size 25 have?

    A. 5
    B. 24
    C. 25

32. Which statistic is appropriate for sampling from a normal distribution with an unknown variance for a large sample size?

    A. t-statistic (use of z-statistic also acceptable)
    B. t-statistic
    C. z-statistic

33. What is the percentage change in quantity demanded divided by the percentage change in price of a substitute or complement?

    A. Price elasticity of demand
    B. Cross elasticity of demand
    C. Income elasticity of demand

34. Which is most likely to lead to equilibrium?

    A. Transaction costs
    B. Invisible hand
    C. Externalities

35. Which is least likely to decrease the supply of an illegal good?

    A. Effective law enforcement
    B. Penalties on sellers
    C. Penalties on buyers

36. Which is least likely to apply to monopolistic competition?

    A. The concentration ratio is low
    B. Firms have considerable control over price
    C. The Herfindahl-Hirschman Index (HHI) is 101 to 999

37. When is economic profit maximized for a perfectly competitive firm?

    A. When marginal costs are less than marginal revenue
    B. When marginal costs equal marginal revenue
    C. When marginal costs are greater than marginal revenue

38. Which best describes marginal-cost pricing for a regulated monopoly?

    A. Efficient but allows natural monopoly an economic gain
    B. Inefficient but would allow natural monopoly an economic gain
    C. Efficient but would leave natural monopoly with an economic loss

39. What happens if the demand for labor is inelastic?

    A. An increase in supply of labor lowers the wage rate and increases labor income
    B. An increase in supply of labor lowers the wage rate and lowers labor income
    C. A change in the supply of labor changes the wage rate but leaves labor income unchanged

40. Which range is closest to the natural unemployment rate?

    A. 0% to 1%
    B. 2% to 3%
    C. 4% to 7%

41. What determines real GDP and the price level?

    A. Aggregate demand and short run aggregate supply
    B. Aggregate demand and long run aggregate supply
    C. Short run and long run aggregate supply

42. What influences the quantity of money that people plan to hold?

    A. Money multiplier, monetary base, discount rate, reserve ratio
    B. Price level, nominal interest rate, real GDP, financial innovation
    C. Price level, real interest rate, nominal GDP, financial innovation

43. Which are most likely goals of monetary policy?

    A. GDP growth and full employment
    B. Tax revenues increase and unemployment insurance payments decrease
    C. Maximum employment, stable prices, and moderate long-term interest rates

44. Which is a decision rule for monetary policy that sets the policy instrument at a level that makes the forecast of the ultimate policy goal the target?

    A. Instrument rule
    B. Targeting rule
    C. k-percent rule

45. Where would information about material events and uncertainties best be found?

    A. Footnotes
    B. Proxy statement
    C. Management's discussion and analysis

46. What is designed to allocate activity to the proper period?

    A. Accrual accounting
    B. Statement of cash flows
    C. Statement of owners' equity

47. Which is the most likely effect on the accounting equation if $10,000 in cash is used to pay $6,000 in prepaid rent and a $4,000 security deposit?

    A. Assets decrease by $10,000
    B. Assets decrease by $6,000
    C. There is no change in assets

48. What are presentation requirements for financial statements under IAS No. 1?

    A. Going concern, accrual basis, consistency, and materiality
    B. Balance sheet, income statement, statement of changes in equity, cash flow statement, and notes
    C. Aggregation where appropriate, no offsetting, classified balance sheet, minimum information on face, minimum note disclosure, and comparative information

49. Under which financial reporting framework is there a broad focus to provide relevant information to a wide range of users?

    A. IFRS but not FASB
    B. FASB but not IFRS
    C. Both IFRS and FASB

50. Which are not included in the calculation of revenue reported on an accrual basis if for the year revenue is $1,000; cost of goods sold equals $800; returns of goods sold are $100; and cash collected is $700?

    A. $100 for return of goods sold and $700 for cash collected
    B. $100 for return of goods sold and $800 for cost of goods sold
    C. $700 for cash collected and $800 for cost of goods sold

51. Which would least likely be considered part of the matching principle of expense recognition?

    A. Expenses are matched either to revenue or the time period in which the expenditure occurs
    B. Expenses are matched to the time period of the expected benefits of the expenditures
    C. Expenses are matched to the present value of the cash flows associated with the expense

52. Which depreciation method would be the most conservative in the first year?

   A. Straight-line depreciation with a short useful life
   B. Straight-line depreciation with a long useful life
   C. Double declining balance method with a short useful life

53. Under U.S. GAAP, which is least likely to be considered other comprehensive income?

   A. Foreign currency translation adjustments
   B. Unrealized holding gains and losses on available-for-sale securities
   C. Realized gains or losses on real estate investments

54. What is the cost of an asset at acquisition?

   A. Fair value
   B. Current cost
   C. Historical cost

55. Receipts from issuing stock would be in what category on a cash flow statement?

   A. Investing
   B. Operating
   C. Financing

56. What are methods for reporting operating cash flow?

   A. Indirect or direct
   B. Income or expense
   C. Financing or investing

57. Which is least likely a prescribed approach for preparing common-size cash flow statements?

   A. Percentage of total assets method
   B. Percentage of net revenues method
   C. Total cash inflows/total cash outflows method

58. Which is closest to inventory expense under IFRS if inventory was purchased for $10 million and $1 million was spent for bringing the inventory to its present location?

   A. $9 million
   B. $10 million
   C. $11 million

59. In a period of rising prices, what is the most likely difference for a company that uses FIFO rather than LIFO?

    A. Lower current assets, lower gross income
    B. Lower current assets, higher gross income
    C. Higher current assets, higher gross income

60. Which estimate regarding an asset results in the lowest cash flow?

    A. Six-year useful life and no salvage value
    B. Seven-year useful life and no salvage value
    C. Seven-year useful life and positive salvage value

61. What can occur at the time a decision is made to sell an asset and before the actual sale?

    A. A gain or loss
    B. A loss but not a gain
    C. A gain but not a loss

62. Which would most likely result from accounting standards requiring an asset to be expensed immediately and tax rules requiring the asset to be capitalized and amortized?

    A. Deferred tax asset
    B. Deferred tax liability
    C. No deferred tax asset or liability

63. Which recognizes a deferred tax asset in full then reduces it by a valuation allowance if it is more likely than not that some or all of the deferred tax asset will not be realized?

    A. U.S. GAAP but not IFRS
    B. IFRS but not U.S. GAAP
    C. Both U.S. GAAP and IFRS

64. What is a comparison of a company with peer companies?

    A. Trend analysis
    B. Time-series analysis
    C. Cross-sectional analysis

65. What is least likely to explain an increase in inventory turnover?

    A. More efficient inventory management system
    B. Large write-offs of inventory at the beginning of the period
    C. Operational difficulties resulting in duplicate orders with suppliers

66. Calculate return on equity (ROE) if sales divided by total assets are 2, net profit margin is 4%, return on total assets is 8%, and total assets divided by equity is 3?

    A. 12%
    B. 24%
    C. 48%

67. Which is a constraint related to the preparation of information in a financial statement?

    A. Timeliness
    B. Neutrality
    C. Accrual basis

68. Under IFRS, which category of marketable securities is most likely to have an asymmetrical treatment of income and changes in value?

    A. Held for trading
    B. Held to maturity
    C. Available for sale

69. If a company paid $10 million for property 5 years ago, the market value of the property is $15 million, and it would cost $2 million to build roads and utilities to get the land ready for building, what is the cost of the land for capital budgeting purposes?

    A. $10 million
    B. $15 million
    C. $17 million

70. Which is least likely to be considered a drawback of the payback period method of capital budgeting?

    A. It is simple
    B. It ignores risk and the time value of money
    C. It ignores cash flows after the payback period

71. Which is preferred if a company must choose one project between two mutually exclusive projects; project A with an NPV of $50 million and an IRR of 35%; and project B with an NPV of $100 million and an IRR of 25%?

   A. Project A because it has a greater IRR
   B. Project B because it has a lower IRR
   C. Project B because it has a greater NPV

72. Which is closest to the weights used for the weighted average cost of capital (WACC) if the a company has bonds with $10 million in face value, 8% coupons with semi-annual payments, five years to maturity, and priced to yield 13.65%; and 1.2 million shares of stock outstanding at $10 per share?

   A. 40% bonds, 60% equity
   B. 50% bonds, 50% equity
   C. 60% bonds, 40% equity

73. Which is closest to the after-tax cost of debt using the debt-rating approach if a company sells a 10-year 4% semi-annual coupon AAA rated bond, the marginal tax rate is 40%, and the yield on debt with the same rating is 5%?

   A. 2.4%
   B. 3.0%
   C. 3.2%

74. What is an estimate of the cost of equity if the expected dividends are $5, the market price is $100, the company's earnings retention rate is 67%, ROE is 6%, and the risk-free rate is 3%?

   A. 9%
   B. 11%
   C. 18%

75. What is the number of days of inventory if annual cost of goods sold is $12 million, accounts receivable are $3 million, and inventory is $4 million?

   A. 91.25
   B. 121.67
   C. 152.09

76. Which company had the highest number of days of inventory if company A had an operating cycle of 176 days, credit sales of $30 million, and an average receivables balance of $12 million; company B had an operating cycle of 142 days, credit sales of $25 million and an average receivables balance of $8 million; and company C had an operating cycle of 108 days, credit sales of $50 million and an average receivables balance of $10 million?

    A. Company A
    B. Company B
    C. Company C

77. Which is least likely to be equal to return on assets using DuPont analysis?

    A. Net profit margin times total asset turnover
    B. Total asset turnover times financial leverage
    C. Net income divided by revenue, times revenue divided by average total assets

78. Which is closest to the total asset turnover if the operating profit margin is 7.7%, the effect of non-operating items is 0.9, the tax effect is 0.8, financial leverage is 1.2, and the return on equity is 10%?

    A. 1.25
    B. 1.33
    C. 1.50

79. Where do new issues of securities occur?

    A. Primary market
    B. Secondary market
    C. Third market

80. Which statement is most accurate regarding continuous markets?

    A. Markets are physical places where traders and dealers gather
    B. Trading takes place at various prices and times as buy and sell orders arrive
    C. Security trades are executed at specific times at a single price after buy and sell orders have accumulated

81. What specifies the buy or sell price?

    A. Short sale
    B. Limit order
    C. Market order

82. What type of security market index is most like investing an equal dollar amount in each stock?

    A. Unweighted
    B. Price-weighted
    C. Value-weighted

83. What is the correlation between investment grade bonds and high-yield bonds?

    A. 19%
    B. 49%
    C. 95%

84. Which form of the efficient market hypothesis (EMH) is tested by performance of insiders, specialists, money managers, and analyst recommendations?

    A. Weak form
    B. Strong form
    C. Semi-strong form

85. Which can result from the retention of people with a good investment record?

    A. Selection bias
    B. Survivorship bias
    C. Incorrect measurement of abnormal return

86. Which is closest to the value of common stock with a current dividend of $1, a dividend growth rate of 7%, and a required rate of return of 12%?

    A. $20.00
    B. $21.40
    C. $22.40

87. Which is most likely to result in a higher value of common stock using the earnings multiplier model?

    A. Higher dividend payout ratio
    B. Higher required rate of return
    C. Lower growth rate of dividends

88. Which is closest to the growth rate of equity earnings without any external financing if the retention rate is 40%, the profit margin is 10%, the total asset turnover is 0.4, the return on assets is 4%, and the financial leverage is 2?

    A. 3.2%
    B. 4.8%
    C. 6.0%

89. What best describes a company whose future earnings are likely to withstand an economic downturn?

    A. Growth company
    B. Defensive company
    C. Speculative company

90. Which is least likely to be considered a drawback of using price to book value (P / B) ratios?

    A. Comparability
    B. Accounting effects such as expensing R&D
    C. Not appropriate for companies not expected to continue as going concern

91. Which is least likely to be a characteristic of a futures contract?

    A. Over-the-counter market
    B. Daily settlement of gains and losses
    C. Clearinghouse guarantee against credit losses

92. Which statement is least accurate regarding Eurodollar time deposits?

    A. The primary Eurodollar rate is called LIBOR
    B. Eurodollar time deposits are loans made in Euros by one bank to another
    C. Eurodollar deposits accrue interest by adding it on to the principal, using a 360-day year assumption

93. What is the ending balance at the end of day 4 for a holder of a long position of 20 futures contracts if the initial futures price on day 0 is $212, the initial margin requirement is $10, the maintenance margin requirement is $8, the settlement price on day 1 is $211, the settlement price on day 2 is $214, the settlement price on day 3 is $209, and the settlement price on day 4 is $210?

    A. $160
    B. $220
    C. $240

94. An investor goes long one futures contract at $50 with 2 days to expiration. The settlement price 1 day before expiration is $52 and the mark to market profit is $2. The settlement price at expiration is $53. How is the futures contract terminated by cash settlement?

   A. Receive $53 - $52 = $1
   B. Pay $52, receive asset worth $53
   C. Sell contract at $53 for a mark to market profit of $53 - $52 = $1

95. What is the value that can be captured if an option is exercised?

   A. Time value
   B. Moneyness
   C. Intrinsic value

96. What is the profit for a covered call option at expiration, for a stock selling for $98 and a call option at $105 selling for $8, if the stock price at expiration is $88?

   A. -$2
   B. $0
   C. $2

97. What is the full price of a bond if the clean price is $1,050 and the accrued interest is $25?

   A. $1,025
   B. $1,050
   C. $1,075

98. Which imbedded option is an advantage to the issuer?

   A. Put provision
   B. Floor on a floater
   C. Accelerated sinking fund

99. What is the price of a bond when the coupon rate is greater than the yield required by the market?

   A. Equal to par value
   B. Less than par value
   C. Greater then par value

100. Which is closest to the duration of a bond if the current price is 102, the price if yields decline by 50 basis points is 109, and the price if yields rise by 50 basis points is 96?

   A. 12.75
   B. 19.12
   C. 25.49

101. Which is least likely to be considered credit risk?

   A. Interest rate risk
   B. Downgrade risk
   C. Credit spread risk

102. What risk is associated with natural disasters?

   A. Event risk
   B. Volatility risk
   C. Purchasing power risk

103. What includes secured bonds, unsecured or debenture bonds, and credit enhanced bonds?

   A. Corporate bonds
   B. Structured notes
   C. Commercial paper

104. How can the Federal Reserve withdraw funds from the market?

   A. Selling Treasury securities
   B. Purchasing Treasury securities
   C. Decreasing the discount rate

105. What do investors require for an issue with a call option with a longer deferred call period compared to a shorter deferred call period?

   A. Larger yield spread
   B. Smaller yield spread
   C. The same yield spread

106. What relates the annual dollar coupon interest to the market price and fails to recognize any capital gain or loss and reinvestment income?

    A. Current yield
    B. Yield to maturity
    C. Bond-equivalent yield

107. If the spot rates on an annual basis are 3.0% for 6 months, 3.3% for 1 year, and 3.5% for 1.5 years, which is closest to the price of a $100 par, 3% coupon 1.5-year Treasury security?

    A. $99
    B. $100
    C. $101

108. Bonds with positive convexity

    A. Are always superior to bonds with negative convexity
    B. Will have less price appreciation than its price decline for a large change in interest rates
    C. Will have greater price appreciation than its price decline for a large change in interest rates

109. What definition of duration should be used for bonds with embedded options?

    A. Modified duration
    B. Effective duration
    C. Macaulay duration

110. Which is closest to percentage price change for a bond with modified duration of 10.66 and convexity of 81.95 if yields increase by 200 basis points?

    A. -18.04%
    B. -14.76%
    C. -11.48%

111. Which is most likely to be considered a disadvantage of exchange-traded funds (ETFs)?

    A. Lack of diversification
    B. Significant premiums or discounts to NAV
    C. Narrow-based market index tracked in some countries

112. A real estate investment project has a first-year NOI of $83,800 that is expected to grow by 5% per year. The purchase price is $700,000 which is financed 20% by equity and 80% by a mortgage loan at 10% pre-tax interest and level annual payments of $59,404. Should the project be recommended based on the NPV of the project using a required rate of return of 16% if the property is sold at the end of the fifth year for $875,000, property sales expenses are 6%, depreciation is $18,700 per year, five years of principal payments total $20,783, the marginal tax rate is 31%, the capital gains tax rate is 20%, and the after-tax cash flow for the first five years are $21,575, $24,361, $27,280, $30,339, and $273,629?

    A. No, based on an NPV of -$61,215
    B. Yes, based on an NPV of $33,461
    C. Yes, based on an NPV of $61,215

113. Which most accurately describes a challenge to venture capital performance measurement?

    A. Too many benchmarks to choose from
    B. Short-term nature of performance feedback
    C. Difficulty in determining precise valuations

114. For a hedge fund index compared to a stock index, most likely the average return is

    A. Overstated and the Sharpe ratio is overstated
    B. Overstated and the Sharpe ratio is understated
    C. Understated and the standard deviation is overstated

115. For which goal would high risk investments be least appropriate?

    A. Lower-priority goals
    B. Near-term, high-priority goals
    C. Long-term, high-priority goals

116. Which is most accurate regarding what asset allocation explains for a single fund?

    A. 40% of the average fund's level of return
    B. 40% of a single fund's variations in returns over time
    C. 90% of a single fund's variations in returns over time

117. What is closest to the correlation coefficient if the sum of the products of the returns minus mean returns for two securities for 12 monthly periods is 5%, and the variances are 0.64% and 1.44%?

    A. 0.43
    B. 0.47
    C. 0.67

118. The optimal portfolio is the efficient portfolio that has

    A. The lowest risk
    B. The highest return
    C. The highest utility

119. Which statement about portfolio risk and diversification is least accurate?

    A. Systematic risk cannot be eliminated through diversification
    B. Unsystematic risk cannot be significantly reduced through diversification
    C. Diversification results from combining securities with less than perfect correlations

120. What relates the expected or required rate of return of an asset to its beta?

    A. CML
    B. SML
    C. Efficient frontier

1. C	41. A	81. B
2. C	42. B	82. A
3. A	43. C	83. B
4. C	44. B	84. B
5. A	45. C	85. B
6. C	46. A	86. B
7. C	47. C	87. A
8. A	48. C	88. A
9. C	49. C	89. B
10. C	50. C	90. C
11. B	51. C	91. A
12. B	52. C	92. B
13. B	53. C	93. B
14. C	54. C	94. A
15. B	55. C	95. C
16. A	56. A	96. A
17. B	57. A	97. C
18. B	58. C	98. C
19. C	59. C	99. C
20. B	60. C	100. A
21. A	61. B	101. A
22. A	62. A	102. A
23. B	63. A	103. A
24. C	64. C	104. A
25. C	65. C	105. B
26. A	66. B	106. A
27. C	67. A	107. A
28. C	68. C	108. C
29. B	69. C	109. B
30. C	70. A	110. A
31. B	71. C	111. C
32. A	72. A	112. C
33. B	73. B	113. C
34. B	74. A	114. A
35. C	75. B	115. B
36. B	76. C	116. C
37. B	77. B	117. B
38. C	78. C	118. C
39. A	79. A	119. B
40. C	80. B	120. B

1. CFA charterholder Amonov's firm advertises its past performance record by showing the 10-year return of a composite of its client accounts. Amonov discovers that former clients have been left off and the result is the performance is overstated. Amonov is asked to use the erroneous promotional material when soliciting new business. What is the most appropriate action for Amonov?

    A. Use the promotional material because she did not calculate the performance
    B. Consider whether her obligation to dissociate from the activity would require her to seek other employment
    *C. Bring the misleading number to the attention of the person responsible for calculating performance, her supervisor, or the compliance department at her firm (Standard I(A) - knowledge of the law)

2. CFA charterholder Wang is an equity analyst with Tong Brokerage who covers the mining industry. He has concluded that the stock of Tapani Mining is overpriced, but is concerned that a negative report will hurt the relationship between Tapani Mining and the investment banking division of his firm, a division that has an outstanding proposal to underwrite a debt offering. Wang needs to issue a report right away and issues a favorable rating. Were any Standards of Professional Conduct violated?

    A. No, the analysis was objective
    B. Yes, Wang violated the standard on duties to employer
    *C. Yes, Wang violated the standard on independence and objectivity (Standard I(B) - independence and objectivity)

3. CFA charterholder Nikitin recommends that risk-averse clients with short investment horizons move their assets from equities to CDs and money market accounts with U.S. banks so the principal will be guaranteed up to a certain amount within the government-insured limit. The interest is not guaranteed. Did Nikitin violate any Standards of Professional Conduct?

    *A. No (Standard I(C) - misrepresentation)
    B. Yes, relating to misrepresentation
    C. Yes, relating to independence and objectivity

4. What occurs when companies discriminate in making material nonpublic information public?

    A. Firewall
    B. Watch list
    *C. Selective disclosure (Standard II(A) - material nonpublic information)

5. CFA charterholder Brenza enters Internet chat rooms to start rumors to try to deflate the price of a stock. Brenza is most likely to have violated the Standards of Professional Conduct relating to

    *A. Market manipulation (Standard II(B) - market manipulation)
    B. Performance presentation
    C. Independence and objectivity

6. Which is least likely a recommended procedure for compliance with the Standard of Professional Conduct relating to fair dealing?

    A. Simultaneous dissemination
    B. Limit the number of people involved
    *C.Lengthen the time frame between decision and dissemination

7. CFA charterholder Gupta distributes a performance sheet claiming compliance with GIPS when not all the requirements of GIPS were met. Did Gupta violate any Standards of Professional Conduct?

    A. No
    B. Yes, relating to records retention
    *C.Yes, relating to performance presentation (Standard III(D) - performance presentation)

8. After departing his former firm, CFA charterholder Volkmann uses public information to contact former clients. Did Volkmann violate any Standards of Professional Conduct?

    *A. No (Standard IV(A) - loyalty)
    B. Yes, relating to loyalty
    C. Yes, relating to preservation of confidentiality

9. CFA charterholder Ganesh sits on a board of directors. Ganesh does not receive monetary compensation but does receive paid club memberships. Ganesh does not disclose the arrangement with his employer. Did Ganesh violate any Standards of Professional Conduct?

    A. No
    B. Yes, relating to independence and objectivity
    *C.Yes, relating to additional compensation arrangements (Standard IV(B) - additional compensation arrangements)

10. CFA charterholder Doyon produces a report that describes an investment strategy for bond trading that will benefit from declines in interest rates. The report states that the strategy is proprietary information and does not describe the characteristics of the strategy. The report does not discuss how the portfolio would perform in periods of rising interest rates. Did Doyon violate any Standards of Professional Conduct?

    A. No
    B. Yes, relating to misrepresentation
    *C. Yes, relating to communications with clients and prospective clients (Standard V(B) - communications with clients and prospective clients)

11. CFA charterholder Potvin accepts additional compensation from a stock promoter for sales of a certain stock without telling his clients or his employer. Potvin is least likely to have violated the Standard of Professional Conduct on

    A. Disclosure of conflicts
    *B. Professional misconduct (Standard VI(A) - disclosure of conflicts and Standard IV(B) - additional compensation arrangements)
    C. Additional compensation arrangements

12. CFA charterholder Laksana attends a closed-circuit broadcast to her firm's branches in which CFA charterholder Khalid makes negative comments about a company. Khalid's comments will be in a report to be published the next day for distribution to clients. Laksana closes out long positions in the stock and buys put options immediately after the broadcast. Which Standard of Professional Conduct did Laksana most likely violate?

    A. Market manipulation
    *B. Priority of transactions (Standard VI(B) - priority of transactions)
    C. Communication with clients and prospective clients

13. CFA charterholder Delo receives compensation and benefits for the recommendation of products or services, and does not mention the arrangement. Did Delo violate any Standards of Professional Conduct?

    A. No
    *B. Yes, related to conflicts of interest (Standard VI(C) - referral fees)
    C. Yes, related to diligence and reasonable basis

14. Kyle Prible, who earned the right to use the CFA designation in 1974, retires. Prible stops paying his CFA Institute dues and does not file a completed Professional Conduct Statement with CFA Institute. According to the Standards of Professional Conduct, how should Prible refer to his affiliation with the CFA program?

   A. Kyle Prible, CFA
   B. Kyle Prible, CFA retired
   *C. I was awarded the CFA charter in 1974 (Standard VII(B) - reference to the CFA Institute, the CFA designation, and the CFA program)

15. The mosaic theory holds that an analyst

   A. Should use all available and relevant information in support of an investment recommendation
   *B. Can use material public information or nonmaterial nonpublic information in the analyst's analysis (Standard II(A) - material nonpublic information)
   C. Violates the Code and Standards if the analyst fails to have knowledge of and comply with applicable laws

16. CFA charterholder Freeman discovers that CFA charterholder Gosselin has been altering trade order records in violation of firm policies, and notifies the firm's compliance officer. Weeks later, Freeman observes that Gosselin is still altering records. Freeman dissociates herself from the unethical activity, but does not report Gosselin to the CFA Institute Professional Conduct Program. Did Freeman violate any Standards of Professional Conduct?

   *A. No (such actions are encouraged but not required)
   B. Yes, related to duties to clients
   C. Yes, related to duties to employers

17. CFA charterholder Neyar attends a luncheon with executives of a company and analysts from other firms. The executives reveal material nonpublic information. Neyar's best course of action is to

   A. Refrain from discussing the information with anyone
   *B. Encourage the company to make the information public (Standard II(A) - material nonpublic information)
   C. Disclose the information to the firm's compliance personnel

18. A firm has met the GIPS requirements if prospective clients receive a compliant presentation within the previous

   A. 3 months
   *B. 12 months
   C. 24 months

19. What is the value a perpetual annuity with $10,000 beginning-of-year payments using a discount rate of 8% per year?

    A. $112,578
    B. $125,000
    *C.$135,000 = $10,000 / (.08 / 1.08) = [$10,000 / .08] + $10,000; approximate a perpetuity using a 999-year annuity; n = 999, i = 8, PMT = 10000; FV = 0; PV (BEG) perpetuity = $135,000

20. What is the annual time-weighted rate of return when one share is purchased for $200 in year 0, a second share is purchased for $300 in year 1, and both are sold for $610 in year 2?

    A. 15%
    *B.23% = [(300/200)(610/600)]^.5 - 1
    C. 53%

21. What is a bar chart of data from a frequency distribution?

    *A. Histogram
    B. Frequency polygon
    C. Cumulative relative frequency

22. What uses the harmonic mean?

    *A. Cost averaging
    B. Chebyshev's inequality
    C. Volatility measurements

23. Investors should be attracted to a return distribution with which type of skew because the mean falls above the median?

    A. Zero skewness
    *B.Positive skewness
    C. Negative skewness

24. What is the sum of the probabilities of mutually exclusive and exhaustive events?

    A. 0.0
    B. 0.5
    *C.1.0

25. If stocks have positive returns 75% of the time, bonds have positive returns 80% of the time, and both have positive returns 65% of the time, what is the probability that at least one of the two asset classes is positive?

    A. 60%
    B. 75%
    *C. 90% = 80% + 75% - 65%

26. If the probability that the change in EPS in the next quarter is 60%, the probability that the change in EPS in the prior quarter is 60%, and the probability that the change is positive in the next quarter given positive change in the prior quarter is 80%, what is the probability of a negative or zero change for the next quarter, given a positive change for the prior quarter?

    *A. 30% = [60% - 80%(60%)] / 60%
    B. 47%
    C. 48%

27. How many ways can five analysts be assigned to each monitor one of five different investment managers?

    A. 25
    B. 32
    *C. 120 = 5! = 5 (4) (3) (2) (1)

28. If the price for a stock in one year is predicted to be in the $50 to $100 range, what is the probability the stock will be under $70 in one year, assuming a continuous uniform distribution?

    A. 10%
    B. 20%
    *C. 40% = 20/50

29. Which allocation is optimal when the minimum acceptable return is 5%: allocation 1 with an expected return of 10% and a standard deviation of 20%, allocation 2 with an expected return of 8% and a standard deviation of 10%, or allocation 3 with an expected return of 11% and a standard deviation of 30%?

    A. 1
    *B. 2, (8%-5%)/10%> (10%-5%)/20%>(11%-5%)/30%
    C. 3

30. When is Monte Carlo simulation least helpful?

    A. Financial risk management
    B. Valuing complex securities
    *C. Providing exact results

31. How many degrees of freedom does a t-distribution for a sample of size 25 have?

    A. 5
    *B. 24 = 25 - 1
    C. 25

32. Which statistic is appropriate for sampling from a normal distribution with an unknown variance for a large sample size?

    *A. t-statistic (use of z-statistic also acceptable)
    B. t-statistic
    C. z-statistic

33. What is the percentage change in quantity demanded divided by the percentage change in price of a substitute or complement?

    A. Price elasticity of demand
    *B. Cross elasticity of demand
    C. Income elasticity of demand

34. Which is most likely to lead to equilibrium?

    A. Transaction costs
    *B. Invisible hand
    C. Externalities

35. Which is least likely to decrease the supply of an illegal good?

    A. Effective law enforcement
    B. Penalties on sellers
    *C. Penalties on buyers

36. Which is least likely to apply to monopolistic competition?

    A. The concentration ratio is low
    *B. Firms have considerable control over price
    C. The Herfindahl-Hirschman Index (HHI) is 101 to 999

37. When is economic profit maximized for a perfectly competitive firm?

    A. When marginal costs are less than marginal revenue
    *B.When marginal costs equal marginal revenue
    C. When marginal costs are greater than marginal revenue

38. Which best describes marginal-cost pricing for a regulated monopoly?

    A. Efficient but allows natural monopoly an economic gain
    B. Inefficient but would allow natural monopoly an economic gain
    *C.Efficient but would leave natural monopoly with an economic loss

39. What happens if the demand for labor is inelastic?

    *A. An increase in supply of labor lowers the wage rate and increases labor income
    B. An increase in supply of labor lowers the wage rate and lowers labor income
    C. A change in the supply of labor changes the wage rate but leaves labor income unchanged

40. Which range is closest to the natural unemployment rate?

    A. 0% to 1%
    B. 2% to 3%
    *C.4% to 7%

41. What determines real GDP and the price level?

    *A. Aggregate demand and short run aggregate supply
    B. Aggregate demand and long run aggregate supply
    C. Short run and long run aggregate supply

42. What influences the quantity of money that people plan to hold?

    A. Money multiplier, monetary base, discount rate, reserve ratio
    *B.Price level, nominal interest rate, real GDP, financial innovation
    C. Price level, real interest rate, nominal GDP, financial innovation

43. Which are most likely goals of monetary policy?

    A. GDP growth and full employment
    B. Tax revenues increase and unemployment insurance payments decrease
    *C.Maximum employment, stable prices, and moderate long-term interest rates

44. Which is a decision rule for monetary policy that sets the policy instrument at a level that makes the forecast of the ultimate policy goal the target?

    A. Instrument rule
    *B. Targeting rule
    C. k-percent rule

45. Where would information about material events and uncertainties best be found?

    A. Footnotes
    B. Proxy statement
    *C. Management's discussion and analysis

46. What is designed to allocate activity to the proper period?

    *A. Accrual accounting
    B. Statement of cash flows
    C. Statement of owners' equity

47. Which is the most likely effect on the accounting equation if $10,000 in cash is used to pay $6,000 in prepaid rent and a $4,000 security deposit?

    A. Assets decrease by $10,000
    B. Assets decrease by $6,000
    *C. There is no change in assets

48. What are presentation requirements for financial statements under IAS No. 1?

    A. Going concern, accrual basis, consistency, and materiality
    B. Balance sheet, income statement, statement of changes in equity, cash flow statement, and notes
    *C. Aggregation where appropriate, no offsetting, classified balance sheet, minimum information on face, minimum note disclosure, and comparative information

49. Under which financial reporting framework is there a broad focus to provide relevant information to a wide range of users?

    A. IFRS but not FASB
    B. FASB but not IFRS
    *C. Both IFRS and FASB

50. Which are not included in the calculation of revenue reported on an accrual basis if for the year revenue is $1,000; cost of goods sold equals $800; returns of goods sold are $100; and cash collected is $700?

    A. $100 for return of goods sold and $700 for cash collected
    B. $100 for return of goods sold and $800 for cost of goods sold
    *C.$700 for cash collected and $800 for cost of goods sold

51. Which would least likely be considered part of the matching principle of expense recognition?

    A. Expenses are matched either to revenue or the time period in which the expenditure occurs
    B. Expenses are matched to the time period of the expected benefits of the expenditures
    *C.Expenses are matched to the present value of the cash flows associated with the expense

52. Which depreciation method would be the most conservative in the first year?

    A. Straight-line depreciation with a short useful life
    B. Straight-line depreciation with a long useful life
    *C.Double declining balance method with a short useful life

53. Under U.S. GAAP, which is least likely to be considered other comprehensive income?

    A. Foreign currency translation adjustments
    B. Unrealized holding gains and losses on available-for-sale securities
    *C.Realized gains or losses on real estate investments

54. What is the cost of an asset at acquisition?

    A. Fair value
    B. Current cost
    *C.Historical cost

55. Receipts from issuing stock would be in what category on a cash flow statement?

    A. Investing
    B. Operating
    *C.Financing

56. What are methods for reporting operating cash flow?

    *A. Indirect or direct
    B. Income or expense
    C. Financing or investing

57. Which is least likely a prescribed approach for preparing common-size cash flow statements?

    *A. Percentage of total assets method
    B. Percentage of net revenues method
    C. Total cash inflows/total cash outflows method

58. Which is closest to inventory expense under IFRS if inventory was purchased for $10 million and $1 million was spent for bringing the inventory to its present location?

    A. $9 million
    B. $10 million
    *C.$11 million

59. In a period of rising prices, what is the most likely difference for a company that uses FIFO rather than LIFO?

    A. Lower current assets, lower gross income
    B. Lower current assets, higher gross income
    *C.Higher current assets, higher gross income

60. Which estimate regarding an asset results in the lowest cash flow?

    A. Six-year useful life and no salvage value
    B. Seven-year useful life and no salvage value
    *C.Seven-year useful life and positive salvage value

61. What can occur at the time a decision is made to sell an asset and before the actual sale?

    A. A gain or loss
    *B.A loss but not a gain
    C. A gain but not a loss

62. Which would most likely result from accounting standards requiring an asset to be expensed immediately and tax rules requiring the asset to be capitalized and amortized?

   *A. Deferred tax asset
   B. Deferred tax liability
   C. No deferred tax asset or liability

63. Which recognizes a deferred tax asset in full then reduces it by a valuation allowance if it is more likely than not that some or all of the deferred tax asset will not be realized?

   *A. U.S. GAAP but not IFRS
   B. IFRS but not U.S. GAAP
   C. Both U.S. GAAP and IFRS

64. What is a comparison of a company with peer companies?

   A. Trend analysis
   B. Time-series analysis
   *C.Cross-sectional analysis

65. What is least likely to explain an increase in inventory turnover?

   A. More efficient inventory management system
   B. Large write-offs of inventory at the beginning of the period
   *C.Operational difficulties resulting in duplicate orders with suppliers

66. Calculate return on equity (ROE) if sales divided by total assets are 2, net profit margin is 4%, return on total assets is 8%, and total assets divided by equity is 3?

   A. 12%
   *B.24% = 4%(2)(3)= 8%(3)
   C. 48%

67. Which is a constraint related to the preparation of information in a financial statement?

   *A. Timeliness
   B. Neutrality
   C. Accrual basis

68. Under IFRS, which category of marketable securities is most likely to have an asymmetrical treatment of income and changes in value?

    A. Held for trading
    B. Held to maturity
    *C.Available for sale

69. If a company paid $10 million for property 5 years ago, the market value of the property is $15 million, and it would cost $2 million to build roads and utilities to get the land ready for building, what is the cost of the land for capital budgeting purposes?

    A. $10 million
    B. $15 million
    *C.$17 million = $15 million + $2 million

70. Which is least likely to be considered a drawback of the payback period method of capital budgeting?

    *A. It is simple
    B. It ignores risk and the time value of money
    C. It ignores cash flows after the payback period

71. Which is preferred if a company must choose one project between two mutually exclusive projects; project A with an NPV of $50 million and an IRR of 35%; and project B with an NPV of $100 million and an IRR of 25%?

    A. Project A because it has a greater IRR
    B. Project B because it has a lower IRR
    *C.Project B because it has a greater NPV

72. Which is closest to the weights used for the weighted average cost of capital (WACC) if the a company has bonds with $10 million in face value, 8% coupons with semi-annual payments, five years to maturity, and priced to yield 13.65%; and 1.2 million shares of stock outstanding at $10 per share?

    *A. 40% bonds, 60% equity; PV of bonds = $8 million where FV = $10 million, n = 10, i = 13.65/2, PMT = $0.4 million; and equity = 1.2 million ($10) = $12 million; $8 / ($8 + $12) = 40%, $12 / ($8 + $12) = 60%
    B. 50% bonds, 50% equity
    C. 60% bonds, 40% equity

73. Which is closest to the after-tax cost of debt using the debt-rating approach if a company sells a 10-year 4% semi-annual coupon AAA rated bond, the marginal tax rate is 40%, and the yield on debt with the same rating is 5%?

    A. 2.4%
    *B.3.0% = 5% (1-40%)
    C. 3.2%

74. What is an estimate of the cost of equity if the expected dividends are $5, the market price is $100, the company's earnings retention rate is 67%, ROE is 6%, and the risk-free rate is 3%?

    *A. 9% = ($5/$100) + [(67%)(6%)]
    B. 11%
    C. 18%

75. What is the number of days of inventory if annual cost of goods sold is $12 million, accounts receivable are $3 million, and inventory is $4 million?

    A. 91.25
    *B.121.67 = $4 / ($12 / 365)
    C. 152.09

76. Which company had the highest number of days of inventory if company A had an operating cycle of 176 days, credit sales of $30 million, and an average receivables balance of $12 million; company B had an operating cycle of 142 days, credit sales of $25 million and an average receivables balance of $8 million; and company C had an operating cycle of 108 days, credit sales of $50 million and an average receivables balance of $10 million?

    A. Company A
    B. Company B
    *C.Company C; 108 - $10 / ($50 / 365) = 35 >176 - $12 / ($30/365) = 30 > 142 - $8 / ($25/365) = 25

77. Which is least likely to be equal to return on assets using DuPont analysis?

    A. Net profit margin times total asset turnover
    *B.Total asset turnover times financial leverage
    C. Net income divided by revenue, times revenue divided by average total assets

78. Which is closest to the total asset turnover if the operating profit margin is 7.7%, the effect of non-operating items is 0.9, the tax effect is 0.8, financial leverage is 1.2, and the return on equity is 10%?

   A. 1.25
   B. 1.33
   *C. 1.50 = 10% / [(7.7%)(0.9)(0.8)(1.2)]

79. Where do new issues of securities occur?

   *A. Primary market
   B. Secondary market
   C. Third market

80. Which statement is most accurate regarding continuous markets?

   A. Markets are physical places where traders and dealers gather
   *B. Trading takes place at various prices and times as buy and sell orders arrive
   C. Security trades are executed at specific times at a single price after buy and sell orders have accumulated

81. What specifies the buy or sell price?

   A. Short sale
   *B. Limit order
   C. Market order

82. What type of security market index is most like investing an equal dollar amount in each stock?

   *A. Unweighted
   B. Price-weighted
   C. Value-weighted

83. What is the correlation between investment grade bonds and high-yield bonds?

   A. 19%
   *B. 49%
   C. 95%

84. Which form of the efficient market hypothesis (EMH) is tested by performance of insiders, specialists, money managers, and analyst recommendations?

    A. Weak form
    *B.Strong form
    C. Semi-strong form

85. Which can result from the retention of people with a good investment record?

    A. Selection bias
    *B.Survivorship bias
    C. Incorrect measurement of abnormal return

86. Which is closest to the value of common stock with a current dividend of $1, a dividend growth rate of 7%, and a required rate of return of 12%?

    A. $20.00
    *B.$21.40 = $1(1.07) / (12% - 7%)
    C. $22.40

87. Which is most likely to result in a higher value of common stock using the earnings multiplier model?

    *A. Higher dividend payout ratio
    B. Higher required rate of return
    C. Lower growth rate of dividends

88. Which is closest to the growth rate of equity earnings without any external financing if the retention rate is 40%, the profit margin is 10%, the total asset turnover is 0.4, the return on assets is 4%, and the financial leverage is 2?

    *A. 3.2% = 40% (10%)(0.4)(2) = 40% (4%)(2)
    B. 4.8%
    C. 6.0%

89. What best describes a company whose future earnings are likely to withstand an economic downturn?

    A. Growth company
    *B.Defensive company
    C. Speculative company

90. Which is least likely to be considered a drawback of using price to book value (P / B) ratios?

    A. Comparability
    B. Accounting effects such as expensing R&D
    *C.Not appropriate for companies not expected to continue as going concern

91. Which is least likely to be a characteristic of a futures contract?

    *A. Over-the-counter market
    B. Daily settlement of gains and losses
    C. Clearinghouse guarantee against credit losses

92. Which statement is least accurate regarding Eurodollar time deposits?

    A. The primary Eurodollar rate is called LIBOR
    *B.Eurodollar time deposits are loans made in Euros by one bank to another
    C. Eurodollar deposits accrue interest by adding it on to the principal, using a 360-day year assumption

93. What is the ending balance at the end of day 4 for a holder of a long position of 20 futures contracts if the initial futures price on day 0 is $212, the initial margin requirement is $10, the maintenance margin requirement is $8, the settlement price on day 1 is $211, the settlement price on day 2 is $214, the settlement price on day 3 is $209, and the settlement price on day 4 is $210?

    A. $160
    *B.$220 = $200 - $20 + $60 - $100 + $60 + $20; where $200 is the initial deposit, $20 is the loss on day 1, $60 is the gain on day 2, $100 is the loss on day 3; triggering a maintenance call, $60 is the deposit on day 3 to bring the balance to $200, $20 is the gain on day 4; the ending balances days 0 through 4 are $200, $180, $240, $140, and $220
    C. $240

94. An investor goes long one futures contract at $50 with 2 days to expiration. The settlement price 1 day before expiration is $52 and the mark to market profit is $2. The settlement price at expiration is $53. How is the futures contract terminated by cash settlement?

    *A. Receive $53 - $52 = $1
    B. Pay $52, receive asset worth $53
    C. Sell contract at $53 for a mark to market profit of $53 - $52 = $1

95. What is the value that can be captured if an option is exercised?

    A. Time value
    B. Moneyness
    *C. Intrinsic value

96. What is the profit for a covered call option at expiration, for a stock selling for $98 and a call option at $105 selling for $8, if the stock price at expiration is $88?

    *A. -$2 = $88 - Max ($0, $88 - $105) - $98 + $8
    B. $0
    C. $2

97. What is the full price of a bond if the clean price is $1,050 and the accrued interest is $25?

    A. $1,025
    B. $1,050
    *C. $1,075

98. Which imbedded option is an advantage to the issuer?

    A. Put provision
    B. Floor on a floater
    *C. Accelerated sinking fund

99. What is the price of a bond when the coupon rate is greater than the yield required by the market?

    A. Equal to par value
    B. Less than par value
    *C. Greater then par value

100. Which is closest to the duration of a bond if the current price is 102, the price if yields decline by 50 basis points is 109, and the price if yields rise by 50 basis points is 96?

    *A. 12.75 = (109 - 96) / [2 (102)(.005)]
    B. 19.12
    C. 25.49

101. Which is least likely to be considered credit risk?

    *A. Interest rate risk
    B. Downgrade risk
    C. Credit spread risk

102. What risk is associated with natural disasters?

    *A. Event risk
    B. Volatility risk
    C. Purchasing power risk

103. What includes secured bonds, unsecured or debenture bonds, and credit enhanced bonds?

    *A. Corporate bonds
    B. Structured notes
    C. Commercial paper

104. How can the Federal Reserve withdraw funds from the market?

    *A. Selling Treasury securities
    B. Purchasing Treasury securities
    C. Decreasing the discount rate

105. What do investors require for an issue with a call option with a longer deferred call period compared to a shorter deferred call period?

    A. Larger yield spread
    *B. Smaller yield spread
    C. The same yield spread

106. What relates the annual dollar coupon interest to the market price and fails to recognize any capital gain or loss and reinvestment income?

    *A. Current yield
    B. Yield to maturity
    C. Bond-equivalent yield

107. If the spot rates on an annual basis are 3.0% for 6 months, 3.3% for 1 year, and 3.5% for 1.5 years, which is closest to the price of a $100 par, 3% coupon 1.5-year Treasury security?

    *A. $99 = 1.5 / 1.015 + 1.5 / 1.0165^2 + 101.5 / 1.0175^3
    B. $100
    C. $101

108. Bonds with positive convexity

    A. Are always superior to bonds with negative convexity
    B. Will have less price appreciation than its price decline for a large change in interest rates
    *C. Will have greater price appreciation than its price decline for a large change in interest rates

109. What definition of duration should be used for bonds with embedded options?

    A. Modified duration
    *B. Effective duration
    C. Macaulay duration

110. Which is closest to percentage price change for a bond with modified duration of 10.66 and convexity of 81.95 if yields increase by 200 basis points?

    *A. -18.04% = -10.66 (.02) + 81.95 (.02)^2
    B. -14.76%
    C. -11.48%

111. Which is most likely to be considered a disadvantage of exchange-traded funds (ETFs)?

    A. Lack of diversification
    B. Significant premiums or discounts to NAV
    *C. Narrow-based market index tracked in some countries

112. A real estate investment project has a first-year NOI of $83,800 that is expected to grow by 5% per year. The purchase price is $700,000 which is financed 20% by equity and 80% by a mortgage loan at 10% pre-tax interest and level annual payments of $59,404. Should the project be recommended based on the NPV of the project using a required rate of return of 16% if the property is sold at the end of the fifth year for $875,000, property sales expenses are 6%, depreciation is $18,700 per year, five years of principal payments total $20,783, the marginal tax rate is 31%, the capital gains tax rate is 20%, and the after-tax cash flow for the first five years are $21,575, $24,361, $27,280, $30,339, and $273,629?

    A. No, based on an NPV of -$61,215
    B. Yes, based on an NPV of $33,461
    *C.Yes, based on an NPV of $61,215 = $21,575/1.16 + $24,361/1.16^2 + $27,280/1.16^3 + $30,339/1.16^4 + $273,629/1.16^5 - 20%($700,000)

113. Which most accurately describes a challenge to venture capital performance measurement?

    A. Too many benchmarks to choose from
    B. Short-term nature of performance feedback
    *C.Difficulty in determining precise valuations

114. For a hedge fund index compared to a stock index, most likely the average return is

    *A. Overstated and the Sharpe ratio is overstated
    B. Overstated and the Sharpe ratio is understated
    C. Understated and the standard deviation is overstated

115. For which goal would high risk investments be least appropriate?

    A. Lower-priority goals
    *B.Near-term, high-priority goals
    C. Long-term, high-priority goals

116. Which is most accurate regarding what asset allocation explains for a single fund?

    A. 40% of the average fund's level of return
    B. 40% of a single fund's variations in returns over time
    *C.90% of a single fund's variations in returns over time

117. What is closest to the correlation coefficient if the sum of the products of the returns minus mean returns for two securities for 12 monthly periods is 5%, and the variances are 0.64% and 1.44%?

    A. 0.43
    *B.0.47 = (5% / 11) / [(0.64%^.5)(1.44%^.5)]
    C. 0.67

118. The optimal portfolio is the efficient portfolio that has

    A. The lowest risk
    B. The highest return
    *C.The highest utility

119. Which statement about portfolio risk and diversification is least accurate?

    A. Systematic risk cannot be eliminated through diversification
    *B.Unsystematic risk cannot be significantly reduced through diversification
    C. Diversification results from combining securities with less than perfect correlations

120. What relates the expected or required rate of return of an asset to its beta?

    A. CML
    *B.SML
    C. Efficient frontier

1. Which statement is least accurate regarding the process for enforcement of CFA Institute Code and Standards?

   A. If a member rejects the proposed sanction from the Designated officer, the matter is referred to a hearing by a panel of CFA Institute members
   B. The Designated Officer may conclude the inquiry with no disciplinary action, issue a cautionary letter, or continue disciplinary proceedings
   C. Candidates in the CFA program who have violated the Code and Standards will be allowed to continue to participate in the CFA program

2. CFA charterholder Wei, an analyst in the corporate finance department of an investment services firm, is making a presentation to a potential new business client that includes the promise that her firm will provide full research coverage of the potential client and provide a favorable recommendation. Were any Standards of Professional Conduct violated?

   A. No, Wei did not actually commit to providing a favorable recommendation
   B. Yes, Wei violated the standard on market manipulation by making a commitment that the research department provide a favorable recommendation
   C. Yes, Wei violated the standard on independence and objectivity by making a commitment that the research department provide a favorable recommendation

3. CFA charterholder Liu wants to include a description of financial concepts in the firm's marketing materials. Liu uses verbatim descriptions from other sources without a reference to the original author. Did Liu violate any Standards of Professional Conduct?

   A. No
   B. Yes, relating to loyalty
   C. Yes, relating to misrepresentation

4. CFA charterholder Barker declares bankruptcy after accumulating large amounts of debt obtained in a fraudulent manner. Did Barker violate any Standards of Professional Conduct?

   A. No
   B. Yes, relating to misconduct
   C. Yes, relating to loyalty, prudence, and care

5. CFA charterholder Zou is an analyst covering South American equities who has her firm use the services of a research firm affiliated with a brokerage house that uses soft dollars from commission income pays for her briefing trip to South America, including five days in Rio de Janeiro during Carnival. Zou does not determine if the commissions are reasonable in relation to the benefit of the research. Zou most likely violated the Standard of Professional Conduct relating to

    A. Loyalty, prudence, and care
    B. Additional compensation arrangements
    C. Communications with clients and prospective clients

6. CFA charterholder Kumar allocates profitable trades to an unhappy client and spreads losing trades to other accounts. Which Standard of Professional Conduct did Kumar most likely violate?

    A. Fair dealing
    B. Market manipulation
    C. Disclosure of conflicts

7. CFA charterholder Case treats all clients the same, and makes the same recommendations for all clients. Which Standard of Professional Conduct did Case most likely violate?

    A. Loyalty
    B. Suitability
    C. Diligence and reasonable basis

8. CFA charterholder O'Cull is leaving his employer and takes employer property. Which Standard of Professional Conduct did O'Cull most likely violate?

    A. Loyalty
    B. Preservation of confidentiality
    C. Additional compensation arrangements

9. To comply with the standard on responsibilities for supervisors, a member who is a supervisor must

    A. Prevent violations of the law
    B. Establish and implement written compliance procedures
    C. Prevent violations of the CFA Code of Ethics and Standards of Professional Conduct

10. As a hobby, CFA charterholder Manning runs a popular internet blog where he makes stock recommendations based on the performance of sports teams. The site lists his bio and employment history. Which Standard of Professional Conduct did Manning least likely violate?

    A. Fair dealing
    B. Duties to employers
    C. Diligence and reasonable basis

11. CFA charterholder Singh owns stock in a company and issues a report with a buy recommendation for the same company, without mentioning her ownership. Singh believes the stock is a good buy. Singh is most likely to have violated the Standard of Professional Conduct on

    A. Disclosure of conflicts
    B. Market manipulation
    C. Additional compensation arrangements

12. Which is least likely to be a recommended procedure for compliance with the standard on priority of transactions?

    A. Blackout / restricted periods
    B. Limited participation in equity IPOs
    C. No restrictions on private placements

13. CFA candidate Ellis takes investment actions on his own behalf rather than on behalf of his clients. Which Standard of Professional Conduct did Ellis least likely violate?

    A. Misconduct
    B. Priority of transactions
    C. Diligence and reasonable basis

14. Which statement conflicts with the recommended procedures for compliance in the Standards of Practice Handbook?

    A. Firms should disclose to clients the personal investing policies and procedures established for their employees
    B. For confidentiality reasons, personal transactions and holdings should not be reported to employers unless mandated by regulatory organizations
    C. Personal transactions should be defined as including securities owned by the employee and members of his or her immediate family and transactions involving securities in which the employee has a financial interest

15. CFA charterholder Scott estimates that Walkton Industries will raise their dividend to $1.50. The increase is contingent on favorable legislation relating to Walkton passing. Scott writes in his research report that the stock price is expected to increase by $8.00 per share and the dividend will increase to $1.50 per share, and investors can expect a 15% total return. Did Scott violate any Standards of Professional Conduct?

    A. No
    B. Yes, by not separating fact from opinion
    C. Yes, by using material nonpublic information

16. CFA charterholder Rooker recommends the purchase of a mutual fund that invests solely in long-term U.S. Treasury bonds. Rooker tells clients that if they invest in the fund, they will earn 8% each year for the next several years. Did Rooker violate any Standards of Professional Conduct?

    A. No
    B. Yes, related to misrepresentation
    C. Yes, related to diligence and reasonable basis

17. To comply with the GIPS, composite returns must be calculated by

    A. Averaging the portfolio returns
    B. Time-weighting the portfolio returns
    C. Asset-weighting the portfolio returns

18. Which is one of the eight major sections of the GIPS?

    A. Input data
    B. Fixed income
    C. Confidentiality

19. Which is closest to the interest rate for an ordinary annuity with a present value of $14 million and payments of $2 million for each of the next ten years?

    A. 6%
    B. 7%
    C. 8%

20. Compare the annual money-weighted and time-weighted rates of return for an account with a value of $400 at the beginning of year 1 and a value of $200 at the end of year 1, cash flows of $300 at the beginning of year 2, and a value at the end year 2 of $1,000?

    A. The money-weighted return will be greater than the time-weighted return
    B. The money-weighted return will be less than the time-weighted return
    C. The money-weighted return and the time-weighted return will be the same

21. Given 1 observation in the 2% to 4% interval, 3 in the 4% to 6% interval, 4 in the 6% to 8% interval, and 2 in the 8% to 10% interval, what is the relative frequency and cumulative relative frequency of the 2% to 4% interval?

    A. Relative frequency = 10%, cumulative relative frequency = 10%
    B. Relative frequency = 20%, cumulative relative frequency = 10%
    C. Relative frequency = 10%, cumulative relative frequency = 90%

22. Which is least likely to be useful as a measure of dispersion?

    A. Standard deviation
    B. Random variable
    C. Mean absolute deviation

23. What is the difference between the mean return on a portfolio and mean return on the risk free rate?

    A. The Sharpe Ratio
    B. Mean excess return
    C. Coefficient of variation

24. What is the approximate geometric return on an investment class if the arithmetic mean was 12% and the standard deviation was 20%?

    A. 8%
    B. 10%
    C. 14%

25. If 60% of portfolio managers who had performance that ranked in the top 50% of all managers for the first year also ranked in the top 50% for the second year, what is the probability that a manager was in the top 50% for both years?

    A. 25%
    B. 30%
    C. 50%

26. What is the expected return for a portfolio with 75% in equities with an expected return of 9% and 25% in bonds with an expected return of 3%?

    A. 7.5%
    B. 7.8%
    C. 8.0%

27. What is a model for calculating a bond's price an example of?

    A. Probability distribution
    B. Discrete random variable
    C. Continuous random variable

28. If an investment manager has a 50% probability of beating a benchmark each year, what is the probability of beating the benchmark in less than or equal to 2 out of 4 years?

    A. 0.6875
    B. 0.8125
    C. 0.9375

29. Which is least accurate regarding a normal distribution?

    A. The normal distribution has a skewness of 3 and kurtosis of 0
    B. The normal distribution is completely described by its mean and standard deviation
    C. A linear combination of two or more normal distributions is also normally distributed

30. Which allocation is optimal when a client with a portfolio of $100,000 would like to withdraw $5,000 at the year end and avoid the balance dropping below $100,000: allocation 1 with an expected return of 10% and a standard deviation of 8%, allocation 2 with an expected return of 11% and a standard deviation of 9%, or allocation 3 with an expected return of 8% and a standard deviation of 5%?

    A. 1
    B. 2
    C. 3

31. What approach would be used to create a bond index by dividing bonds into categories by issuer, maturity, and imbedded options, then selecting bonds from the subpopulations?

    A. Simple random sampling
    B. Systematic sampling
    C. Stratified random sampling

32. What sampling issue comes from using data not available at the time market participants act?

    A. Look-ahead bias
    B. Time-period bias
    C. Data-mining bias

33. What happens to demand for a resource when the price of a substitute resource increases?

    A. Increases
    B. Decreases
    C. Stays the same

34. Which group is most likely to have greater unemployment as a result of an increase in the minimum wage?

    A. Teachers
    B. Low-skilled workers
    C. High-skilled workers

35. What is a firm with two or more owners with unlimited liability?

    A. Proprietorship
    B. Partnership
    C. Corporation

36. What is least likely a reason firms are more efficient than markets as coordinators of economic activity?

    A. Higher transaction costs
    B. Economies of team production
    C. Economies of scope

37. Which is the least likely monopoly price-setting strategy?

    A. Market price
    B. Single price
    C. Price discrimination

38. What is the least likely outcome when a monopoly adopts perfect price discrimination?

    A. The total surplus is shared with consumers
    B. Price for marginal unit less than for other units
    C. Output increases to where price equals marginal cost

39. What is the supply of a given piece of land?

    A. Perfectly inelastic
    B. Perfectly elastic
    C. Elastic

40. Which is least likely to lower real GDP?

    A. Hurricane
    B. Terrorist attack
    C. Technology shock

41. Which is the most likely long-run effect of an increase in government spending if the economy is operating at full employment?

    A. The price level stays the same and real GDP increases
    B. The price level increases and real GDP stays the same
    C. The price level increases and real GDP increases

42. An increase in the natural unemployment rate most likely shifts

    A. The long-run and short-run Phillips curves to the left
    B. The long-run and short-run Phillips curves to the right
    C. The long-run Phillips curve to the right and the short-run Phillips curve to the left

43. Which is least likely to increase during an expansion?

    A. Growth
    B. Unemployment
    C. Inflation

44. Which is least likely to result from the Federal Reserve System selling securities in the open market?

    A. Fed assets and liabilities increase
    B. Buying bank exchanges reserves for securities
    C. Reduces bank reserves

45. What would be best to evaluate to determine a company's current financial position?

    A. Balance sheet
    B. Income statement
    C. Cash flow statement

46. The most likely initial effect on the accounting equation if a group of investors form a new company with an investment of $100,000 is an increase in cash and

    A. Revenue
    B. Liabilities
    C. Contributed capital

47. Under IFRS, what is the preparation of a complete set of financial statements best described as?

    A. Objective of financial reporting
    B. General requirement of financial reporting
    C. Qualitative framework of IFRS framework

48. What is the center of the IFRS framework?

    A. The enforcement of financial reporting rules
    B. The objective of fair presentation of useful information
    C. Reliance on the judgment of financial statement preparers

49. Which is a characteristic of an effective financial reporting framework?

    A. Accuracy
    B. Timeliness
    C. Comprehensiveness

50. Under IFRS, which is least likely a condition that must be met for revenue to be recognized?

    A. Goods have been delivered
    B. Costs can be reasonably measured
    C. Revenue can be reasonably measured

51. Which is closest to the profit that will be reported in the first year under the installment method if property purchased for $5 million was sold for $6 million with $4 million payable the first year and the remaining $2 million payable the second year?

    A. $0.0 million
    B. $0.5 million
    C. $0.7 million

52. Which is closest to the second year depreciation using the straight line method for equipment costing $50,000 with a residual value of $5,000 and a useful life of 10 years?

    A. $4,000
    B. $4,500
    C. $5,000

53. How is diluted EPS calculated for a company with a simple capital structure?

    A. The treasury stock method
    B. The if-converted method
    C. The same as basic EPS

54. What best describes amounts paid by a company to acquire certain rights that are not represented by the possession of physical assets?

    A. Tangible assets
    B. Noncurrent assets
    C. Intangible assets

55. What measures whether a company can meet its long-term debt and other obligations?

    A. Acid test
    B. Liquidity ratio
    C. Solvency ratio

56. What method for reporting cash flow activities reconciles net income to cash flow from operating activities by adjusting net income for all noncash items and the net changes in the operating working capital accounts?

    A. Direct
    B. Indirect
    C. Common-size

57. What would most likely be measured by the sum of cash flow from operating activities divided by net revenue, assets, equity, or operating income?

    A. Solvency
    B. Coverage
    C. Performance

58. Which is closest to inventory reported on the balance sheet under U.S. GAAP if an art dealer purchased inventory for $2 million, later wrote-it down to $1 million, then it was discovered that one item was extremely more valuable than thought and the inventory was now worth $3 million?

    A. $1 million
    B. $2 million
    C. $3 million

59. Which is least likely to have occurred if company A uses U.S. GAAP and company B uses IFRS?

    A. Company A reversed an inventory write-down
    B. Company B reversed an inventory write-down
    C. Company A and company B both use FIFO

60. A longer useful life and greater salvage value

    A. Increase the initial amount of annual depreciation
    B. Decrease the initial amount of annual depreciation
    C. Have no impact on the initial amount of annual depreciation

61. What is the amount that will be deductible for tax purposes as an expense in the calculation of taxable income as the company expenses the tax basis?

    A. Tax base of an asset
    B. Carrying amount of an asset
    C. Carrying amount of a liability

62. How are deferred tax liabilities treated as when both timing and amount of tax payment is uncertain?

    A. Liabilities
    B. Equity
    C. Neither liabilities nor equity

63. Which permits offset of deferred tax assets and liabilities only when the entity has a legally enforceable right to offset and the balance relates to tax levied by the same authority?

    A. U.S. GAAP but not IFRS
    B. IFRS but not U.S. GAAP
    C. Both U.S. GAAP and IFRS

64. How do solvency ratios appear if financial instruments with characteristics of both debt and equity are treated as equity?

    A. Weaker
    B. Stronger
    C. The same

65. If days of inventory on hand increased, day's sales outstanding decreased, and number of days payables increased, which was least likely to have contributed to improved liquidity?

    A. Inventory management
    B. Management of payables
    C. Management of receivables

66. Which would decrease ROA with all other variables constant?

    A. Decrease in tax rate
    B. Increase in average assets
    C. Decrease in interest expense

67. Which would most likely be added to total liabilities to evaluate solvency?

    A. LIFO inventory
    B. The present value of future operating lease payments
    C. The present value of future capital lease payments

68. Which is used by IFRS to determine need for consolidation when accounting for investments?

    A. Model based on voting control but not economic control
    B. Model based on economic control but not voting control
    C. Model based on both voting control and economic control

69. What are categories of projects susceptible to the capital budgeting process?

    A. Generating ideas, analyzing individual proposals, planning, and monitoring and post auditing
    B. Replacement, expansion, new products and services, and regulatory, safety, and environmental
    C. Net present value, internal rate of return, payback period, and discounted payback period

70. Which is least likely to be considered a drawback of the average accounting rate of return method of capital budgeting?

    A. It is easy to calculate
    B. It ignores the time value of money
    C. It does not distinguish between profitable and unprofitable investments

71. Which capital budgeting problem can arise for a project with cash flows of positive $100 at time 0, negative $300 at time 1, and positive $250 at time 2?

    A. The multiple IRR problem but not the no IRR problem
    B. The no IRR problem but not the multiple IRR problem
    C. Both the multiple IRR problem and the no IRR problem

72. Which is closest to the after-tax cost of debt if a company sells a $1,000 face value 20-year 6% semi-annual coupon bond for $900 and the marginal tax rate is 35%?

    A. 4.5%
    B. 4.8%
    C. 5.0%

73. What is the cost of common stock using the CAPM?

    A. Beta times the risk-free rate plus alpha
    B. Risk-free rate plus beta times the equity risk premium
    C. Beta times the risk-free rate plus the equity risk premium

74. Which is closest to the project beta using the pure-play method if the comparable asset beta is 1.4, the project is financed 60% with debt, and the marginal tax rate is 20%?

    A. 3
    B. 4
    C. 5

75. Which is closest to the cost of equity for a project if the comparable asset beta is 1.1, the project is financed 80% with debt, the marginal tax rate is 30%, the risk-free rate is 3%, the domestic equity risk premium is 5%, and the country risk premium for the country of the project is 2%?

    A. 18%
    B. 28%
    C. 32%

76. What is the bond equivalent yield for a 182-day $10,000 U.S. T-bill with a purchase price of $9,750?

    A. 4.95%
    B. 5.07%
    C. 5.14%

77. Given the net profit margin is 3.6%, operating profit margin is 5.0%, effect of non-operating items is 0.9, the tax effect is 0.8, total asset turnover is 2.0, and financial leverage is 1.5; which is closest to the expected return on equity using DuPont analysis if financial leverage increases to 2.1, reducing the effect of non-operating items to 0.86?

    A. 10%
    B. 11%
    C. 14%

78. Which shareowner voting practice is least likely to be supportive of shareowner protection?

    A. Public voting
    B. Cumulative voting
    C. Voting on changes to by-laws

79. What is an asset's likelihood of being sold quickly regardless of whether or not the price is known?

    A. Liquidity
    B. Marketability
    C. Price continuity

80. What are alternate trading systems (ATSs) including Electronic Communication Networks (ECNs) and Electronic Crossing Systems (ECSs) associated with?

    A. Secondary market
    B. Third market
    C. Fourth market

81. When would a short sale most likely be used?

    A. A zero uptick
    B. To limit losses
    C. When the price is expected to decline

82. For a margin account with an initial margin requirement of 50%, a purchase of 100 shares at $30, and a maintenance margin of 25%, what is the price at which the investor will get a margin call?

    A. $15
    B. $20
    C. $25

83. Which is least accurate regarding the correlations between the S&P 500 and world equity indexes?

    A. U.S. - U.K. correlation about 0.67
    B. U.S. - Japan correlation about 0.38
    C. U.S. - Canada correlation about 0.25

84. Autocorrelation tests

    A. Are a test of trading rules
    B. Study the correlation of stock price changes over time
    C. Have confirmed the strong form of the efficient market hypothesis

85. If short selling is more difficult than buying long, then prices are likely to be

    A. Unbiased
    B. Biased upward
    C. Biased downward

86. Which is least likely to explain why a mispricing would persist?

    A. Arbitrage is too costly
    B. Profit potential is insufficient
    C. The mispricing is well understood

87. Which is closest to the P/E ratio of a common stock with a dividend payout ratio of 50%, a dividend growth rate of 8%, and a required rate of return of 13%?

    A. 8
    B. 9
    C. 10

88. Which is closest to price of a share using the dividend discount model (DDM) with a dividend payout ratio of 60%, a dividend growth rate of 6%, beta of 1.2, a market risk premium of 5%, a risk-free rate of 3%, a weighted-average cost of capital of 10%, and current earnings per share of $2?

    A. $31.80
    B. $42.40
    C. $47.70

89. What best describes a company that invests in projects with returns above the cost of capital?

    A. Growth stock
    B. Growth company
    C. Defensive company

90. A company had EPS of $1 for 2004, $1 for 2005, $1 for 2006, $2 for 2007, and -$1 for 2008; book value per share (BVPS) of $8 for 2004, $9 for 2005, $16 for 2006, $19 for 2007, and $16 for 2008; and ROE of 12% for 2004, 6% for 2005, 8% for 2006, and 8% for 2007. If the current market price is $50, what is the normalized P/E based on the method of average ROE?

    A. 36.8
    B. 38.4
    C. 40.0

91. What is an over-the-counter transaction consisting of a series of forward commitments?

    A. Swap
    B. Option
    C. Futures contract

92. What is the main risk for an investor who enters into a forward contract to buy the S&P 500 index?

    A. The market may rise
    B. The market may fall
    C. Market volatility may rise

93. Which is least accurate regarding futures contracts?

    A. Trade on exchange
    B. Have a secondary market
    C. Not guaranteed against default

94. If the IMM index price for a Treasury bill futures contract is 93.75, which is closest to the change in price of the contract if the IMM index declines to 93.50?

    A. $500
    B. $625
    C. $2,500

95. An asset manager enters into a $50 million equity swap and agrees to pay a dealer the return on a small-cap index and the dealer agrees to pay a fixed rate of 5.5%. Payments are made semi-annually based on 180 days out of a 365-day year. The value of the small-cap index starts at 234.10. In six months, the small cap index is at 241.27. Which party pays what amount after the payments are netted?

    A. The asset manager pays the dealer $175,233
    B. The dealer pays the asset manager $175,233
    C. The dealer pays the asset manager $2,887,561

96. Which is least accurate regarding the graphs of covered calls and protective put values and profits compared to the value of the underlying security at expiration?

    A. For covered calls, the graph changes from a line with an upward slope to a horizontal line
    B. For protective puts, the graph changes from a horizontal line to a line with an downward slope
    C. For covered calls and protective puts, the value at expiration line is above the profit line

97. Callable bonds are more likely to be called if

    A. Interest rates increase
    B. Interest rates decrease
    C. Interest rates are stable

98. What provision allows the issuer to retire more of the issue each year than required?

    A. Sinking fund
    B. Make-whole premium
    C. Accelerated sinking fund

99. Which is least likely to explain why the price of a floating rate security will fluctuate?

    A. The required margin that investors demand in the market changes
    B. The shorter the time to the next coupon reset date, the greater the potential price fluctuation
    C. Floating-rate securities typically have a cap, and once the cap is reached, the price reacts much the same as a fixed-rate security

100. Which is closest to the dollar price change for a 25 basis point change in yield for a bond with a par value of $5 million, market value of $4.875 million, and a duration of 5.6?

    A. $68,250
    B. $70,000
    C. $71,750

101. Option-free bonds are least likely exposed to

    A. Liquidity risk
    B. Volatility risk
    C. Reinvestment risk

102. How are Treasury securities sold in the primary market?

    A. Ad hoc auction system
    B. Over-the-counter market
    C. Sealed bid auction system on a regular cycle using a single-price method

103. The rating of an asset-backed securities can be improved by transferring assets to a

    A. Bank
    B. Collateralized debt obligation
    C. Special purpose corporation

104. What shape of the yield curve reflects an expectation that future short-term rates will fall?

   A. Flat
   B. Inverted
   C. Upward sloping

105. Which is closest to the change in present value of a 5-year security with a 7% annual coupon and a par value of $100, using a discount rate of 9% rather than 7%?

   A. Decrease of $8.66
   B. Decrease of $7.78
   C. Increase of $8.66

106. Which is closest to the yield to put for a 7% 8-year bond selling for $94.17, callable at 101 in 4 years and putable at 100 in 4 years?

   A. 8.6%
   B. 8.8%
   C. 9.0%

107. Which spread measure uses all points the Treasury spot rate curve as a benchmark, reflects compensation for credit risk, liquidity risk, and adjusts for volatility?

   A. Bid-ask
   B. Nominal
   C. Option-adjusted

108. For a 9% coupon option-free bond, the price changes by 12% if market yields decrease 100 basis points. What is the price change if yields increase 100 basis points?

   A. Decrease by less than 12%
   B. Decrease exactly 12%
   C. Decrease by more than 12%

109. What is the approximate percentage change in a bond's price for a 100 basis point change in yield assuming that the bond's expected cash flows do change when the yield changes?

   A. Convexity
   B. Modified duration
   C. Effective duration

110. Which is closest to percentage price change if yields decrease by 200 basis points for a callable bond with an effective duration of 4 and a convexity adjustment for a 200 basis point change of -1.2%??

    A. -9.2%
    B. -8.0%
    C. -6.8%

111. An investor is considering 3 classes of mutual funds: class A has a 3% sales load on purchases, no deferred sales charge on redemptions, and 1.25% in annual expenses; class B has no sales load on purchases, a deferred sales charge on redemptions of 5% in the first year declining by 1 percentage point each year thereafter, and 1.50% in annual expenses for the first 6 years then 1.25% per year thereafter; and class C has no sales load on purchases, a deferred sales charge on redemptions of 1% per year for the initial two years, and 1.50% in annual expenses. Which class would provide the greatest net return for an investor who must liquidate after 1 year with a gross return of 8%?

    A. Class C ($1.0532), followed by class A ($1.0345), and class B ($1.0106)
    B. Class A ($1.0345), followed by class C ($1.0332), and class B ($1.0106)
    C. Class C ($1.0532), followed by class B ($1.0345), and class A ($1.0106)

112. A real estate investment project has a first-year NOI of $83,800 that is expected to grow by 5% per year. The purchase price is $700,000 which is financed 20% by equity and 80% by a mortgage loan at 10% pre-tax interest and level annual payments of $59,404. Which is closest to the first-year after-tax cash flow if depreciation is $18,700 per year, the marginal tax rate is 31%, and the first year mortgage interest is $56,000?

    A. $21,575
    B. $24,361
    C. $24,979

113. Which venture capital investments are most likely to be considered expansion stage financing?

    A. Seed stage and early stage financing
    B. Second stage and third stage financing
    C. All stages, seed through mezzanine

114. How do commodities complement the investment opportunities offered by shares of corporations that extensively use these raw materials in their production processes?

   A. As a vehicle for investing in production and consumption
   B. As a result of their extremely high positive correlations with inflation and stock and bond returns
   C. As a result of their extremely high negative correlations with inflation and stock and bond returns

115. Which portfolio is most appropriate for a 65-year old investor with moderate risk tolerance?

   A. 100% cash
   B. 15% to 25% bonds, 75% to 85% stocks
   C. 55% to 65% bonds, 35% to 45% stocks

116. Which is least likely to be a legal constraint on institutional investors?

   A. No more than 10% of pension fund assets in the company's stock
   B. No more than 10% of assets in companies doing business in unfriendly nations
   C. No more than 5% of mutual fund assets in any one company's stock

117. What is the covariance closest to if the sum of products of returns minus mean returns for two securities for 6 monthly periods is 2.22%?

   A. 0.317%
   B. 0.370%
   C. 0.444%

118. Which is closest to the standard deviation of a portfolio with a 50% weight in each of two securities, one with an expected return of 15% and a standard deviation of 10%, and the other with an expected return of 20% and a standard deviation of 20%, if the correlation coefficient is 0.6?

   A. 8.1%
   B. 9.7%
   C. 13.6%

119. What is point of tangency of the capital market line (CML) with the efficient frontier?

   A. Risky portfolio
   B. Market portfolio
   C. Risk-free portfolio

120. Which statement is least accurate regarding the zero-beta model?

    A. A minimum variance zero-beta portfolio has no unsystematic risk
    B. Several portfolios exist where the returns are completely uncorrelated with the market portfolio
    C. From among the several zero-beta portfolios, investors should choose one with minimum variance

1. C	41. B	81. C
2. C	42. B	82. B
3. C	43. B	83. C
4. B	44. A	84. B
5. A	45. A	85. B
6. A	46. C	86. C
7. B	47. B	87. C
8. A	48. B	88. B
9. B	49. C	89. B
10. A	50. A	90. A
11. A	51. C	91. A
12. C	52. B	92. B
13. C	53. C	93. C
14. B	54. C	94. B
15. B	55. C	95. A
16. B	56. B	96. B
17. C	57. C	97. B
18. A	58. A	98. C
19. B	59. A	99. B
20. A	60. B	100. A
21. A	61. A	101. B
22. B	62. C	102. C
23. B	63. C	103. C
24. B	64. B	104. B
25. B	65. A	105. B
26. A	66. B	106. B
27. A	67. B	107. C
28. A	68. A	108. A
29. A	69. B	109. C
30. B	70. A	110. A
31. C	71. B	111. A
32. A	72. A	112. A
33. A	73. A	113. B
34. B	74. A	114. A
35. B	75. C	115. C
36. A	76. C	116. B
37. A	77. C	117. C
38. A	78. A	118. C
39. A	79. B	119. B
40. C	80. C	120. A

1. Which statement is least accurate regarding the process for enforcement of CFA Institute Code and Standards?

    A. If a member rejects the proposed sanction from the Designated officer, the matter is referred to a hearing by a panel of CFA Institute members

    B. The Designated Officer may conclude the inquiry with no disciplinary action, issue a cautionary letter, or continue disciplinary proceedings

    *C.Candidates in the CFA program who have violated the Code and Standards will be allowed to continue to participate in the CFA program

2. CFA charterholder Wei, an analyst in the corporate finance department of an investment services firm, is making a presentation to a potential new business client that includes the promise that her firm will provide full research coverage of the potential client and provide a favorable recommendation. Were any Standards of Professional Conduct violated?

    A. No, Wei did not actually commit to providing a favorable recommendation

    B. Yes, Wei violated the standard on market manipulation by making a commitment that the research department provide a favorable recommendation

    *C.Yes, Wei violated the standard on independence and objectivity by making a commitment that the research department provide a favorable recommendation (Standard I(B) - independence and objectivity)

3. CFA charterholder Liu wants to include a description of financial concepts in the firm's marketing materials. Liu uses verbatim descriptions from other sources without a reference to the original author. Did Liu violate any Standards of Professional Conduct?

    A. No

    B. Yes, relating to loyalty

    *C.Yes, relating to misrepresentation (Standard I(C) - misrepresentation)

4. CFA charterholder Barker declares bankruptcy after accumulating large amounts of debt obtained in a fraudulent manner. Did Barker violate any Standards of Professional Conduct?

    A. No

    *B.Yes, relating to misconduct (Standard I(D) - misconduct)

    C. Yes, relating to loyalty, prudence, and care

5. CFA charterholder Zou is an analyst covering South American equities who has her firm use the services of a research firm affiliated with a brokerage house that uses soft dollars from commission income pays for her briefing trip to South America, including five days in Rio de Janeiro during Carnival. Zou does not determine if the commissions are reasonable in relation to the benefit of the research. Zou most likely violated the Standard of Professional Conduct relating to

   *A. Loyalty, prudence, and care (Standard III(A) - loyalty, prudence, and care)
   B. Additional compensation arrangements
   C. Communications with clients and prospective clients

6. CFA charterholder Kumar allocates profitable trades to an unhappy client and spreads losing trades to other accounts. Which Standard of Professional Conduct did Kumar most likely violate?

   *A. Fair dealing (Standard III(B) - fair dealing)
   B. Market manipulation
   C. Disclosure of conflicts

7. CFA charterholder Case treats all clients the same, and makes the same recommendations for all clients. Which Standard of Professional Conduct did Case most likely violate?

   A. Loyalty
   *B.Suitability (Standard III(C) - suitability)
   C. Diligence and reasonable basis

8. CFA charterholder O'Cull is leaving his employer and takes employer property. Which Standard of Professional Conduct did O'Cull most likely violate?

   *A. Loyalty (Standard IV(A) - loyalty)
   B. Preservation of confidentiality
   C. Additional compensation arrangements

9. To comply with the standard on responsibilities for supervisors, a member who is a supervisor must

   A. Prevent violations of the law
   *B.Establish and implement written compliance procedures (Standard IV(C) - responsibilities of supervisors)
   C. Prevent violations of the CFA Code of Ethics and Standards of Professional Conduct

10. As a hobby, CFA charterholder Manning runs a popular internet blog where he makes stock recommendations based on the performance of sports teams. The site lists his bio and employment history. Which Standard of Professional Conduct did Manning least likely violate?

   *A. Fair dealing (Standard V(A) - diligence and reasonable basis and Standard IV - duties to employers)
   B. Duties to employers
   C. Diligence and reasonable basis

11. CFA charterholder Singh owns stock in a company and issues a report with a buy recommendation for the same company, without mentioning her ownership. Singh believes the stock is a good buy. Singh is most likely to have violated the Standard of Professional Conduct on

   *A. Disclosure of conflicts (Standard VI(A) - disclosure of conflicts and Standard I(B) - independence and objectivity)
   B. Market manipulation
   C. Additional compensation arrangements

12. Which is least likely to be a recommended procedure for compliance with the standard on priority of transactions?

   A. Blackout / restricted periods
   B. Limited participation in equity IPOs
   *C. No restrictions on private placements (Standard VI(B) - priority of transactions)

13. CFA candidate Ellis takes investment actions on his own behalf rather than on behalf of his clients. Which Standard of Professional Conduct did Ellis least likely violate?

   A. Misconduct
   B. Priority of transactions
   *C. Diligence and reasonable basis (Standard VI(B) - priority of transactions, Standard I(D) - misconduct, and Standard IV(A) - loyalty)

14. Which statement conflicts with the recommended procedures for compliance in the Standards of Practice Handbook?

    A. Firms should disclose to clients the personal investing policies and procedures established for their employees
    *B. For confidentiality reasons, personal transactions and holdings should not be reported to employers unless mandated by regulatory organizations (Standard IV(C) - responsibilities of supervisors)
    C. Personal transactions should be defined as including securities owned by the employee and members of his or her immediate family and transactions involving securities in which the employee has a financial interest

15. CFA charterholder Scott estimates that Walkton Industries will raise their dividend to $1.50. The increase is contingent on favorable legislation relating to Walkton passing. Scott writes in his research report that the stock price is expected to increase by $8.00 per share and the dividend will increase to $1.50 per share, and investors can expect a 15% total return. Did Scott violate any Standards of Professional Conduct?

    A. No
    *B. Yes, by not separating fact from opinion (Standard V(B) - communication with clients and prospective clients)
    C. Yes, by using material nonpublic information

16. CFA charterholder Rooker recommends the purchase of a mutual fund that invests solely in long-term U.S. Treasury bonds. Rooker tells clients that if they invest in the fund, they will earn 8% each year for the next several years. Did Rooker violate any Standards of Professional Conduct?

    A. No
    *B. Yes, related to misrepresentation (Standard I(C) - misrepresentation)
    C. Yes, related to diligence and reasonable basis

17. To comply with the GIPS, composite returns must be calculated by

    A. Averaging the portfolio returns
    B. Time-weighting the portfolio returns
    *C. Asset-weighting the portfolio returns

18. Which is one of the eight major sections of the GIPS?

    *A. Input data
    B. Fixed income
    C. Confidentiality

19. Which is closest to the interest rate for an ordinary annuity with a present value of $14 million and payments of $2 million for each of the next ten years?

    A. 6%
    *B. 7% because $14/$2 = [(1 - (1/1.07)^10] / .07; n = 10, PV = 14,000,000, PMT = 2,000,000, FV = 0; i = 7.07 percent = 7.07%
    C. 8%

20. Compare the annual money-weighted and time-weighted rates of return for an account with a value of $400 at the beginning of year 1 and a value of $200 at the end of year 1, cash flows of $300 at the beginning of year 2, and a value at the end year 2 of $1,000?

    *A. The money-weighted return will be greater than the time-weighted return; money-weighted = 25% where 400 + 300/(1+r) = 1000/(1+r)^2; CF0 = -400, CF1 = -300, CF2 = 1000; IRR = 25.0 percent = 25%; Time-weighted = 0%; [(200/400)(1000/500)]^.5 - 1 = 0.00%
    B. The money-weighted return will be less than the time-weighted return
    C. The money-weighted return and the time-weighted return will be the same

21. Given 1 observation in the 2% to 4% interval, 3 in the 4% to 6% interval, 4 in the 6% to 8% interval, and 2 in the 8% to 10% interval, what is the relative frequency and cumulative relative frequency of the 2% to 4% interval?

    *A. Relative frequency = 10%, cumulative relative frequency = 10%
    B. Relative frequency = 20%, cumulative relative frequency = 10%
    C. Relative frequency = 10%, cumulative relative frequency = 90%

22. Which is least likely to be useful as a measure of dispersion?

    A. Standard deviation
    *B. Random variable
    C. Mean absolute deviation

23. What is the difference between the mean return on a portfolio and mean return on the risk free rate?

    A. The Sharpe Ratio
    *B. Mean excess return
    C. Coefficient of variation

24. What is the approximate geometric return on an investment class if the arithmetic mean was 12% and the standard deviation was 20%?

    A. 8%
    *B. 10% = 12% - .5 (.2)^2
    C. 14%

25. If 60% of portfolio managers who had performance that ranked in the top 50% of all managers for the first year also ranked in the top 50% for the second year, what is the probability that a manager was in the top 50% for both years?

    A. 25%
    *B. 30% = 60% (50%)
    C. 50%

26. What is the expected return for a portfolio with 75% in equities with an expected return of 9% and 25% in bonds with an expected return of 3%?

    *A. 7.5% = .75 (9%) + .25 (3%)
    B. 7.8%
    C. 8.0%

27. What is a model for calculating a bond's price an example of?

    *A. Probability distribution
    B. Discrete random variable
    C. Continuous random variable

28. If an investment manager has a 50% probability of beating a benchmark each year, what is the probability of beating the benchmark in less than or equal to 2 out of 4 years?

    *A. 0.6875 = .5^4 + 4 (.5^4) + 6 (.5^4)
    B. 0.8125
    C. 0.9375

29. Which is least accurate regarding a normal distribution?

    *A. The normal distribution has a skewness of 3 and kurtosis of 0
    B. The normal distribution is completely described by its mean and standard deviation
    C. A linear combination of two or more normal distributions is also normally distributed

30. Which allocation is optimal when a client with a portfolio of $100,000 would like to withdraw $5,000 at the year end and avoid the balance dropping below $100,000: allocation 1 with an expected return of 10% and a standard deviation of 8%, allocation 2 with an expected return of 11% and a standard deviation of 9%, or allocation 3 with an expected return of 8% and a standard deviation of 5%?

   A. 1
   *B.2, (11%-5%)/9%>(10%-5%)/8%>(8%-5%)/5%
   C. 3

31. What approach would be used to create a bond index by dividing bonds into categories by issuer, maturity, and imbedded options, then selecting bonds from the subpopulations?

   A. Simple random sampling
   B. Systematic sampling
   *C.Stratified random sampling

32. What sampling issue comes from using data not available at the time market participants act?

   *A. Look-ahead bias
   B. Time-period bias
   C. Data-mining bias

33. What happens to demand for a resource when the price of a substitute resource increases?

   *A. Increases
   B. Decreases
   C. Stays the same

34. Which group is most likely to have greater unemployment as a result of an increase in the minimum wage?

   A. Teachers
   *B.Low-skilled workers
   C. High-skilled workers

35. What is a firm with two or more owners with unlimited liability?

   A. Proprietorship
   *B.Partnership
   C. Corporation

36. What is least likely a reason firms are more efficient than markets as coordinators of economic activity?

   *A. Higher transaction costs
   B. Economies of team production
   C. Economies of scope

37. Which is the least likely monopoly price-setting strategy?

   *A. Market price
   B. Single price
   C. Price discrimination

38. What is the least likely outcome when a monopoly adopts perfect price discrimination?

   *A. The total surplus is shared with consumers
   B. Price for marginal unit less than for other units
   C. Output increases to where price equals marginal cost

39. What is the supply of a given piece of land?

   *A. Perfectly inelastic
   B. Perfectly elastic
   C. Elastic

40. Which is least likely to lower real GDP?

   A. Hurricane
   B. Terrorist attack
   *C.Technology shock

41. Which is the most likely long-run effect of an increase in government spending if the economy is operating at full employment?

   A. The price level stays the same and real GDP increases
   *B.The price level increases and real GDP stays the same
   C. The price level increases and real GDP increases

42. An increase in the natural unemployment rate most likely shifts

   A. The long-run and short-run Phillips curves to the left
   *B.The long-run and short-run Phillips curves to the right
   C. The long-run Phillips curve to the right and the short-run Phillips curve to the left

43. Which is least likely to increase during an expansion?

    A. Growth
    *B.Unemployment
    C. Inflation

44. Which is least likely to result from the Federal Reserve System selling securities in the open market?

    *A. Fed assets and liabilities increase
    B. Buying bank exchanges reserves for securities
    C. Reduces bank reserves

45. What would be best to evaluate to determine a company's current financial position?

    *A. Balance sheet
    B. Income statement
    C. Cash flow statement

46. The most likely initial effect on the accounting equation if a group of investors form a new company with an investment of $100,000 is an increase in cash and

    A. Revenue
    B. Liabilities
    *C.Contributed capital

47. Under IFRS, what is the preparation of a complete set of financial statements best described as?

    A. Objective of financial reporting
    *B.General requirement of financial reporting
    C. Qualitative framework of IFRS framework

48. What is the center of the IFRS framework?

    A. The enforcement of financial reporting rules
    *B.The objective of fair presentation of useful information
    C. Reliance on the judgment of financial statement preparers

49. Which is a characteristic of an effective financial reporting framework?

    A. Accuracy
    B. Timeliness
    *C.Comprehensiveness

50. Under IFRS, which is least likely a condition that must be met for revenue to be recognized?

    *A. Goods have been delivered
    B. Costs can be reasonably measured
    C. Revenue can be reasonably measured

51. Which is closest to the profit that will be reported in the first year under the installment method if property purchased for $5 million was sold for $6 million with $4 million payable the first year and the remaining $2 million payable the second year?

    A. $0.0 million
    B. $0.5 million
    *C.$0.7 million = ($4/$6) ($6 - $5)

52. Which is closest to the second year depreciation using the straight line method for equipment costing $50,000 with a residual value of $5,000 and a useful life of 10 years?

    A. $4,000
    *B.$4,500 = ($50,000 - $5,000) / 10
    C. $5,000

53. How is diluted EPS calculated for a company with a simple capital structure?

    A. The treasury stock method
    B. The if-converted method
    *C.The same as basic EPS

54. What best describes amounts paid by a company to acquire certain rights that are not represented by the possession of physical assets?

    A. Tangible assets
    B. Noncurrent assets
    *C.Intangible assets

55. What measures whether a company can meet its long-term debt and other obligations?

    A. Acid test
    B. Liquidity ratio
    *C.Solvency ratio

56. What method for reporting cash flow activities reconciles net income to cash flow from operating activities by adjusting net income for all noncash items and the net changes in the operating working capital accounts?

    A. Direct
    *B.Indirect
    C. Common-size

57. What would most likely be measured by the sum of cash flow from operating activities divided by net revenue, assets, equity, or operating income?

    A. Solvency
    B. Coverage
    *C.Performance

58. Which is closest to inventory reported on the balance sheet under U.S. GAAP if an art dealer purchased inventory for $2 million, later wrote-it down to $1 million, then it was discovered that one item was extremely more valuable than thought and the inventory was now worth $3 million?

    *A. $1 million
    B. $2 million
    C. $3 million

59. Which is least likely to have occurred if company A uses U.S. GAAP and company B uses IFRS?

    *A. Company A reversed an inventory write-down
    B. Company B reversed an inventory write-down
    C. Company A and company B both use FIFO

60. A longer useful life and greater salvage value

    A. Increase the initial amount of annual depreciation
    *B.Decrease the initial amount of annual depreciation
    C. Have no impact on the initial amount of annual depreciation

61. What is the amount that will be deductible for tax purposes as an expense in the calculation of taxable income as the company expenses the tax basis?

    *A. Tax base of an asset
    B. Carrying amount of an asset
    C. Carrying amount of a liability

62. How are deferred tax liabilities treated as when both timing and amount of tax payment is uncertain?

   A. Liabilities
   B. Equity
   *C. Neither liabilities nor equity

63. Which permits offset of deferred tax assets and liabilities only when the entity has a legally enforceable right to offset and the balance relates to tax levied by the same authority?

   A. U.S. GAAP but not IFRS
   B. IFRS but not U.S. GAAP
   *C. Both U.S. GAAP and IFRS

64. How do solvency ratios appear if financial instruments with characteristics of both debt and equity are treated as equity?

   A. Weaker
   *B. Stronger
   C. The same

65. If days of inventory on hand increased, day's sales outstanding decreased, and number of days payables increased, which was least likely to have contributed to improved liquidity?

   *A. Inventory management
   B. Management of payables
   C. Management of receivables

66. Which would decrease ROA with all other variables constant?

   A. Decrease in tax rate
   *B. Increase in average assets
   C. Decrease in interest expense

67. Which would most likely be added to total liabilities to evaluate solvency?

   A. LIFO inventory
   *B. The present value of future operating lease payments
   C. The present value of future capital lease payments

68. Which is used by IFRS to determine need for consolidation when accounting for investments?

    *A. Model based on voting control but not economic control
    B. Model based on economic control but not voting control
    C. Model based on both voting control and economic control

69. What are categories of projects susceptible to the capital budgeting process?

    A. Generating ideas, analyzing individual proposals, planning, and monitoring and post auditing
    *B.Replacement, expansion, new products and services, and regulatory, safety, and environmental
    C. Net present value, internal rate of return, payback period, and discounted payback period

70. Which is least likely to be considered a drawback of the average accounting rate of return method of capital budgeting?

    *A. It is easy to calculate
    B. It ignores the time value of money
    C. It does not distinguish between profitable and unprofitable investments

71. Which capital budgeting problem can arise for a project with cash flows of positive $100 at time 0, negative $300 at time 1, and positive $250 at time 2?

    A. The multiple IRR problem but not the no IRR problem
    *B.The no IRR problem but not the multiple IRR problem
    C. Both the multiple IRR problem and the no IRR problem

72. Which is closest to the after-tax cost of debt if a company sells a $1,000 face value 20-year 6% semi-annual coupon bond for $900 and the marginal tax rate is 35%?

    *A. 4.5% = 2(3.47%)(1-35%) where PV = -$900, FV = $1,000, PMT = $30, and n = 40; i = 3.47
    B. 4.8%
    C. 5.0%

73. What is the cost of common stock using the CAPM?

    *A. Beta times the risk-free rate plus alpha
    B. Risk-free rate plus beta times the equity risk premium
    C. Beta times the risk-free rate plus the equity risk premium

74. Which is closest to the project beta using the pure-play method if the comparable asset beta is 1.4, the project is financed 60% with debt, and the marginal tax rate is 20%?

    *A. 3 = 1.4[1 + ((1-20%)(60%/40%))]
    B. 4
    C. 5

75. Which is closest to the cost of equity for a project if the comparable asset beta is 1.1, the project is financed 80% with debt, the marginal tax rate is 30%, the risk-free rate is 3%, the domestic equity risk premium is 5%, and the country risk premium for the country of the project is 2%?

    A. 18%
    B. 28%
    *C. 32% = 3% + {1.1[1 + ((1-30%)(80%/20%))]}(5% + 2%)

76. What is the bond equivalent yield for a 182-day $10,000 U.S. T-bill with a purchase price of $9,750?

    A. 4.95%
    B. 5.07%
    *C. 5.14% = [($10,000 - $9,750)/$9,750](365/182)

77. Given the net profit margin is 3.6%, operating profit margin is 5.0%, effect of non-operating items is 0.9, the tax effect is 0.8, total asset turnover is 2.0, and financial leverage is 1.5; which is closest to the expected return on equity using DuPont analysis if financial leverage increases to 2.1, reducing the effect of non-operating items to 0.86?

    A. 10%
    B. 11%
    *C. 14% = 5.0% (0.86)(0.8)(2.0)(2.1)

78. Which shareowner voting practice is least likely to be supportive of shareowner protection?

    *A. Public voting
    B. Cumulative voting
    C. Voting on changes to by-laws

79. What is an asset's likelihood of being sold quickly regardless of whether or not the price is known?

    A. Liquidity
    *B.Marketability
    C. Price continuity

80. What are alternate trading systems (ATSs) including Electronic Communication Networks (ECNs) and Electronic Crossing Systems (ECSs) associated with?

    A. Secondary market
    B. Third market
    *C.Fourth market

81. When would a short sale most likely be used?

    A. A zero uptick
    B. To limit losses
    *C.When the price is expected to decline

82. For a margin account with an initial margin requirement of 50%, a purchase of 100 shares at $30, and a maintenance margin of 25%, what is the price at which the investor will get a margin call?

    A. $15
    *B.$20 = $30 (1 - 50%) / (1 - 25%); [100($20) - $1,500] / [100($20)] = 25%
    C. $25

83. Which is least accurate regarding the correlations between the S&P 500 and world equity indexes?

    A. U.S. - U.K. correlation about 0.67
    B. U.S. - Japan correlation about 0.38
    *C.U.S. - Canada correlation about 0.25

84. Autocorrelation tests

    A. Are a test of trading rules
    *B.Study the correlation of stock price changes over time
    C. Have confirmed the strong form of the efficient market hypothesis

85. If short selling is more difficult than buying long, then prices are likely to be

    A. Unbiased
    *B.Biased upward
    C. Biased downward

86. Which is least likely to explain why a mispricing would persist?

    A. Arbitrage is too costly
    B. Profit potential is insufficient
    *C.The mispricing is well understood

87. Which is closest to the P/E ratio of a common stock with a dividend payout ratio of 50%, a dividend growth rate of 8%, and a required rate of return of 13%?

    A. 8
    B. 9
    *C.10 = 50% / (13% - 8%)

88. Which is closest to price of a share using the dividend discount model (DDM) with a dividend payout ratio of 60%, a dividend growth rate of 6%, beta of 1.2, a market risk premium of 5%, a risk-free rate of 3%, a weighted-average cost of capital of 10%, and current earnings per share of $2?

    A. $31.80
    *B.$42.40 = [$2 (60%)(1.06) / (9% - 6%)] where 9% = 3% + 5%(1.2)
    C. $47.70

89. What best describes a company that invests in projects with returns above the cost of capital?

    A. Growth stock
    *B.Growth company
    C. Defensive company

90. A company had EPS of $1 for 2004, $1 for 2005, $1 for 2006, $2 for 2007, and -$1 for 2008; book value per share (BVPS) of $8 for 2004, $9 for 2005, $16 for 2006, $19 for 2007, and $16 for 2008; and ROE of 12% for 2004, 6% for 2005, 8% for 2006, and 8% for 2007. If the current market price is $50, what is the normalized P/E based on the method of average ROE?

    *A. 36.8 = $50 / {[(12% + 6% + 8% + 8%) / 4]($16)}
    B. 38.4
    C. 40.0

91. What is an over-the-counter transaction consisting of a series of forward commitments?

    *A. Swap
    B. Option
    C. Futures contract

92. What is the main risk for an investor who enters into a forward contract to buy the S&P 500 index?

    A. The market may rise
    *B.The market may fall
    C. Market volatility may rise

93. Which is least accurate regarding futures contracts?

    A. Trade on exchange
    B. Have a secondary market
    *C.Not guaranteed against default

94. If the IMM index price for a Treasury bill futures contract is 93.75, which is closest to the change in price of the contract if the IMM index declines to 93.50?

    A. $500
    *B.$625 = $1,000,000[(1 - (1 - .9375)(90/360))] - $1,000,000[(1 - (1 - .9350)(90/360))] = 25 ($25)
    C. $2,500

95. An asset manager enters into a $50 million equity swap and agrees to pay a dealer the return on a small-cap index and the dealer agrees to pay a fixed rate of 5.5%. Payments are made semi-annually based on 180 days out of a 365-day year. The value of the small-cap index starts at 234.10. In six months, the small cap index is at 241.27. Which party pays what amount after the payments are netted?

    *A. The asset manager pays the dealer $175,233 = $50,000,000(241.27/234.10 - 1) - $50,000,000(5.5%) (180/365)
    B. The dealer pays the asset manager $175,233
    C. The dealer pays the asset manager $2,887,561

96. Which is least accurate regarding the graphs of covered calls and protective put values and profits compared to the value of the underlying security at expiration?

  A. For covered calls, the graph changes from a line with an upward slope to a horizontal line
  *B.For protective puts, the graph changes from a horizontal line to a line with an downward slope
  C. For covered calls and protective puts, the value at expiration line is above the profit line

97. Callable bonds are more likely to be called if

  A. Interest rates increase
  *B.Interest rates decrease
  C. Interest rates are stable

98. What provision allows the issuer to retire more of the issue each year than required?

  A. Sinking fund
  B. Make-whole premium
  *C.Accelerated sinking fund

99. Which is least likely to explain why the price of a floating rate security will fluctuate?

  A. The required margin that investors demand in the market changes
  *B.The shorter the time to the next coupon reset date, the greater the potential price fluctuation
  C. Floating-rate securities typically have a cap, and once the cap is reached, the price reacts much the same as a fixed-rate security

100. Which is closest to the dollar price change for a 25 basis point change in yield for a bond with a par value of $5 million, market value of $4.875 million, and a duration of 5.6?

  *A. $68,250 = [(5.6%)/4] ($4.875 million)
  B. $70,000
  C. $71,750

101. Option-free bonds are least likely exposed to

  A. Liquidity risk
  *B.Volatility risk
  C. Reinvestment risk

102. How are Treasury securities sold in the primary market?

    A. Ad hoc auction system
    B. Over-the-counter market
    *C.Sealed bid auction system on a regular cycle using a single-price method

103. The rating of an asset-backed securities can be improved by transferring assets to a

    A. Bank
    B. Collateralized debt obligation
    *C.Special purpose corporation

104. What shape of the yield curve reflects an expectation that future short-term rates will fall?

    A. Flat
    *B.Inverted
    C. Upward sloping

105. Which is closest to the change in present value of a 5-year security with a 7% annual coupon and a par value of $100, using a discount rate of 9% rather than 7%?

    A. Decrease of $8.66
    *B.Decrease of $7.78; where n = 5, i = 9, PMT = 7, FV = 100, resulting in PV = -92.22; $100 - $108.65 = $7.88
    C. Increase of $8.66

106. Which is closest to the yield to put for a 7% 8-year bond selling for $94.17, callable at 101 in 4 years and putable at 100 in 4 years?

    A. 8.6%
    *B.8.8%; where n = 8, PV = -94.17, PMT = 3.5, FV = 100, resulting in i = 4.38, 2(4.38%) = 8.8%
    C. 9.0%

107. Which spread measure uses all points the Treasury spot rate curve as a benchmark, reflects compensation for credit risk, liquidity risk, and adjusts for volatility?

    A. Bid-ask
    B. Nominal
    *C.Option-adjusted

108. For a 9% coupon option-free bond, the price changes by 12% if market yields decrease 100 basis points. What is the price change if yields increase 100 basis points?

    *A. Decrease by less than 12%
    B. Decrease exactly 12%
    C. Decrease by more than 12%

109. What is the approximate percentage change in a bond's price for a 100 basis point change in yield assuming that the bond's expected cash flows do change when the yield changes?

    A. Convexity
    B. Modified duration
    *C.Effective duration

110. Which is closest to percentage price change if yields decrease by 200 basis points for a callable bond with an effective duration of 4 and a convexity adjustment for a 200 basis point change of -1.2%??

    *A. -9.2% = -8.0% - 1.2%
    B. -8.0%
    C. -6.8%

111. An investor is considering 3 classes of mutual funds: class A has a 3% sales load on purchases, no deferred sales charge on redemptions, and 1.25% in annual expenses; class B has no sales load on purchases, a deferred sales charge on redemptions of 5% in the first year declining by 1 percentage point each year thereafter, and 1.50% in annual expenses for the first 6 years then 1.25% per year thereafter; and class C has no sales load on purchases, a deferred sales charge on redemptions of 1% per year for the initial two years, and 1.50% in annual expenses. Which class would provide the greatest net return for an investor who must liquidate after 1 year with a gross return of 8%?

    *A. Class C ($1.0532), followed by class A ($1.0345), and class B ($1.0106); .A: $0.97(1.08)(1-.0125)=$1.0345; B: $1(1.08)(1-0.015)(1-0.05)=$1.0106; C: $1(1.08)(1-0.015)(1-0.01)=$1.0532
    B. Class A ($1.0345), followed by class C ($1.0332), and class B ($1.0106)
    C. Class C ($1.0532), followed by class B ($1.0345), and class A ($1.0106)

112. A real estate investment project has a first-year NOI of $83,800 that is expected to grow by 5% per year. The purchase price is $700,000 which is financed 20% by equity and 80% by a mortgage loan at 10% pre-tax interest and level annual payments of $59,404. Which is closest to the first-year after-tax cash flow if depreciation is $18,700 per year, the marginal tax rate is 31%, and the first year mortgage interest is $56,000?

   *A. $21,575 = ($83,800 - $18,700 - $56,000)(1 - 31%) + $18,700 - ($59,404 - $56,000)
   B. $24,361
   C. $24,979

113. Which venture capital investments are most likely to be considered expansion stage financing?

   A. Seed stage and early stage financing
   *B. Second stage and third stage financing
   C. All stages, seed through mezzanine

114. How do commodities complement the investment opportunities offered by shares of corporations that extensively use these raw materials in their production processes?

   *A. As a vehicle for investing in production and consumption
   B. As a result of their extremely high positive correlations with inflation and stock and bond returns
   C. As a result of their extremely high negative correlations with inflation and stock and bond returns

115. Which portfolio is most appropriate for a 65-year old investor with moderate risk tolerance?

   A. 100% cash
   B. 15% to 25% bonds, 75% to 85% stocks
   *C. 55% to 65% bonds, 35% to 45% stocks

116. Which is least likely to be a legal constraint on institutional investors?

   A. No more than 10% of pension fund assets in the company's stock
   *B. No more than 10% of assets in companies doing business in unfriendly nations
   C. No more than 5% of mutual fund assets in any one company's stock

117. What is the covariance closest to if the sum of products of returns minus mean returns for two securities for 6 monthly periods is 2.22%?

   A. 0.317%
   B. 0.370%
   *C.0.444% = 2.22% / 5

118. Which is closest to the standard deviation of a portfolio with a 50% weight in each of two securities, one with an expected return of 15% and a standard deviation of 10%, and the other with an expected return of 20% and a standard deviation of 20%, if the correlation coefficient is 0.6?

   A. 8.1%
   B. 9.7%
   *C.13.6% = [(50%^2)(10%^2) + (50%^2)(20%^2) +
       2(50%)(50%)(0.6)(10%)(20%)]^.5

119. What is point of tangency of the capital market line (CML) with the efficient frontier?

   A. Risky portfolio
   *B.Market portfolio
   C. Risk-free portfolio

120. Which statement is least accurate regarding the zero-beta model?

   *A. A minimum variance zero-beta portfolio has no unsystematic risk
   B. Several portfolios exist where the returns are completely uncorrelated with the market portfolio
   C. From among the several zero-beta portfolios, investors should choose one with minimum variance

1. Which statement is most accurate related to the Standard of Professional Conduct on knowledge of the law?

    A. In the event of conflict, members must comply with the more strict law, rule, or regulation

    B. The member's responsibility to respond shall be subject to applicable restrictions on confidential information and those imposed by law

    C. A member is not expected to discuss an apparent unresolved material violation with another member if either member is prohibited by law from doing so

2. CFA charterholder Takagi supports the sales effort of her corporate bond department and offers credit guidance to fixed-income security buyers. Her compensation is linked to the compensation of the corporate bond department. Salespeople have asked her to contact large clients to push the bonds of Surles, Ltd. because the company has a large position it has been unable to sell because of Surles' recent announcement of an operating problem, and Takagi agrees despite being unable to justify that the market price has already adjusted for the operating problem. Were any Standards of Professional Conduct violated?

    A. No

    B. Yes, relating to duties to employers

    C. Yes, relating to independence and objectivity

3. Which statement is least accurate related to the Standard of Professional Conduct on professionalism?

    A. Members and candidates must act for the benefit of their clients and place their clients' interests before their employer's or their own interests

    B. Members and candidates must not knowingly make any misrepresentations relating to investment analysis, recommendations, actions, or other professional activities

    C. Members and candidates must not engage in any professional conduct involving dishonesty, fraud, or deceit or commit any act that reflects adversely on their professional reputation, integrity, or competence

4. The president of a company accepts a tender offer and decides to sell his family business at a significant premium over the current share price. The president tells his sister, who tells her daughter, who tells her husband, CFA charterholder Kazun. Kazun tells his broker, CFA charterholder Jumani. Jumani buys shares for himself. Who violated the Standards of Professional Conduct?

    A. Kazun only

    B. Jumani only

    C. Kazun and Jumani

5. Which statement is least accurate related to the Standard of Professional Conduct on duties to clients?

    A. Members and candidates have a duty of loyalty to their clients and must act with reasonable care and exercise prudent judgment

    B. Members and candidates must act for the benefit of their clients and place their clients' interests before their employer's or their own interests

    C. Members and candidates who possess material nonpublic information that could affect the value of an investment must not act or cause others to act on the information

6. When making investments in new offerings or secondary financings, CFA charterholder Brack allocates issues to new accounts first and discloses the policy to all current and prospective clients. Did Brack violate any Standards of Professional Conduct?

    A. No

    B. Yes, all discretionary accounts were not treated equally

    C. Yes, disclosure of the policy does not fulfill the duty regarding equitable allocation methods

7. CFA charterholder Dutta joins a new firm and prepares marketing material for his new firm including his performance at his previous employer without identifying the performance as having been while with another firm. Did Dutta violate and Standards of Professional Conduct?

    A. No

    B. Yes, relating to duty to employers

    C. Yes, relating to performance presentation

8. Compiling a list of contacts based on a client list used with a previous employer is most likely to violate which Standard of Professional Conduct?

    A. None

    B. Loyalty

    C. Preservation of confidentiality

9. CFA charterholder Essaheb supervises CFA charterholder Dabrowski at a registered investment advisory and registered broker/dealer firm. Dabrowski makes S&P 500 futures trades so that the most profitable trades go to the company's profit sharing plan and the least profitable trades go to the other funds. The firm has no documented procedures for futures trading. Essaheb most likely violated which Standard of Professional Conduct?

    A. Priority of transactions
    B. Responsibilities of supervisors
    C. Diligence and reasonable basis

10. CFA charterholder Shapsis is a junior analyst. Shapsis prepares a report for the firm's investment committee to review. The committee does not agree with the report and makes changes. What is the least appropriate action for Shapsis?

    A. Document her differences
    B. Ask to have her name removed
    C. Insist that the report be changed back

11. Regarding the Standard of Professional Conduct related to record retention, the CFA institute recommends maintaining records in hard copy

    A. For a minimum of 7 years
    B. Or electronic format for a minimum of 7 years
    C. Or electronic format for a minimum of 10 years

12. CFA charterholder Greffet is a senior portfolio manager at an investment firm. He serves on several boards of not-for-profit organizations. He does not receive any compensation for serving on the boards and does not tell his employer about serving on the boards. Which Standard of Professional Conduct did Greffet least likely violate?

    A. Loyalty
    B. Conflicts of interest
    C. Independence and objectivity

13. CFA charterholder Glowacki does not inform clients of a referral fee arrangement. Did Glowacki violate any Standards of Professional Conduct?

    A. No
    B. Yes, related to loyalty
    C. Yes, related to referral fees

14. Which is an improper reference to the CFA Institute, the CFA designation, or the CFA program?

    A. CFA degree expected in 2015
    B. Level I candidate in the CFA program
    C. Passed Level I of the CFA examination in 2008

15. Jeong is a portfolio manager. One of her firm's clients told her he will compensate her beyond that provided by her firm on the basis of the capital appreciation of his portfolio. Jeong accepts the arrangement and does not notify her employer. Jeong most likely violated which Standard of Professional Conduct?

    A. Fair dealing
    B. Referral fees
    C. Additional compensation arrangements

16. Which statement is most accurate regarding a member's or candidate's duty under the Standards of Professional Conduct?

    A. A member must comply with the CFA Institute Code and Standards when they conflict with local law
    B. In the absence of specific applicable law or other regulatory requirements, the Code and Standards govern the member's or candidate's actions
    C. A member is only required to comply with local laws, rules, and regulations even though the CFA Institute code and Standards may impose a higher degree of responsibility

17. Verification of GIPS compliance is performed with respect to

    A. One fund
    B. An entire firm
    C. A specific composite

18. To comply with the GIPS, if a firm previously claimed compliance with an Investment Performance Council-endorsed Country Version of GIPS (CVG), at a minimum, the firm must continue to show the historical CVG-compliant track record up to

    A. 5 years or since inception
    B. 7 years or since inception
    C. 10 years or since inception

19. What is the value of a $100,000 deposit after three years of earning 3% compounded continuously?

    A. $109,381
    B. $109,405
    C. $109,417

20. Is the internal rate of return (IRR) rule or the net present value (NPV) rule preferable for mutually exclusive projects?

    A. The IRR rule is preferable
    B. The NPV rule is preferable; NPV represents the addition to shareholder wealth
    C. The IRR and NPV rules give the same results

21. Is the S&P 500 a population or sample?

    A. Sample
    B. Population
    C. Both a sample and a population

22. Why is the geometric mean always less than or equal to the arithmetic mean?

    A. Volatility
    B. Cost averaging
    C. Chebyshev's inequality

23. Using Chebyshev's inequality, at least what proportion of 1,000 observations must lie within 1.5 standard deviations of the mean?

    A. 33.3%
    B. 44.4%
    C. 55.6%

24. What is the kurtosis of a sample of 1000 observations with a sum of the cubed deviation of 168.75%, a sum of the deviations to the fourth power of 182.25%, and a sample standard deviation 15%?

    A. 0.5
    B. 0.6
    C. 3.6

25. What type of probability determines if the S&P 500 return is over 10%?

    A. Joint probability
    B. Conditional probability
    C. Unconditional probability

26. If Treasury bonds are yielding 2% and the expected default rate on corporate bonds of the same maturity is 9%, approximately what is the expected yield on corporate bonds?

    A. 10%
    B. 11%
    C. 12%

27. If the prior probabilities are 50% that EPS exceeded expectations, 30% that EPS met expectations, and 20% that EPS fell short of expectations; the new probabilities of an expansion are 70% given that EPS exceeded expectations, 20% given that EPS met expectations, and 10% given that EPS fell short of expectations, how would the probability that EPS exceeded expectations be adjusted?

    A. It would increase
    B. It would remain the same
    C. It would decrease

28. What is tracking error?

    A. Total return on the portfolio gross of fees minus the risk-free rate
    B. Total return on the portfolio gross of fees minus the total return on the benchmark index
    C. The standard deviation of the differences between the portfolio's and the EAFE

29. Approximately what percent of observations in a normal distribution fall in the interval of the mean plus or minus 2/3 of the standard deviation?

    A. 50%
    B. 68%
    C. 95%

30. Which mutual fund category minimizes the risk of earning less than the risk-free rate of return: category 1 with standard deviation of 20% and Sharpe ratio of 0.36, category 2 with standard deviation of 25% and Sharpe ratio of 0.16, or category 3 with standard deviation of 15% and Sharpe ratio of 0.25?

    A. 1
    B. 2
    C. 3

31. What is the approximate reliability factor for a 95% confidence interval?

    A. 1.65
    B. 1.96
    C. 2.58

32. Which uses Dow theory, total quantity traded, support and resistance levels, moving-average lines, and charts?

    A. Stock price and volume techniques
    B. Follow-the-smart-money tactics
    C. Momentum indicators

33. What is the income demand elasticity when the percentage decrease in quantity demanded is 10% when incomes are increased 5%?

    A. Income elastic demand
    B. Income inelastic demand
    C. Negative income elastic demand

34. When what sum is maximized is it most likely to indicate that resources are being used efficiently?

    A. Supply + demand
    B. Marginal cost + marginal benefit
    C. Producer surplus + consumer surplus

35. What are wages that an owner forgoes considered?

    A. Interest forgone
    B. Explicit costs
    C. Opportunity costs

36. What is least likely to happen with an increase in the price of a factor of production such as wages or other component of variable costs?

    A. Leaves the fixed cost curves unchanged
    B. Leaves the total cost curve unchanged
    C. Shifts the variable cost curves and the marginal cost curves upward

37. Which is least likely to apply to the price charged by a single-price monopoly?

    A. Price is higher when demand is inelastic
    B. Price exceeds marginal revenue
    C. Price exceeds marginal cost

38. Which is least accurate regarding advertising by firms in monopolistic competition?

    A. Advertising increases total cost but average cost might decrease if the quantity sold increases by enough
    B. Advertising might increase demand but demand might decrease if competition increases
    C. Advertising always increases the markup and the price

39. What happens to the quantity of labor supplied as the wage rate increases?

    A. It increases, and at high wage rates, the supply curve increases more rapidly
    B. It increases, but at high wage rates, the supply curve eventually bends backward
    C. It decreases, but at high wage rates, the supply curve increases

40. What does a change in the money wage rate change?

    A. Only the short run aggregate supply (SAS) curve
    B. Only the long run aggregate supply (LAS) curve
    C. Both the SAS and the LAS curves

41. The view that by stimulating aggregate demand in a recession, full employment can be restored is most likely held by which school of thought?

    A. Classical
    B. Keynesian
    C. Monetarist

42. Which is least likely to be considered a liability of the Federal Reserve?

    A. Banks' deposits
    B. Federal Reserve notes
    C. U.S. government securities

43. Which is most likely to be an idea associated with the Laffer curve?

    A. Taxes increase employment and potential GDP
    B. Tax cuts could increase government revenue
    C. Tax increases increase government revenue

44. Which is least likely a reason why the Federal Reserve System would find a money targeting rule unreliable?

    A. Stable demand for money
    B. Technological change in the banking industry
    C. Unpredictable fluctuations in the demand for money

45. Who must express an opinion on the effectiveness of a company's internal control systems?

    A. Auditor
    B. Chairman
    C. Board of Directors

46. Which is a financing activity?

    A. Paying dividends
    B. Cost of providing goods and services
    C. Purchase of property, plant, and equipment

47. What is the most likely effect on the accounting equation of $5,000 in depreciation expense?

    A. Assets decrease by $5,000
    B. Liabilities increase by $5,000
    C. There is no change in assets or liabilities

48. Which is an inherent constraint of the IFRS framework?

    A. Timeliness
    B. Accrual basis
    C. Understandability

49. What does the income statement present?

    A. Assets and liabilities
    B. Other comprehensive income
    C. Revenue, expenses, and net income

50. Which is closest to the revenue that will be reported in the third year under the percentage-of-completion method if the revenue is $3 million the first year, $4 million the second year, and $5 million the third year; and the costs are $5 million the first year, $3 million the second year, and $2 million the third year?

    A. $2.4 million
    B. $3.6 million
    C. $4.0 million

51. If an Internet retailer sells $1,000 worth of books from a supplier for a commission of $450, what are the revenues using gross reporting?

    A. $450
    B. $550
    C. $1,000

52. Which best describes extraordinary items under U.S. GAAP and IFRS?

    A. Permitted under both U.S. GAAP and IFRS
    B. Permitted under IFRS but prohibited under U.S. GAAP
    C. Permitted under U.S. GAAP but prohibited under IFRS

53. What are closest to the basic and diluted EPS using the if-converted method if a company had $500,000 in net income; a weighted average of 400,000 shares outstanding, 10,000 shares of convertible preferred; and preferred dividends of $5 per share; with each share of preferred convertible into 3 shares?

    A. EPS = $1.13; diluted EPS = $1.13
    B. EPS = $1.13; diluted EPS = $1.16
    C. EPS = $1.16, diluted EPS = $1.13

54. What is debt due within one year?

    A. Current
    B. Tangible
    C. Noncurrent

55. Where would gains or losses from derivatives that qualify as net investment hedges or cash flow hedges most likely be reported?

    A. Income statement
    B. Statement of cash flows
    C. Statement of changes in equity

56. Which is a way to classify interest paid on a cash flow statement?

    A. Operating or financing under U.S. GAAP
    B. Operating or financing under IFRS
    C. Only in financing under both IRFS and U.S. GAAP

57. Which is closest to cash flows from operations in 2009 if for 2008, retained earnings were $100,000; accounts receivable were $38,000; inventory was $45,000; and accounts payable were $23,000; for 2009, retained earnings were $125,000; accounts receivable were $35,000; inventory was $40,000; and accounts payable were $30,000; and in 2009, the company declared and paid $10,000 in cash dividends and recorded $25,000 in depreciation expense?

    A. $45,000
    B. $55,000
    C. $75,000

58. Which is the most likely to result in a higher current ratio if prices are generally rising?

    A. LIFO
    B. FIFO
    C. Weighted average cost

59. What is the 2009 gross profit closest to if a company had used FIFO instead of LIFO; given 2009 sales of $200,000; cost of goods sold of $150,000; ending inventory under LIFO of $50,000 for 2008 and $60,000 for 2009; and the inventory under FIFO would have been $6,000 higher for 2008 and $4,000 greater for 2009?

    A. $44,000
    B. $48,000
    C. $52,000

60. When is the immediate write-off of in process research and development acquired in a business combination required?

    A. Under IFRS but not under U.S. GAAP
    B. Under U.S. GAAP but not under IFRS
    C. Under both U.S. GAAP and IFRS

61. Obligations of ownership that must be fulfilled at the end of an asset's service life are treated like debt by analysts and referred to as

    A. Asset retirement obligations
    B. Intangible assets with finite lives
    C. Intangible assets without a finite useful life

62. Which would most likely result from higher reported tax expense relative to taxes paid?

    A. Increase the deferred tax asset
    B. Increase the deferred tax liability
    C. Decrease the valuation allowance

63. Which is least likely to be a debt covenant?

    A. Maintain minimum profit margin
    B. Limitations on future borrowing
    C. Maintain minimum debt-to-equity ratio

64. Under what type of lease does a lessor earn both interest revenue and a profit (or loss) on the sale of the leased asset?

    A. Sales-types leases
    B. Direct financing leases
    C. Direct financing leases or sales-types leases

65. Which would most likely explain a decrease in receivables turnover?

    A. Large write-offs of receivables
    B. Offering credit to customers with weak credit histories
    C. Payment terms changed to require net payment within 15 days rather than 30 days

66. If ROE is 15%, which is closest to the profit margin if a company has sales of $120 million, assets of $70 million, and liabilities of $25 million?

    A. 5.625%
    B. 8.750%
    C. 23.333%

67. If a company reports 2008 gross investment in fixed assets of $2.8 million and 2008 accumulated depreciation of $1.2 million, and 2009 gross investment in fixed assets of $2.8 million and 2009 accumulated depreciation of $1.6 million, which is closest to the average age of the company's fixed assets in 2009?

   A. 2 years
   B. 4 years
   C. 7 years

68. What would an analyst use to adjust a U.S. company using LIFO to compare with an IFRS company using FIFO?

   A. FIFO reserve note disclosures
   B. LIFO reserve note disclosures
   C. Weighted average cost method

69. What type of project interaction for capital budgeting relates to a decision for a project contingent on the outcome of another project?

   A. Project sequencing
   B. Independent versus mutually exclusive
   C. Unlimited funds versus capital rationing

70. What is the present value of a project's future cash flow divided by the initial investment?

   A. Profitability index
   B. Internal rate of return
   C. Average accounting rate of return

71. What would happen if the all the cash flows, including the initial investment and all future cash flows, doubled for a profitable conventional project?

   A. The IRR would increase but the NPV would stay the same
   B. The NPV would increase but the IRR would stay the same
   C. Both the IRR and the NPV would increase

72. What is the weighted average cost of capital (WACC) for a company with a capital structure of 20% debt, 10% preferred stock, and 70% equity; a before-tax cost of debt of 7%; cost of preferred stock of 8%; cost of equity of 10%; and a 20% tax rate?

   A. 7.36%
   B. 8.76%
   C. 8.92%

73. What is an estimate of the cost of retained earnings using the discounted cash flow (DCF) approach if the current dividends are $2, the market price is $30, ROE is 15%, the dividend payout rate is 40%, the risk-free rate is 4%, beta is 1.175, and the expected return on the market portfolio is 12%?

    A. 13.4%
    B. 13.8%
    C. 16.3%

74. Which is closest to the new equity beta of a company using the pure-play method if the beta of equity for the company before the change in capital structure is 1.5, the debt to equity ratio is 0.4 before the change and 0.5 after the change, and the marginal tax rate is 30%?

    A. 1.58
    B. 1.88
    C. 2.03

75. What is the current ratio if current assets are $10 million, cash is $2 million, short-term marketable investments are $3 million, receivables are $3 million, and current liabilities are $5 million?

    A. 1.6
    B. 2.0
    C. 3.6

76. Which is least likely to indicate greater liquidity?

    A. Greater current ratio and quick ratio
    B. Greater number of days of payables
    C. Greater number of days of inventory and greater number of days of receivables

77. A company changing credit terms from 1/10, net 60 to 1/10, net 30 will most likely experience a decrease in

    A. Cash
    B. Uncollectable accounts
    C. Average collection period

78. A company has a 12-person board, the chairman is the past president of the company, the board includes 6 outside directors, half the members are elected for 2-year terms each year, and 3 members of the audit committee are outside directors. Which is the best action to improve corporate governance?

   A. The chairman should be an independent director
   B. All members should stand for election every year
   C. The company's VP of finance should be added to the audit committee

79. What type of underwriting of corporate issues is usually done with speculative new issues?

   A. Negotiated
   B. Competitive bid
   C. Best-efforts arrangements

80. Accounting for 9 to 10 percent of total exchange volume in the United States, shares of local firms are traded on

   A. Over-the-counter markets
   B. National stock exchanges
   C. Regional stock exchanges

81. Security lending enables what type of trade?

   A. Short sale
   B. Stop order
   C. Limit order

82. An investor purchased 100 shares for $10,000 and posted an initial margin of 50%. If the maintenance margin requirement is 35%, which is closest to the price at which the investor will get a margin call?

   A. $70.00
   B. $76.92
   C. $82.50

83. Which is closest to the return on the unweighted index using the geometric mean for three stocks with prices at the beginning of the year for stocks A, B, and C of $100, $50, and $30, respectively, and prices at the end of the year for stocks A, B, and C of $110, $53, and $36, respectively?

   A. 10.6%
   B. 11.8%
   C. 12.0%

84. If semi-strong form efficiency holds, technical analysis

    A. And fundamental analysis produce a performance advantage
    B. And fundamental analysis produce no performance advantage
    C. Produces a performance advantage but fundamental analysis does not

85. What could justify a pricing anomaly?

    A. Fusion investing
    B. Transaction costs
    C. Flaws in the discovery process

86. What is the preferred security valuation process?

    A. Bottom-up analysis
    B. Top-down, two step approach
    C. Top-down, three step approach

87. What is the discount rate for calculating the present value of operating free cash flow?

    A. Real risk-free rate
    B. Required rate of return on equity
    C. Weighted average cost of capital

88. Which is most likely to result in a higher P/E ratio using the earnings multiplier model?

    A. Higher dividend payout ratio
    B. Higher required rate of return
    C. Lower growth rate of dividends

89. If in 2005 sales were $62 million, net profit margin (NPM) was 5%, and there were 5 million shares outstanding; and in 2009 sales were $100 million, net profit margin (NPM) was 6%, and there were 5 million shares outstanding; what is closest to the estimated EPS for 2010 if the growth rate is the same as from 2002 through 2009 and the number of shares is the same?

    A. $1.10
    B. $1.32
    C. $2.20

90. Which is least likely to be considered a drawback of using price to sales value (P / S) ratios?

    A. Overemphasizes a company's expenses
    B. Potential manipulation of revenue recognition
    C. Business may show high growth in sales but not be profitable

91. Which is a forward commitment created in the over-the-counter market?

    A. Option
    B. Futures contract
    C. Forward contract

92. Which is closest to the payoff of a 3 x 6 FRA if the notional principal is $15 million, the underlying rate at expiration is 4.5%, and the forward contract rate is 5%?

    A. -$18,750
    B. -$18,541
    C. $18,750

93. Which most accurately describes margin in the futures market?

    A. Loan
    B. Layaway
    C. Down payment

94. What has a payoff of the greater of zero, or the underlying price minus the exercise price?

    A. Put option
    B. Call option
    C. Interest rate option

95. A longer term American put must be worth

    A. Less than a corresponding shorter-term American put
    B. Less than a corresponding shorter-term American call
    C. At least as much as a corresponding shorter-term American put

96. What is the payment at expiration for an investor who went long a $10 million 3 x 9 FRA where the 180-LIBOR at expiration is 4.8% and the forward contract rate was set at 5.2%?

    A. -$588,235
    B. -$19,531
    C. $19,531

97. What type of bond could have a coupon of 20% minus double the 5-year Treasury rate?

    A. Step-up note
    B. Inverse floater
    C. Floating-rate security

98. A U.S. investor who plans to hold a security for 6 years is considering purchasing a Treasury security that matures in 6 years, or, alternatively, purchasing an Italian government security that matures in 6 years and is denominated in lira. Which best describes the difference in the major risks associated with the investment alternatives?

    A. The Italian bond exposes the investor to greater credit risk and exchange rate risk
    B. The Italian bond exposes the investor to greater liquidity risk and inflation risk
    C. The Treasury security exposes the investor to greater reinvestment risk and interest rate risk

99. Duration captures the true price effects for

    A. Parallel shifts in the yield curve
    B. Non-parallel shifts in the yield curve
    C. Both parallel and non-parallel shifts in the yield curve

100. Which would have the least reinvestment risk?

    A. T-bill
    B. Zero-coupon bond
    C. Prepayable amortizing bond

101. What is the value of the embedded call option if the price of a callable bond is $920 and the price an option free bond with the same yield, rating, and maturity is $980?

    A. -$60
    B. $20
    C. $60

102. An investor purchases $10,000 of par value of a Treasury inflation protection security (TIPS). The real rate determined at the auction is 3.8%. If at the end of six months the CPI-U is 2.4% on an annual rate, what is the inflation-adjusted principal at the end of six months?

    A. $10,120.00
    B. $10,192.28
    C. $10,240.00

103. Which are government sponsored enterprises (GSEs)?

    A. Ginnie Mae and Fannie Mae
    B. Fannie Mae, Freddie Mac, and Sallie Mae
    C. Ginnie Mae, TVA, and the Private Export Funding Corporation

104. How are bonds issued in the primary market?

    A. Over-the counter market
    B. Electronic trading and trading on exchanges
    C. Bought deal, auction process, or private placement

105. What do larger fixed income issues most likely have?

    A. Less liquidity and larger yield spreads
    B. Greater liquidity and larger yield spreads
    C. Greater liquidity and smaller yield spreads

106. Which is closest to the market value of a bond maturing in 2 years with a face value of $1,000 and a 5% annual coupon, if the 2-year Treasury rate is 3.75% for years 1 and 2; and the Treasury spot rate is 3.0% for year 1, and 3.5% for year 2?

    A. $1,024
    B. $1,029
    C. $1,038

107. The basic principle underlying the bootstrap method is that the value of a Treasury coupon security is equal to

    A. The difference between the Z-spread and the option-adjusted spread (OAS)
    B. The value of the package of zero-coupon securities that duplicates the coupon bond's cash flows
    C. The spread that the investor will realize over the entire Treasury spot rate curve if the bond is held to maturity

108. What do putable bonds exhibit?

    A. Positive convexity
    B. Negative convexity
    C. Positive convexity at high yield levels and negative convexity at low yield levels

109. How good is an estimated new price using duration likely to be for a 200 basis point increase in yield?

    A. Overestimates new price
    B. Underestimates new price
    C. Estimated price close to new price

110. Which is closest to percentage price change for a 5% 25-year bond with duration of 14.19 and convexity of 141.68 if yields increase by 200 basis points?

    A. -34.05%
    B. -28.38%
    C. -22.71%

111. Which is most accurate regarding advantages of open-end exchange-traded funds (ETFs)?

    A. More immediate dividend reinvestment than for index funds
    B. More cost-effective way for large institutions to enter emerging markets
    C. Greater exposure to capital gains taxes than traditional mutual funds

112. Which real estate valuation approach is least likely to be accurate for an office building in poor condition with a large vacancy rate in a bad neighborhood?

    A. Cost approach
    B. Income approach
    C. Sales comparison approach

113. Which is most accurate regarding real estate appraisals?

    A. An appraisal-based index overstates volatility
    B. A spuriously high volatility inflates the attractiveness of real estate
    C. Real estate appraisals show relatively few changes compared to changes in market value

114. Which classification of hedge funds is a form of long/short funds that attempt to be hedged against market movements?

    A. Market-neutral funds
    B. Emerging-market funds
    C. Distressed securities funds

115. Which investment strategy is most appropriate for risk-takers?

    A. Total return
    B. Capital preservation
    C. Capital appreciation

116. Which is most likely related to unique needs and preferences?

    A. Liquidity
    B. Social investing
    C. Fiduciary responsibility

117. What is the correlation coefficient closest to if the variance of security A is 9%, the variance of security B is 16%, and the covariance is 6%?

    A. 0.4
    B. 0.5
    C. 0.6

118. Which is closest to weights that would give a portfolio standard deviation of 3% if security A has an expected return of 10% and a standard deviation of 7%, and security B has an expected return of 20% and a standard deviation of 10%, if the correlation coefficient is -1.0?

    A. 41.2% in security A and 58.8% in security B
    B. 50.0% in security A and 50.0% in security B
    C. 58.8% in security A and 41.2% in security B

119. Which is least likely to be considered an assumption of capital market theory?

    A. Capital markets are in equilibrium
    B. There are taxes and transaction costs
    C. There is no inflation or changes in interest rates

120. What is a regression line that indicates the beta of a risky asset, using an equation where the rate of return for an asset equals alpha, plus beta times the return on the market portfolio, plus an error term?

    A. CML
    B. SML
    C. Characteristic line

1. A	41. B	81. A
2. C	42. C	82. B
3. A	43. B	83. B
4. C	44. A	84. B
5. C	45. A	85. C
6. C	46. A	86. C
7. C	47. A	87. C
8. B	48. A	88. A
9. B	49. C	89. B
10. C	50. A	90. A
11. B	51. C	91. C
12. A	52. C	92. B
13. C	53. A	93. C
14. A	54. A	94. B
15. C	55. C	95. C
16. B	56. B	96. B
17. B	57. C	97. B
18. C	58. B	98. A
19. C	59. B	99. A
20. B	60. B	100. B
21. A	61. A	101. C
22. A	62. B	102. A
23. C	63. A	103. B
24. C	64. A	104. C
25. C	65. B	105. C
26. C	66. A	106. B
27. A	67. B	107. B
28. B	68. B	108. A
29. A	69. A	109. B
30. A	70. A	110. C
31. B	71. B	111. A
32. A	72. C	112. A
33. C	73. C	113. C
34. C	74. A	114. A
35. C	75. B	115. C
36. B	76. C	116. B
37. A	77. C	117. B
38. C	78. A	118. A
39. B	79. C	119. B
40. A	80. C	120. C

1. Which statement is most accurate related to the Standard of Professional Conduct on knowledge of the law?

    *A. In the event of conflict, members must comply with the more strict law, rule, or regulation

    B. The member's responsibility to respond shall be subject to applicable restrictions on confidential information and those imposed by law

    C. A member is not expected to discuss an apparent unresolved material violation with another member if either member is prohibited by law from doing so

2. CFA charterholder Takagi supports the sales effort of her corporate bond department and offers credit guidance to fixed-income security buyers. Her compensation is linked to the compensation of the corporate bond department. Salespeople have asked her to contact large clients to push the bonds of Surles, Ltd. because the company has a large position it has been unable to sell because of Surles' recent announcement of an operating problem, and Takagi agrees despite being unable to justify that the market price has already adjusted for the operating problem. Were any Standards of Professional Conduct violated?

    A. No

    B. Yes, relating to duties to employers

    *C. Yes, relating to independence and objectivity (Standard I(B) - independence and objectivity)

3. Which statement is least accurate related to the Standard of Professional Conduct on professionalism?

    *A. Members and candidates must act for the benefit of their clients and place their clients' interests before their employer's or their own interests

    B. Members and candidates must not knowingly make any misrepresentations relating to investment analysis, recommendations, actions, or other professional activities

    C. Members and candidates must not engage in any professional conduct involving dishonesty, fraud, or deceit or commit any act that reflects adversely on their professional reputation, integrity, or competence

4. The president of a company accepts a tender offer and decides to sell his family business at a significant premium over the current share price. The president tells his sister, who tells her daughter, who tells her husband, CFA charterholder Kazun. Kazun tells his broker, CFA charterholder Jumani. Jumani buys shares for himself. Who violated the Standards of Professional Conduct?

    A. Kazun only

    B. Jumani only

    *C. Kazun and Jumani (Standard II(A) - material nonpublic information)

5. Which statement is least accurate related to the Standard of Professional Conduct on duties to clients?

    A. Members and candidates have a duty of loyalty to their clients and must act with reasonable care and exercise prudent judgment

    B. Members and candidates must act for the benefit of their clients and place their clients' interests before their employer's or their own interests

    *C. Members and candidates who possess material nonpublic information that could affect the value of an investment must not act or cause others to act on the information

6. When making investments in new offerings or secondary financings, CFA charterholder Brack allocates issues to new accounts first and discloses the policy to all current and prospective clients. Did Brack violate any Standards of Professional Conduct?

    A. No

    B. Yes, all discretionary accounts were not treated equally

    *C. Yes, disclosure of the policy does not fulfill the duty regarding equitable allocation methods (Standard III(B) - fair dealing)

7. CFA charterholder Dutta joins a new firm and prepares marketing material for his new firm including his performance at his previous employer without identifying the performance as having been while with another firm. Did Dutta violate and Standards of Professional Conduct?

    A. No

    B. Yes, relating to duty to employers

    *C. Yes, relating to performance presentation (Standard III(D) - performance presentation)

8. Compiling a list of contacts based on a client list used with a previous employer is most likely to violate which Standard of Professional Conduct?

    A. None

    *B. Loyalty (Standard IV(A) - loyalty)

    C. Preservation of confidentiality

9. CFA charterholder Essaheb supervises CFA charterholder Dabrowski at a registered investment advisory and registered broker/dealer firm. Dabrowski makes S&P 500 futures trades so that the most profitable trades go to the company's profit sharing plan and the least profitable trades go to the other funds. The firm has no documented procedures for futures trading. Essaheb most likely violated which Standard of Professional Conduct?

    A. Priority of transactions
    *B.Responsibilities of supervisors (Standard IV(C) - responsibilities of supervisors)
    C. Diligence and reasonable basis

10. CFA charterholder Shapsis is a junior analyst. Shapsis prepares a report for the firm's investment committee to review. The committee does not agree with the report and makes changes. What is the least appropriate action for Shapsis?

    A. Document her differences
    B. Ask to have her name removed
    *C.Insist that the report be changed back (Standard V(A) - diligence and reasonable basis)

11. Regarding the Standard of Professional Conduct related to record retention, the CFA institute recommends maintaining records in hard copy

    A. For a minimum of 7 years
    *B.Or electronic format for a minimum of 7 years (Standard V(C) - record retention)
    C. Or electronic format for a minimum of 10 years

12. CFA charterholder Greffet is a senior portfolio manager at an investment firm. He serves on several boards of not-for-profit organizations. He does not receive any compensation for serving on the boards and does not tell his employer about serving on the boards. Which Standard of Professional Conduct did Greffet least likely violate?

    *A. Loyalty (Standard VI(A) - disclosure of conflicts and Standard I(B) - independence and objectivity)
    B. Conflicts of interest
    C. Independence and objectivity

13. CFA charterholder Glowacki does not inform clients of a referral fee arrangement. Did Glowacki violate any Standards of Professional Conduct?

    A. No
    B. Yes, related to loyalty
    *C.Yes, related to referral fees (Standard VI(C) - referral fees)

14. Which is an improper reference to the CFA Institute, the CFA designation, or the CFA program?

    *A. CFA degree expected in 2015 (Standard VII(B) - reference to the CFA Institute, the CFA designation, and the CFA program)
    B. Level I candidate in the CFA program
    C. Passed Level I of the CFA examination in 2008

15. Jeong is a portfolio manager. One of her firm's clients told her he will compensate her beyond that provided by her firm on the basis of the capital appreciation of his portfolio. Jeong accepts the arrangement and does not notify her employer. Jeong most likely violated which Standard of Professional Conduct?

    A. Fair dealing
    B. Referral fees
    *C. Additional compensation arrangements (Standard IV(B) - additional compensation arrangements)

16. Which statement is most accurate regarding a member's or candidate's duty under the Standards of Professional Conduct?

    A. A member must comply with the CFA Institute Code and Standards when they conflict with local law
    *B. In the absence of specific applicable law or other regulatory requirements, the Code and Standards govern the member's or candidate's actions (Standard I(A) - knowledge of the law)
    C. A member is only required to comply with local laws, rules, and regulations even though the CFA Institute code and Standards may impose a higher degree of responsibility

17. Verification of GIPS compliance is performed with respect to

    A. One fund
    *B. An entire firm
    C. A specific composite

18. To comply with the GIPS, if a firm previously claimed compliance with an Investment Performance Council-endorsed Country Version of GIPS (CVG), at a minimum, the firm must continue to show the historical CVG-compliant track record up to

    A. 5 years or since inception
    B. 7 years or since inception
    *C. 10 years or since inception

19. What is the value of a $100,000 deposit after three years of earning 3% compounded continuously?

    A. $109,381
    B. $109,405
    *C.$109,417 = $100,000 (e^((.03)(3))); continuous compounding can be approximated using 1,000 compounding periods per year; n = 3,000, i = 0.003, PV = -100,000, PMT = 0; FV = $109,417

20. Is the internal rate of return (IRR) rule or the net present value (NPV) rule preferable for mutually exclusive projects?

    A. The IRR rule is preferable
    *B.The NPV rule is preferable; NPV represents the addition to shareholder wealth
    C. The IRR and NPV rules give the same results

21. Is the S&P 500 a population or sample?

    *A. Sample
    B. Population
    C. Both a sample and a population

22. Why is the geometric mean always less than or equal to the arithmetic mean?

    *A. Volatility
    B. Cost averaging
    C. Chebyshev's inequality

23. Using Chebyshev's inequality, at least what proportion of 1,000 observations must lie within 1.5 standard deviations of the mean?

    A. 33.3%
    B. 44.4%
    *C.55.6% = 1 - 1/(1.5)^2

24. What is the kurtosis of a sample of 1000 observations with a sum of the cubed deviation of 168.75%, a sum of the deviations to the fourth power of 182.25%, and a sample standard deviation 15%?

    A. 0.5
    B. 0.6
    *C.3.6 = (1/1000) 1.8225 / (0.15^4)

25. What type of probability determines if the S&P 500 return is over 10%?

    A. Joint probability
    B. Conditional probability
    *C.Unconditional probability

26. If Treasury bonds are yielding 2% and the expected default rate on corporate bonds of the same maturity is 9%, approximately what is the expected yield on corporate bonds?

    A. 10%
    B. 11%
    *C.12% = [1.02/(1-.09)] - 1

27. If the prior probabilities are 50% that EPS exceeded expectations, 30% that EPS met expectations, and 20% that EPS fell short of expectations; the new probabilities of an expansion are 70% given that EPS exceeded expectations, 20% given that EPS met expectations, and 10% given that EPS fell short of expectations, how would the probability that EPS exceeded expectations be adjusted?

    *A. It would increase
    B. It would remain the same
    C. It would decrease

28. What is tracking error?

    A. Total return on the portfolio gross of fees minus the risk-free rate
    *B.Total return on the portfolio gross of fees minus the total return on the benchmark index
    C. The standard deviation of the differences between the portfolio's and the EAFE

29. Approximately what percent of observations in a normal distribution fall in the interval of the mean plus or minus 2/3 of the standard deviation?

    *A. 50%
    B. 68%
    C. 95%

30. Which mutual fund category minimizes the risk of earning less than the risk-free rate of return: category 1 with standard deviation of 20% and Sharpe ratio of 0.36, category 2 with standard deviation of 25% and Sharpe ratio of 0.16, or category 3 with standard deviation of 15% and Sharpe ratio of 0.25?

    *A. 1; .36>.25>.16
    B. 2
    C. 3

31. What is the approximate reliability factor for a 95% confidence interval?

    A. 1.65
    *B. 1.96
    C. 2.58

32. Which uses Dow theory, total quantity traded, support and resistance levels, moving-average lines, and charts?

    *A. Stock price and volume techniques
    B. Follow-the-smart-money tactics
    C. Momentum indicators

33. What is the income demand elasticity when the percentage decrease in quantity demanded is 10% when incomes are increased 5%?

    A. Income elastic demand
    B. Income inelastic demand
    *C. Negative income elastic demand

34. When what sum is maximized is it most likely to indicate that resources are being used efficiently?

    A. Supply + demand
    B. Marginal cost + marginal benefit
    *C. Producer surplus + consumer surplus

35. What are wages that an owner forgoes considered?

    A. Interest forgone
    B. Explicit costs
    *C. Opportunity costs

36. What is least likely to happen with an increase in the price of a factor of production such as wages or other component of variable costs?

    A. Leaves the fixed cost curves unchanged
    *B.Leaves the total cost curve unchanged
    C. Shifts the variable cost curves and the marginal cost curves upward

37. Which is least likely to apply to the price charged by a single-price monopoly?

    *A. Price is higher when demand is inelastic
    B. Price exceeds marginal revenue
    C. Price exceeds marginal cost

38. Which is least accurate regarding advertising by firms in monopolistic competition?

    A. Advertising increases total cost but average cost might decrease if the quantity sold increases by enough
    B. Advertising might increase demand but demand might decrease if competition increases
    *C.Advertising always increases the markup and the price

39. What happens to the quantity of labor supplied as the wage rate increases?

    A. It increases, and at high wage rates, the supply curve increases more rapidly
    *B.It increases, but at high wage rates, the supply curve eventually bends backward
    C. It decreases, but at high wage rates, the supply curve increases

40. What does a change in the money wage rate change?

    *A. Only the short run aggregate supply (SAS) curve
    B. Only the long run aggregate supply (LAS) curve
    C. Both the SAS and the LAS curves

41. The view that by stimulating aggregate demand in a recession, full employment can be restored is most likely held by which school of thought?

    A. Classical
    *B.Keynesian
    C. Monetarist

42. Which is least likely to be considered a liability of the Federal Reserve?

    A. Banks' deposits
    B. Federal Reserve notes
    *C.U.S. government securities

43. Which is most likely to be an idea associated with the Laffer curve?

    A. Taxes increase employment and potential GDP
    *B.Tax cuts could increase government revenue
    C. Tax increases increase government revenue

44. Which is least likely a reason why the Federal Reserve System would find a money targeting rule unreliable?

    *A. Stable demand for money
    B. Technological change in the banking industry
    C. Unpredictable fluctuations in the demand for money

45. Who must express an opinion on the effectiveness of a company's internal control systems?

    *A. Auditor
    B. Chairman
    C. Board of Directors

46. Which is a financing activity?

    *A. Paying dividends
    B. Cost of providing goods and services
    C. Purchase of property, plant, and equipment

47. What is the most likely effect on the accounting equation of $5,000 in depreciation expense?

    *A. Assets decrease by $5,000
    B. Liabilities increase by $5,000
    C. There is no change in assets or liabilities

48. Which is an inherent constraint of the IFRS framework?

    *A. Timeliness
    B. Accrual basis
    C. Understandability

49. What does the income statement present?

    A. Assets and liabilities
    B. Other comprehensive income
    *C.Revenue, expenses, and net income

50. Which is closest to the revenue that will be reported in the third year under the percentage-of-completion method if the revenue is $3 million the first year, $4 million the second year, and $5 million the third year; and the costs are $5 million the first year, $3 million the second year, and $2 million the third year?

    *A. $2.4 million = ($2/$10) $12 million
    B. $3.6 million
    C. $4.0 million

51. If an Internet retailer sells $1,000 worth of books from a supplier for a commission of $450, what are the revenues using gross reporting?

    A. $450
    B. $550
    *C.$1,000

52. Which best describes extraordinary items under U.S. GAAP and IFRS?

    A. Permitted under both U.S. GAAP and IFRS
    B. Permitted under IFRS but prohibited under U.S. GAAP
    *C.Permitted under U.S. GAAP but prohibited under IFRS

53. What are closest to the basic and diluted EPS using the if-converted method if a company had $500,000 in net income; a weighted average of 400,000 shares outstanding, 10,000 shares of convertible preferred; and preferred dividends of $5 per share; with each share of preferred convertible into 3 shares?

    *A. EPS = $1.13; diluted EPS = $1.13; $1.13 = {$500,000 - [$5(10,000)]}/ 400,000;
        $1.16 = $500,000 / (400,000 + 30,000) > $1.13
    B.   EPS = $1.13; diluted EPS = $1.16
    C.   EPS = $1.16, diluted EPS = $1.13

54. What is debt due within one year?

    *A. Current
    B. Tangible
    C. Noncurrent

55. Where would gains or losses from derivatives that qualify as net investment hedges or cash flow hedges most likely be reported?

    A. Income statement
    B. Statement of cash flows
    *C.Statement of changes in equity

56. Which is a way to classify interest paid on a cash flow statement?

    A. Operating or financing under U.S. GAAP
    *B.Operating or financing under IFRS
    C. Only in financing under both IRFS and U.S. GAAP

57. Which is closest to cash flows from operations in 2009 if for 2008, retained earnings were $100,000; accounts receivable were $38,000; inventory was $45,000; and accounts payable were $23,000; for 2009, retained earnings were $125,000; accounts receivable were $35,000; inventory was $40,000; and accounts payable were $30,000; and in 2009, the company declared and paid $10,000 in cash dividends and recorded $25,000 in depreciation expense?

    A. $45,000
    B. $55,000
    *C.$75,000 = $125,000 - $100,000 + $10,000 + $25,000 - ($35,000 - $38,000) - ($40,000 - $45,000) + ($30,000 - $23,000)

58. Which is the most likely to result in a higher current ratio if prices are generally rising?

    A. LIFO
    *B.FIFO
    C. Weighted average cost

59. What is the 2009 gross profit closest to if a company had used FIFO instead of LIFO; given 2009 sales of $200,000; cost of goods sold of $150,000; ending inventory under LIFO of $50,000 for 2008 and $60,000 for 2009; and the inventory under FIFO would have been $6,000 higher for 2008 and $4,000 greater for 2009?

    A. $44,000
    *B.$48,000 = $50,000 + ($4,000 - $6,000)
    C. $52,000

60. When is the immediate write-off of in process research and development acquired in a business combination required?

    A. Under IFRS but not under U.S. GAAP
    *B.Under U.S. GAAP but not under IFRS
    C. Under both U.S. GAAP and IFRS

61. Obligations of ownership that must be fulfilled at the end of an asset's service life are treated like debt by analysts and referred to as

    *A. Asset retirement obligations
    B. Intangible assets with finite lives
    C. Intangible assets without a finite useful life

62. Which would most likely result from higher reported tax expense relative to taxes paid?

    A. Increase the deferred tax asset
    *B.Increase the deferred tax liability
    C. Decrease the valuation allowance

63. Which is least likely to be a debt covenant?

    *A. Maintain minimum profit margin
    B. Limitations on future borrowing
    C. Maintain minimum debt-to-equity ratio

64. Under what type of lease does a lessor earn both interest revenue and a profit (or loss) on the sale of the leased asset?

    *A. Sales-types leases
    B. Direct financing leases
    C. Direct financing leases or sales-types leases

65. Which would most likely explain a decrease in receivables turnover?

    A. Large write-offs of receivables
    *B.Offering credit to customers with weak credit histories
    C. Payment terms changed to require net payment within 15 days rather than 30 days

66. If ROE is 15%, which is closest to the profit margin if a company has sales of $120 million, assets of $70 million, and liabilities of $25 million?

    *A. 5.625% = 15%/[(120/70)(70/(70-25))]
    B. 8.750%
    C. 23.333%

67. If a company reports 2008 gross investment in fixed assets of $2.8 million and 2008 accumulated depreciation of $1.2 million, and 2009 gross investment in fixed assets of $2.8 million and 2009 accumulated depreciation of $1.6 million, which is closest to the average age of the company's fixed assets in 2009?

    A. 2 years
    *B. 4 years = $1.6 / ($1.6 - $1.2)
    C. 7 years

68. What would an analyst use to adjust a U.S. company using LIFO to compare with an IFRS company using FIFO?

    A. FIFO reserve note disclosures
    *B. LIFO reserve note disclosures
    C. Weighted average cost method

69. What type of project interaction for capital budgeting relates to a decision for a project contingent on the outcome of another project?

    *A. Project sequencing
    B. Independent versus mutually exclusive
    C. Unlimited funds versus capital rationing

70. What is the present value of a project's future cash flow divided by the initial investment?

    *A. Profitability index
    B. Internal rate of return
    C. Average accounting rate of return

71. What would happen if the all the cash flows, including the initial investment and all future cash flows, doubled for a profitable conventional project?

    A. The IRR would increase but the NPV would stay the same
    *B. The NPV would increase but the IRR would stay the same
    C. Both the IRR and the NPV would increase

72. What is the weighted average cost of capital (WACC) for a company with a capital structure of 20% debt, 10% preferred stock, and 70% equity; a before-tax cost of debt of 7%; cost of preferred stock of 8%; cost of equity of 10%; and a 20% tax rate?

    A. 7.36%
    B. 8.76%
    *C. 8.92% = .2(7%)(1-.2) + .1(8%) + .7(10%)

73. What is an estimate of the cost of retained earnings using the discounted cash flow (DCF) approach if the current dividends are $2, the market price is $30, ROE is 15%, the dividend payout rate is 40%, the risk-free rate is 4%, beta is 1.175, and the expected return on the market portfolio is 12%?

    A. 13.4%
    B. 13.8%
    *C.16.3% = (1-40%)(15%) + ($2)(1.09)/$30; 1+ (1-40%)(15%) = 1.09

74. Which is closest to the new equity beta of a company using the pure-play method if the beta of equity for the company before the change in capital structure is 1.5, the debt to equity ratio is 0.4 before the change and 0.5 after the change, and the marginal tax rate is 30%?

    *A. 1.58 = [1.5 / (1+(1-30%)0.4)] [1 + ((1-30%)(0.5)]
    B.   1.88
    C.   2.03

75. What is the current ratio if current assets are $10 million, cash is $2 million, short-term marketable investments are $3 million, receivables are $3 million, and current liabilities are $5 million?

    A. 1.6
    *B.2.0 = $10 / $5
    C. 3.6

76. Which is least likely to indicate greater liquidity?

    A. Greater current ratio and quick ratio
    B. Greater number of days of payables
    *C.Greater number of days of inventory and greater number of days of receivables

77. A company changing credit terms from 1/10, net 60 to 1/10, net 30 will most likely experience a decrease in

    A. Cash
    B. Uncollectable accounts
    *C.Average collection period

78. A company has a 12-person board, the chairman is the past president of the company, the board includes 6 outside directors, half the members are elected for 2-year terms each year, and 3 members of the audit committee are outside directors. Which is the best action to improve corporate governance?

    *A. The chairman should be an independent director
    B. All members should stand for election every year
    C. The company's VP of finance should be added to the audit committee

79. What type of underwriting of corporate issues is usually done with speculative new issues?

    A. Negotiated
    B. Competitive bid
    *C.Best-efforts arrangements

80. Accounting for 9 to 10 percent of total exchange volume in the United States, shares of local firms are traded on

    A. Over-the-counter markets
    B. National stock exchanges
    *C.Regional stock exchanges

81. Security lending enables what type of trade?

    *A. Short sale
    B. Stop order
    C. Limit order

82. An investor purchased 100 shares for $10,000 and posted an initial margin of 50%. If the maintenance margin requirement is 35%, which is closest to the price at which the investor will get a margin call?

    A. $70.00
    *B.$76.92 = ($10,000/100) (1 - 50%) / (1 - 35%); [100($76.92) - $5,000] / [100($76.92)] = 35%
    C. $82.50

83. Which is closest to the return on the unweighted index using the geometric mean for three stocks with prices at the beginning of the year for stocks A, B, and C of $100, $50, and $30, respectively, and prices at the end of the year for stocks A, B, and C of $110, $53, and $36, respectively?

    A. 10.6%
    *B.11.8% = [(110%)(106%)(120%)]^(1/3) - 1
    C. 12.0%

84. If semi-strong form efficiency holds, technical analysis

    A. And fundamental analysis produce a performance advantage
    *B.And fundamental analysis produce no performance advantage
    C. Produces a performance advantage but fundamental analysis does not

85. What could justify a pricing anomaly?

    A. Fusion investing
    B. Transaction costs
    *C.Flaws in the discovery process

86. What is the preferred security valuation process?

    A. Bottom-up analysis
    B. Top-down, two step approach
    *C.Top-down, three step approach

87. What is the discount rate for calculating the present value of operating free cash flow?

    A. Real risk-free rate
    B. Required rate of return on equity
    *C.Weighted average cost of capital

88. Which is most likely to result in a higher P/E ratio using the earnings multiplier model?

    *A. Higher dividend payout ratio
    B. Higher required rate of return
    C. Lower growth rate of dividends

89. If in 2005 sales were $62 million, net profit margin (NPM) was 5%, and there were 5 million shares outstanding; and in 2009 sales were $100 million, net profit margin (NPM) was 6%, and there were 5 million shares outstanding; what is closest to the estimated EPS for 2010 if the growth rate is the same as from 2002 through 2009 and the number of shares is the same?

   A. $1.10
   *B.$1.32 = $100 (1.10) 6% / 5 where 10% = ($100 / $62)^(1/5) - 1
   C. $2.20

90. Which is least likely to be considered a drawback of using price to sales value (P / S) ratios?

   *A. Overemphasizes a company's expenses
   B. Potential manipulation of revenue recognition
   C. Business may show high growth in sales but not be profitable

91. Which is a forward commitment created in the over-the-counter market?

   A. Option
   B. Futures contract
   *C.Forward contract

92. Which is closest to the payoff of a 3 x 6 FRA if the notional principal is $15 million, the underlying rate at expiration is 4.5%, and the forward contract rate is 5%?

   A. -$18,750
   *B.-$18,541 = $15,000,000{[(4.5% - 5%)(90/360)] / [1+4.5%(90/360)]}
   C. $18,750

93. Which most accurately describes margin in the futures market?

   A. Loan
   B. Layaway
   *C.Down payment

94. What has a payoff of the greater of zero, or the underlying price minus the exercise price?

   A. Put option
   *B.Call option
   C. Interest rate option

95. A longer term American put must be worth

    A. Less than a corresponding shorter-term American put
    B. Less than a corresponding shorter-term American call
    *C. At least as much as a corresponding shorter-term American put

96. What is the payment at expiration for an investor who went long a $10 million 3 x 9 FRA where the 180-LIBOR at expiration is 4.8% and the forward contract rate was set at 5.2%?

    A. -$588,235
    *B. -$19,531 = $10,000,000{(4.8% - 5.2%)(180/360) / [1 + 4.8%(180/360)]
    C. $19,531

97. What type of bond could have a coupon of 20% minus double the 5-year Treasury rate?

    A. Step-up note
    *B. Inverse floater
    C. Floating-rate security

98. A U.S. investor who plans to hold a security for 6 years is considering purchasing a Treasury security that matures in 6 years, or, alternatively, purchasing an Italian government security that matures in 6 years and is denominated in lira. Which best describes the difference in the major risks associated with the investment alternatives?

    *A. The Italian bond exposes the investor to greater credit risk and exchange rate risk
    B. The Italian bond exposes the investor to greater liquidity risk and inflation risk
    C. The Treasury security exposes the investor to greater reinvestment risk and interest rate risk

99. Duration captures the true price effects for

    *A. Parallel shifts in the yield curve
    B. Non-parallel shifts in the yield curve
    C. Both parallel and non-parallel shifts in the yield curve

100. Which would have the least reinvestment risk?

    A. T-bill
    *B. Zero-coupon bond
    C. Prepayable amortizing bond

101. What is the value of the embedded call option if the price of a callable bond is $920 and the price an option free bond with the same yield, rating, and maturity is $980?

    A. -$60
    B. $20
    *C.$60

102. An investor purchases $10,000 of par value of a Treasury inflation protection security (TIPS). The real rate determined at the auction is 3.8%. If at the end of six months the CPI-U is 2.4% on an annual rate, what is the inflation-adjusted principal at the end of six months?

    *A. $10,120.00 = $10,000[1+ (2.4%) / 2]
    B. $10,192.28
    C. $10,240.00

103. Which are government sponsored enterprises (GSEs)?

    A. Ginnie Mae and Fannie Mae
    *B.Fannie Mae, Freddie Mac, and Sallie Mae
    C. Ginnie Mae, TVA, and the Private Export Funding Corporation

104. How are bonds issued in the primary market?

    A. Over-the counter market
    B. Electronic trading and trading on exchanges
    *C.Bought deal, auction process, or private placement

105. What do larger fixed income issues most likely have?

    A. Less liquidity and larger yield spreads
    B. Greater liquidity and larger yield spreads
    *C.Greater liquidity and smaller yield spreads

106. Which is closest to the market value of a bond maturing in 2 years with a face value of $1,000 and a 5% annual coupon, if the 2-year Treasury rate is 3.75% for years 1 and 2; and the Treasury spot rate is 3.0% for year 1, and 3.5% for year 2?

    A. $1,024
    *B.$1,029 = $50 / 1.03 + $1,050 / 1.035^2
    C. $1,038

107. The basic principle underlying the bootstrap method is that the value of a Treasury coupon security is equal to

    A. The difference between the Z-spread and the option-adjusted spread (OAS)
    *B.The value of the package of zero-coupon securities that duplicates the coupon bond's cash flows
    C. The spread that the investor will realize over the entire Treasury spot rate curve if the bond is held to maturity

108. What do putable bonds exhibit?

    *A. Positive convexity
    B. Negative convexity
    C. Positive convexity at high yield levels and negative convexity at low yield levels

109. How good is an estimated new price using duration likely to be for a 200 basis point increase in yield?

    A. Overestimates new price
    *B.Underestimates new price
    C. Estimated price close to new price

110. Which is closest to percentage price change for a 5% 25-year bond with duration of 14.19 and convexity of 141.68 if yields increase by 200 basis points?

    A. -34.05%
    B. -28.38%
    *C.-22.71% = -14.19 (.02) + 141.68 (.02)^2

111. Which is most accurate regarding advantages of open-end exchange-traded funds (ETFs)?

    *A. More immediate dividend reinvestment than for index funds
    B. More cost-effective way for large institutions to enter emerging markets
    C. Greater exposure to capital gains taxes than traditional mutual funds

112. Which real estate valuation approach is least likely to be accurate for an office building in poor condition with a large vacancy rate in a bad neighborhood?

    *A. Cost approach
    B. Income approach
    C. Sales comparison approach

113. Which is most accurate regarding real estate appraisals?

    A. An appraisal-based index overstates volatility
    B. A spuriously high volatility inflates the attractiveness of real estate
    *C.Real estate appraisals show relatively few changes compared to changes in market value

114. Which classification of hedge funds is a form of long/short funds that attempt to be hedged against market movements?

    *A. Market-neutral funds
    B. Emerging-market funds
    C. Distressed securities funds

115. Which investment strategy is most appropriate for risk-takers?

    A. Total return
    B. Capital preservation
    *C.Capital appreciation

116. Which is most likely related to unique needs and preferences?

    A. Liquidity
    *B.Social investing
    C. Fiduciary responsibility

117. What is the correlation coefficient closest to if the variance of security A is 9%, the variance of security B is 16%, and the covariance is 6%?

    A. 0.4
    *B.0.5 = 6% / [((9%)^.5) ((16%)^.5)]
    C. 0.6

118. Which is closest to weights that would give a portfolio standard deviation of 3% if security A has an expected return of 10% and a standard deviation of 7%, and security B has an expected return of 20% and a standard deviation of 10%, if the correlation coefficient is -1.0?

    *A. 41.2% in security A and 58.8% in security B; 3% = [(41.2%^2)(7%^2) + (58.8%^2)(10%^2) + 2(41.2%)(58.8%)(-1.0)(7%)(10%)]^.5, 7%/17% = 41.2%, 10%/17% = 58.8%
    B. 50.0% in security A and 50.0% in security B
    C. 58.8% in security A and 41.2% in security B

119. Which is least likely to be considered an assumption of capital market theory?

    A. Capital markets are in equilibrium
    *B.There are taxes and transaction costs
    C. There is no inflation or changes in interest rates

120. What is a regression line that indicates the beta of a risky asset, using an equation where the rate of return for an asset equals alpha, plus beta times the return on the market portfolio, plus an error term?

    A. CML
    B. SML
    *C.Characteristic line

1. Which topic of the CFA Institute's Standards of Professional Conduct includes loyalty; additional compensation arrangements; and responsibility of supervisors?

    A. Professionalism
    B. Duties to clients
    C. Duties to employers

2. CFA charterholder Stopnicki is a securities analyst following airline stocks. Her boss has been carrying a buy recommendation on Transglobal Airlines and asks Stopnicki to take over coverage of that airline. The boss tells Stopnicki that under no circumstances should the buy recommendation be changed, and Stopnicki tells the boss that she cannot cover the company under those constraints. Did Stopnicki violate any Standards of Professional Conduct?

    A. No
    B. Yes, relating to loyalty
    C. Yes, relating to independence and objectivity

3. CFA charterholder Mumford is an analyst in the research department of Mucha and Company. Lufi Corporation has asked Mucha to prepare a report on Campbell Company because Lufi is considering them for an acquisition. Lufi provides a report on Campbell prepared by another investment firm. Mumford uses some information from the other firm's report, cites the source, adds her own analysis and conclusions, signs her name, and gets it out. Did Mumford violate any Standards of Professional Conduct?

    A. No
    B. Yes, relating to misrepresentation
    C. Yes, relating to independence and objectivity

4. CFA charterholder Jiang is on an elevator and overhears a pizza delivery man say that he just delivered pizzas to the headquarters of Iddings Furniture Company and they did not give him as big of a tip as he wanted, so they must not be making that much money. Jiang calls her broker and tells him to sell her Iddings stock in her personal account. Did Jiang violate any Standards of Professional Conduct?

    A. No
    B. Yes, relating to misconduct
    C. Yes, relating to material nonpublic information

5. CFA charterholder Arora works for a bank that serves as the trustee for a pension fund. Arora uses pension fund assets to invest in companies that he finds socially responsible and divests in companies that he finds socially irresponsible. Did Arora violate any Standards of Professional Conduct?

    A. No
    B. Yes, relating to loyalty, prudence, and care
    C. Yes, relating to independence and objectivity

6. When determining the suitability of an investment, the primary focus should be on

    A. The characteristics of the client's total portfolio and on an issue-by-issue basis
    B. An issue-by-issue basis, not on the characteristics of the client's total portfolio
    C. The characteristics of the client's total portfolio, not on an issue-by-issue basis

7. Members and candidates must keep information about current, former, and prospective clients confidential

    A. At all times
    B. Unless disclosure is required by law
    C. Unless the supervisor permits disclosure of the information

8. CFA charterholder Chen finds evidence of illegal activity when working on an acquisition in a country with strict confidentiality laws. What is Chen's most appropriate initial response?

    A. Inform the CFA Institute
    B. Consult outside counsel
    C. Disclose the evidence to government officials

9. According to the standards, members and candidates must make reasonable efforts to detect and prevent violations of applicable laws, rules, regulations, and the Code and Standards by anyone

    A. Subject to their direct supervision
    B. In a position of supervision or authority
    C. Subject to their supervision or authority

10. If a member or candidate does not agree with the conclusions of group research and decision making but is satisfied with the process, they

    A. Must dissociate from the report and document their differences
    B. Do not need to dissociate from the report but should document their differences
    C. Must make reasonable and diligent efforts to determine whether such secondary or third-party research is sound

11. With the introduction of a new and different valuation model that represents a material change in the investment process, a firm must

    A. File notice of the change with regulatory authorities
    B. Communicate the change to the firm's prospective clients
    C. Communicate the change to the firm's clients and prospective clients

12. CFA charterholder Linton is a stock analyst. Linton is asked to write a report about a construction company that is a client of his firm's investment banking division, and half of Linton's compensation comes from his firm's investment banking. Linton has concerns about the construction industry and the company, but writes a very favorable report. Which Standard of Professional Conduct did Linton least likely violate?

    A. Loyalty to employers
    B. Disclosure of conflicts
    C. Loyalty, prudence, and care

13. CFA charterholder Delo receives referral fees, and fully discloses the arrangement to his employer and clients. Did Delo violate any Standards of Professional Conduct?

    A. No
    B. Yes, related to misconduct
    C. Yes, related to conflicts of interest

14. CFA charterholder Spetko mentions to a friend who is considering enrolling in the CFA program that she learned a great deal from the CFA program and that many firms require their employees to be CFA charterholders. Spetko recommends the CFA program to anyone interested in a career in investment management. Did Spetko violate any Standards of Professional Conduct?

    A. No
    B. Yes, related to conduct as members and candidates in the CFA program
    C. Yes, related to reference to the CFA Institute, the CFA designation, and the CFA program

15. CFA charterholder Shewarega manages the assets of the Ganesh Corporation Profit Sharing Plan. The president of Ganesh asks that Shewarega vote shares in the profit sharing plan in favor of the company-nominated board of directors and against the slate nominated by a dissident stockholder group. Shewarega conducts an independent investigation and concludes the dissident group's slate is better for the long-term prospects of the company than the company nominated slate, but votes based on the president's request in favor of the company-nominated board. Did Shewarega violate any Standards of Professional Conduct?

A. No
B. Yes, related to loyalty, prudence, and care
C. Yes, related to diligence and reasonable basis

16. CFA charterholder Palatnick completes an initial report recommending the purchase of shares of McLachlan and distributes it within his firm. Then he finds out his wife has just inherited a substantial amount of stock in McLachlan. Before he has a chance to tell his employer about the inheritance, he is asked to write a follow-up report on McLachlan. Palatnick does not mention the inheritance, and modifies the report to make it even more favorable. Did Palatnick violate any Standards of Professional Conduct?

A. No
B. Yes, related to loyalty
C. Yes, related to disclosure of conflicts

17. Which is least appropriate relating to the standard on responsibilities of supervisors? Members with supervisory responsibilities should encourage their employers to adopt codes of ethics that are

A. Stand-alone codes
B. Applicable to all the firm's employees
C. Confidential and not shared with the firm's clients

18. The GIPS section on private equity applies to

A. Open-end funds
B. Evergreen funds
C. Fund-of-funds investing

19. Which is closest to the growth rate if sales doubled in 10 years?

A. 7%
B. 12%
C. 20%

20. What is the annual time-weighted rate of return for an account with a beginning value of $20, with cash inflow of $1 at the beginning of the first quarter, a value of $16 at the end of the first quarter, cash outflow of $1 at the beginning of the second quarter, a value of $14 at the end of the second quarter, cash inflow of $5 at the beginning of the third quarter, a value at the end of the third quarter of $20, cash outflow at the beginning of the fourth quarter of $5, and a value at the end of the fourth quarter of $20?

    A. -0.2%
    B. 0.0%
    C. 0.2%

21. What measurement scale would be used for bond maturity in years?

    A. Ordinal scale
    B. Ratio scale
    C. Nominal scale

22. Percentiles divide distributions into how many parts?

    A. 99
    B. 100
    C. 101

23. If small caps had a mean return of 12% with a standard deviation of 20%, large caps had a mean return of 10% with a standard deviation of 16%, and the risk-free rate is 2%, which had superior risk-adjusted performance as measured by the Sharpe Ratio?

    A. Small caps
    B. Large caps
    C. They are the same

24. What type of distribution is less peaked than the normal distribution?

    A. Leptokurtic
    B. Mesokurtic
    C. Platykurtic

25. What are the odds of a gain on the S&P 500 if the probability of a loss is 25%?

    A. 1 to 3
    B. 3 to 1
    C. 4 to 1

26. What is the correlation between the S&P 500 and bonds for a portfolio with 75% in the S&P 500 with a variance of 2.25%, and 25% in bonds with a variance of 0.25%, given the covariance between the S&P 500 and bonds of 0.60%?

    A. -0.4
    B. 0.4
    C. 0.8

27. How many ways can 5 stocks be selected from a group of 12?

    A. 792
    B. 19,008
    C. 95,040

28. If high yield bonds can be expected to default 20% of the time, what is the mean and standard deviation (SD) of the number of high yield bonds out of 50 that are expected to default?

    A. Mean = 10, SD =8
    B. Mean = 10, SD = 2.8
    C. Mean = 8, SD = 10

29. Approximately what percent of normally distributed stock returns with a mean return of 10% and a standard deviation of 15% have a return that exceeds 20%?

    A. 16%
    B. 25%
    C. 32%

30. What is the probability that the return on the optimal portfolio will be less than the threshold level when a client with a portfolio of $100,000 would like to withdraw $3,000 at the year end and avoid the balance dropping below $100,000: allocation 1 with an expected return of 12% and a standard deviation of 12%, allocation 2 with an expected return of 9% and a standard deviation of 7%, or allocation 3 with an expected return of 11% and a standard deviation of 8%, given that $P(Z<=0.00) = 0.5000$; $P(Z<=0.25) = 0.5987$; $P(Z<=0.50) = 0.6915$; $P(Z<=0.75) = 0.7734$; and $P(Z<=1.00) = 0.8413$?

    A. 16%
    B. 18%
    C. 25%

31. Which is least likely to apply to a sampling distribution of the sample mean based on the Central Limit Theorem when the sample size is large (n>=30)?

    A. The distribution will be normal only if the population is normally distributed
    B. The sample mean will approximate the population mean
    C. The variance of the distribution of the sample mean will be the population variance divided by the sample size

32. What applies to a null hypothesis that the correlation coefficient is zero, given that the value of the test statistic is 1 and the critical value at the 0.05 significance level is 2?

    A. Reject the null hypothesis of the one-tailed test
    B. Reject the null hypothesis of the two-tailed test
    C. Do not reject the null hypothesis of the two-tailed test

33. What happens to demand for a resource when the price of a close substitute resource decreases?

    A. Large increase
    B. Small increase
    C. Decrease

34. Which is most likely to involve the free-rider problem, an obstacle to efficiency?

    A. Price and quantity regulations
    B. Public goods
    C. Externality

35. What is total revenue minus opportunity costs?

    A. Implicit and explicit costs
    B. Normal profit
    C. Economic profit

36. Which is least likely to be considered an advantage of a proprietorship or partnership?

    A. Easy to set up
    B. Limited liability
    C. Profits only taxed once

37. What is the least likely result of long-run equilibrium in a market in perfect competition?

    A. Economic profit is zero
    B. The entrepreneur makes no profit
    C. There is no entry, exit, plant expansion, or downsizing

38. What is the demand for a factor of production called?

    A. Demand for money
    B. Factor price
    C. Derived demand

39. Which is least likely part of the total income of a factor of production?

    A. Opportunity cost
    B. Economic rent
    C. Flow supply

40. What does an increase in potential GDP increase?

    A. Only the short run aggregate supply
    B. Only the long run aggregate supply
    C. Both the short run and the long run aggregate supply

41. What includes currency, traveler's checks, checking deposits, times deposits, savings deposits, money market mutual funds, and other deposits?

    A. M1
    B. M2
    C. Quantity of real money

42. How would financial innovation most likely impact the demand for money?

    A. Generally increases demand as a result of movement along the demand curve
    B. Always increases demand as a result of a shift of the demand curve
    C. Generally decreases demand as a result of a shift of the demand curve

43. Which is most likely a generational effect of fiscal policy?

    A. Generational accounting and present values show that Social Security and Medicare obligations have been and will remain actuarially sound
    B. Budget deficits improve intergenerational equity
    C. The international debt of the US means that in the future the US will need a surplus of exports over imports

44. Which decision rule for monetary policy sets the federal funds rate at 2% plus the inflation rate plus one-half the deviation of inflation from its target of 2% plus one-half of the output gap?

   A. McCallum rule
   B. Taylor rule
   C. Targeting rule

45. On which would an analyst assessing a company's financial position most likely focus?

   A. Balance sheet
   B. Statement of cash flows
   C. Statement of owners' equity

46. If assets are $500 million and liabilities are $200 million, what is owners' equity?

   A. $300 million
   B. $500 million
   C. $700 million

47. What is reducing operating expense by recharacterizing certain expenses as operating activities?

   A. Judgment
   B. Creativity
   C. Manipulation

48. What is the amount at which an asset could be exchanged or a liability settled?

   A. Fair value
   B. Present value
   C. Historical cost

49. Which of these elements of financial statement is most closely related to the measurement of financial position?

   A. Income
   B. Expenses
   C. Liabilities

50. Which is included in income as defined under IFRS?

    A. Increase in liabilities related to contributions from equity participants
    B. Enhancement of assets not related to contributions from equity participants
    C. Enhancement of assets related to contributions from equity participants

51. Under IFRS, revenue from barter transactions is measured based on the fair value of revenue from

    A. Similar barter transactions with unrelated parties
    B. Similar nonbarter transactions with related parties
    C. Similar nonbarter transactions with unrelated parties

52. Which is closest to the weighted average number of shares outstanding for calculating EPS for a calendar year if a company had $2 million in net income; paid $200,000 in preferred dividends; had 1,000,000 shares outstanding on January 1st; issued 800,000 shares on April 1st; and repurchased 200,000 shares on July 1?

    A. 1,500,000
    B. 1,600,000
    C. 1,700,000

53. What are obligations of a company as a result of past events?

    A. Equity
    B. Assets
    C. Liabilities

54. What type of balance sheet distinguishes between current and noncurrent items and presents a subtotal for current assets and liabilities?

    A. Report format
    B. Account format
    C. Classified balance sheet

55. If total long-term debt is $500; total debt is $1,000; total equity is $500; and total assets are $1,500; which is closest to the total debt ratio?

    A. 1/3
    B. 1/2
    C. 2/3

56. Which permits greater discretion in classifying some cash flow items as operating, investing, or financing activities?

    A. IFRS
    B. U.S. GAAP
    C. IFRS and U.S. GAAP are the same in this regard

57. How much cash did a company pay in wages if the wage expense was $200,000; the beginning balance of wages payable was $10,000; and the ending balance of wages payable was $30,000?

    A. $180,000
    B. $220,000
    C. $240,000

58. In a period of rising prices, which is most likely greater for a company that uses LIFO compared to a company that uses FIFO?

    A. Gross margin
    B. Current ratio
    C. Inventory turnover

59. When are research costs most likely to be expensed rather than capitalized and development costs most likely allowed to be capitalized under certain conditions?

    A. Under U.S. GAAP but not under IFRS
    B. Under IFRS but not under U.S. GAAP
    C. Under both U.S. GAAP and IFRS

60. What would most likely be decreased in the early periods of an asset's life for a company uses accelerated depreciation rather than straight-line depreciation?

    A. Asset turnover ratios and expenses
    B. Expenses and cash flow from operations
    C. Retained earnings and shareholders' equity

61. Which allows impairment losses to be reversed?

    A. U.S. GAAP but not IFRS
    B. IFRS but not U.S. GAAP
    C. Both U.S. GAAP and IFRS

62. If a company has a net deferred tax asset, what would a reduction in the statutory tax rate most likely benefit?

    A. Income statement but not the balance sheet
    B. Balance sheet but not the income statement
    C. Both the balance sheet and income statement

63. If a company issues zero-coupon bonds rather than coupon bearing bonds, what will the company's debt-to-equity ratio do as the maturity date approaches?

    A. Rise
    B. Decline
    C. Remain constant

64. How much should an analyst increase reported liabilities to treat all leases as debt if a company has financial leases of $10 million including $2 million in interest payments and operating leases of $15 million?

    A. $12 million
    B. $15 million
    C. $25 million

65. Which is the most appropriate conclusion if ROE stayed the same, the tax burden increased, the interest burden stayed the same, the EBIT margin stayed the same, asset turnover decreased, and leverage stayed the same?

    A. Profitability and liquidity decreased
    B. The lower tax rate offset the decrease in efficiency, leaving ROE unchanged
    C. The higher tax rate offset the increase in efficiency, leaving ROE unchanged

66. Which is least likely to increase cash flow from operations?

    A. Securitizing assets receivable
    B. Delaying payments to suppliers
    C. Using short term debt for accounts payable

67. Which is not allowed under IFRS?

    A. FIFO
    B. LIFO
    C. Weighted average cost

68. Which is allowed under IFRS?

    A. Revaluations of property, plant, and equipment but not intangible assets
    B. Revaluations of property, plant, and equipment as well as intangible assets
    C. Revaluations of intangible assets but not property, plant, and equipment

69. Which is least likely to factor into a capital budgeting decision?

    A. Sunk cost
    B. Opportunity cost
    C. Incremental cash flow

70. Which project should be chosen if mutually exclusive projects are ranked differently by the NPV and IRR?

    A. The one with the higher NPV
    B. The one with the higher IRR
    C. The one with the lower IRR

71. What is the crossover rate for the NPV profiles for two projects?

    A. Where the NPVs are equal
    B. Where the IRRs are equal
    C. Where the NPVs go from negative to positive

72. Which would most likely be used to discount the value a project using the net present value (NPV) method?

    A. IRR
    B. WACC
    C. Cost of debt

73. What is an estimate of the sustainable growth rate using the dividend discount model if the dividend next year will be $2.30, the payout ratio is 30%, ROE is 15%, and the stock price is $45?

    A. 5.38%
    B. 10.50%
    C. 15.61%

74. What is an estimate of the cost of equity using the bond yield plus risk premium approach if the before-tax cost of debt is 4%, the risk premium is 8%, and the tax rate is 25%?

    A. 10%
    B. 11%
    C. 12%

75. Which is graphed on the marginal cost of capital schedule?

    A. CAPM for different amounts of new capital
    B. WACC for different amounts of new capital
    C. WACC for different amounts of new debt

76. Which is most likely to indicate greater liquidity?

    A. Shorter operating cycle and shorter net operating cycle
    B. Shorter operating cycle and longer net operating cycle
    C. Longer operating cycle and longer net operating cycle

77. Which is closest to return on equity using DuPont analysis if net profit margin is 4.90%, operating profit margin is 7.79%, effect of non-operating items is 0.9909, the tax effect is 0.6350, total asset turnover is 2.0433, and financial leverage is 1.7184?

    A. 10.83%
    B. 17.21%
    C. 27.36%

78. Which is the system of internal controls by which companies are managed?

    A. Code of ethics
    B. Pro forma analysis
    C. Corporate governance

79. Liquidity includes

    A. Marketability and efficiency
    B. Efficiency and price continuity
    C. Marketability and price continuity

80. The minimum number of holders of round lots for a stock listed on the NYSE in 2004 was two

    A. Thousand
    B. Million
    C. Billion

81. What is executed at the lowest ask price for a buy order?

    A. Short sale
    B. Limit order
    C. Market order

82. An investor buys 100 shares at $70 using 50% margin. If the price increases 15%, the total market value of the position is

    A. $4,550 and the equity is $3,500
    B. $8,050 and the equity is $3,500
    C. $8,050 and the equity is $4,550

83. What is closest to the return on the unweighted index using the geometric mean for three stocks with prices at the beginning of the year for stocks A, B, and C of $11, $20, and $17, respectively, prices at the end of the year for stocks A, B, and C of $14, $25, and $15, respectively, and 3 million shares of stock A, 20 million shares of stock B, and 6 million shares of stock C?

    A. 12.0%
    B. 12.5%
    C. 13.5%

84. Event studies such as stock splits and initial public offerings (IPOs) support the

    A. Weak form of the EMH
    B. Strong form of the EMH
    C. Semi-strong form of the EMH

85. What explains why investors fear losses more than they value gains, and would hold onto losers too long and sell winners too soon?

    A. Selection bias and confirmation bias
    B. Confirmation bias and data mining bias
    C. Loss aversion, utility, and prospect theory

86. Which is closest to the value of common stock with an estimated dividend of $2 payable at year end and an estimated year-end sale price of $30 with a risk free rate of 4%, a market return of 10.67%, and a beta of 1.2?

    A. $26.78
    B. $28.57
    C. $32.00

87. Which is closest to value of a common stock with a dividend payout ratio of 50%, a dividend growth rate of 9%, a required rate of return of 12%, and current earnings per share of $2?

    A. $32.44
    B. $33.33
    C. $36.33

88. What is the growth rate of equity earnings without any external financing if the dividend payout ratio is 75% and the ROE is 10%?

    A. 2.5%
    B. 5.0%
    C. 7.5%

89. What is the estimated price of a stock using the dividend discount model if the earnings retention ratio is 60%, the ROE is 20%, the current dividends are $2 per share, and the required rate of return is 15%?

    A. $30.86
    B. $44.00
    C. $74.67

90. What is the price to book (P/B) ratio for a company with $100 million in common shareholders' equity, 20 million common shares outstanding, and a closing price of $9?

    A. 0.6
    B. 0.9
    C. 1.8

91. Which are best described as a contingent claims?

    A. Swap agreements and convertible bonds
    B. Convertible bonds and asset-backed securities
    C. Asset backed securities and swap agreements

92. The credit risk of a forward contract most likely be eliminated by entering into an opposite position with

    A. The same counterparty
    B. A different counterparty
    C. The same counterparty or a different counterparty

93. What type of FRA is a contract expiring in 3 months on a 180-day LIBOR?

    A. 1 x 3
    B. 3 x 6
    C. 3 x 9

94. What are call options on interest rates?

    A. Caps
    B. Floors
    C. Collars

95. The lower bound on a European call price the greater of zero or

    A. The price of an American put option
    B. The present value of the exercise price minus the underlying price
    C. The underlying price minus the present value of the exercise price

96. What is the profit on a call option, where the exercise price is X and the price of the underlying security is S?

    A. Max (0, S - X)
    B. Max (0, X - S) - option cost
    C. Max (0, S - X) - option cost

97. What is the price of a bond plus accrued interest?

    A. Price or clean price
    B. Full price or dirty price
    C. Full price or clean price

98. Which imbedded option is an advantage to the bondholder?

    A. Put provision
    B. Cap on a floater
    C. Accelerated sinking fund

99. Which bond has the greatest interest rate risk?

    A. Floating rate bond
    B. Zero-coupon bond
    C. 7% fixed coupon bond

100. Which is closest to the dollar price change of a bond, with a market value of $8 million and a duration of 5, for a 50 basis point change in yield?

    A. $100,000
    B. $200,000
    C. $400,000

101. What is the risk that the issuer will not make timely payments of interest and principal?

    A. Default risk
    B. Downgrade risk
    C. Credit spread risk

102. A decrease in expected yield volatility will cause the price of

    A. Putable bonds to decrease
    B. Callable bonds to decrease
    C. Embedded put and call options to increase

103. Which is a bank obligation used in importing and exporting that exposes an investor to credit risk and liquidity risk?

    A. Commercial paper
    B. Bankers acceptances
    C. Index amortizing note

104. What is the shape of the yield curve when yield increases with maturity?

    A. Flat
    B. Upward sloping
    C. Downward sloping

105. For an investor considering a taxable bond with a yield of 6.0%, and a tax-exempt security with a yield of 4.0%, what is the tax rate at which the investor is indifferent?

    A. 33%
    B. 50%
    C. 67%

106. Which is closest to the change in price due to the change in maturity of a bond maturing in 6 years with an 8% annual coupon, a par value of $100, a price of $95.51, and a yield of 9%; if the price one year earlier was $90.26 and the yield was 10%?

   A. $1.03
   B. $4.22
   C. $5.25

107. Which is closest to the bond-equivalent yield if the yield to maturity on an annual pay bond is 6%?

   A. 5.91%
   B. 6.00%
   C. 6.09%

108. Which is least accurate regarding interest rate risk?

   A. Two bonds with the same duration can have different convexities
   B. The duration / convexity approach does not take into consideration how the yield curve can shift
   C. If two bonds have the same duration, then the percentage change in price of the two bonds will be exactly the same for any given change in interest rates

109. Which is closest to the duration of a portfolio with $0.5 million in 11% coupon bonds with a duration of 6.2; $1.2 million in 6% coupon bonds with a duration of 5.7; and $0.3 million in 9% coupon bonds with a duration of 3.0?

   A. 5.42
   B. 5.73
   C. 6.85

110. Which is closest to percentage price change if yields increase by 10 basis points based on duration and the convexity adjustment of a 6% coupon 20-year option-free bond selling at par of 100 to yield 6%, if the price increases to 101.1651 at a yield of 5.8%, and the price decreases to 98.8535 at a yield of 6.2%?

   A. -1.17%
   B. -1.16%
   C. -1.15%

111. Which is least accurate regarding investment styles of investment companies?

    A. International ETFs are an insignificant segment of ETFs offered in the U.S
    B. Some ETFs track a specific investment style, such as value or growth
    C. Some ETFs track a specific index or invest in stocks from a specific industry sector

112. Which is closest to the value of a real estate investment if rents are $2,018,250, operating expenses are $1.2 million, the mortgage rate is 6%, financing is 90%, the required rate of return is 15%, the holding period is 5 years, and the tax rate is 25%?

    A. $4.000 million
    B. $5.455 million
    C. $6.133 million

113. Which set of characteristics is least accurate in describing venture capital investing?

    A. Illiquidity, long-term commitment period, and difficulty in determining market values
    B. Limited historical risk and return data, limited information, and entrepreneurial/management mismatches
    C. Fund manager incentive alignment, publicly available information on competitors, stability, and only routine operations analysis and advice required

114. Which is closest to the NPV of a project with a $500,000 initial investment and an expected $15.5 million payoff at the end of 5 years if it survives, with a probability of survival for 5 years of 25%, and a required rate of return of 19%?

    A. $0.129 million
    B. $1.124 million
    C. $2.104 million

115. Which phase occurs before age 36 to 38?

    A. Gifting
    B. Spending
    C. Accumulation

116. Which is most likely related to tax concerns?

    A. Liquidity
    B. Time horizon
    C. Capital gains

117. Which is closest to the variance for an individual asset with a 35% probability of an 8% return, 50% probability of an 11% return, and a 15% probability of a 14% return?

    A. 0.04%
    B. 2.03%
    C. 21.96%

118. Which is closest to the standard deviation of a portfolio with a 41.2% weight in a security with an expected return of 10% and a standard deviation of 7%, and a 58.8% weight in a security with an expected return of 20% and a standard deviation of 10%, if the correlation coefficient is -1.0?

    A. 0%
    B. 3%
    C. 4%

119. Which is closest to the standard deviation of a leveraged portfolio with an investor borrowing 50% of the original wealth to buy more of a risky asset with an expected return of 8% and a standard deviation of 10%, if the risk-free asset has an expected return of 3%?

    A. 10%
    B. 11%
    C. 15%

120. Which assumption would most likely only be made if the CAPM assumptions were relaxed?

    A. No taxes
    B. Transaction costs exist
    C. Equal borrowing and lending rates

1. C	41. B	81. C
2. A	42. C	82. C
3. A	43. C	83. A
4. A	44. B	84. C
5. B	45. A	85. C
6. C	46. A	86. A
7. B	47. C	87. C
8. B	48. A	88. A
9. C	49. C	89. C
10. B	50. B	90. C
11. C	51. C	91. B
12. A	52. A	92. A
13. A	53. C	93. C
14. A	54. C	94. A
15. B	55. C	95. C
16. C	56. A	96. C
17. C	57. A	97. B
18. C	58. C	98. A
19. A	59. B	99. B
20. A	60. C	100. B
21. B	61. B	101. A
22. B	62. A	102. A
23. C	63. A	103. B
24. C	64. A	104. B
25. B	65. B	105. A
26. C	66. C	106. A
27. A	67. B	107. A
28. B	68. B	108. C
29. B	69. A	109. A
30. A	70. A	110. C
31. A	71. A	111. A
32. C	72. B	112. B
33. A	73. B	113. C
34. B	74. C	114. B
35. C	75. B	115. C
36. B	76. A	116. C
37. B	77. B	117. A
38. C	78. C	118. B
39. C	79. C	119. C
40. C	80. A	120. B

1. Which topic of the CFA Institute's Standards of Professional Conduct includes loyalty; additional compensation arrangements; and responsibility of supervisors?

    A. Professionalism
    B. Duties to clients
    *C. Duties to employers

2. CFA charterholder Stopnicki is a securities analyst following airline stocks. Her boss has been carrying a buy recommendation on Transglobal Airlines and asks Stopnicki to take over coverage of that airline. The boss tells Stopnicki that under no circumstances should the buy recommendation be changed, and Stopnicki tells the boss that she cannot cover the company under those constraints. Did Stopnicki violate any Standards of Professional Conduct?

    *A. No (Standard I(B) - independence and objectivity)
    B. Yes, relating to loyalty
    C. Yes, relating to independence and objectivity

3. CFA charterholder Mumford is an analyst in the research department of Mucha and Company. Lufi Corporation has asked Mucha to prepare a report on Campbell Company because Lufi is considering them for an acquisition. Lufi provides a report on Campbell prepared by another investment firm. Mumford uses some information from the other firm's report, cites the source, adds her own analysis and conclusions, signs her name, and gets it out. Did Mumford violate any Standards of Professional Conduct?

    *A. No (Standard I(C) - misrepresentation)
    B. Yes, relating to misrepresentation
    C. Yes, relating to independence and objectivity

4. CFA charterholder Jiang is on an elevator and overhears a pizza delivery man say that he just delivered pizzas to the headquarters of Iddings Furniture Company and they did not give him as big of a tip as he wanted, so they must not be making that much money. Jiang calls her broker and tells him to sell her Iddings stock in her personal account. Did Jiang violate any Standards of Professional Conduct?

    *A. No (Standard II(A) - material nonpublic information)
    B. Yes, relating to misconduct
    C. Yes, relating to material nonpublic information

5. CFA charterholder Arora works for a bank that serves as the trustee for a pension fund. Arora uses pension fund assets to invest in companies that he finds socially responsible and divests in companies that he finds socially irresponsible. Did Arora violate any Standards of Professional Conduct?

    A. No
    *B. Yes, relating to loyalty, prudence, and care (Standard III(A) - loyalty, prudence, and care)
    C. Yes, relating to independence and objectivity

6. When determining the suitability of an investment, the primary focus should be on

    A. The characteristics of the client's total portfolio and on an issue-by-issue basis
    B. An issue-by-issue basis, not on the characteristics of the client's total portfolio
    *C. The characteristics of the client's total portfolio, not on an issue-by-issue basis (Standard III(C) - suitability)

7. Members and candidates must keep information about current, former, and prospective clients confidential

    A. At all times
    *B. Unless disclosure is required by law (Standard III(E) - preservation of confidentiality)
    C. Unless the supervisor permits disclosure of the information

8. CFA charterholder Chen finds evidence of illegal activity when working on an acquisition in a country with strict confidentiality laws. What is Chen's most appropriate initial response?

    A. Inform the CFA Institute
    *B. Consult outside counsel (Standard III(E) - preservation of confidentiality)
    C. Disclose the evidence to government officials

9. According to the standards, members and candidates must make reasonable efforts to detect and prevent violations of applicable laws, rules, regulations, and the Code and Standards by anyone

    A. Subject to their direct supervision
    B. In a position of supervision or authority
    *C. Subject to their supervision or authority (Standard IV(C) - responsibilities of supervisors)

10. If a member or candidate does not agree with the conclusions of group research and decision making but is satisfied with the process, they

    A. Must dissociate from the report and document their differences
    *B.Do not need to dissociate from the report but should document their differences (Standard V(A) - diligence and reasonable basis)
    C. Must make reasonable and diligent efforts to determine whether such secondary or third-party research is sound

11. With the introduction of a new and different valuation model that represents a material change in the investment process, a firm must

    A. File notice of the change with regulatory authorities
    B. Communicate the change to the firm's prospective clients
    *C.Communicate the change to the firm's clients and prospective clients (Standard V(B) - communications with clients and prospective clients)

12. CFA charterholder Linton is a stock analyst. Linton is asked to write a report about a construction company that is a client of his firm's investment banking division, and half of Linton's compensation comes from his firm's investment banking. Linton has concerns about the construction industry and the company, but writes a very favorable report. Which Standard of Professional Conduct did Linton least likely violate?

    *A. Loyalty to employers (Standard VI(A) - disclosure of conflicts, Standard III(A) - loyalty, prudence and care, and Standard I(B) - independence and objectivity)
    B. Disclosure of conflicts
    C. Loyalty, prudence, and care

13. CFA charterholder Delo receives referral fees, and fully discloses the arrangement to his employer and clients. Did Delo violate any Standards of Professional Conduct?

    *A. No (Standard VI(C) - referral fees)
    B. Yes, related to misconduct
    C. Yes, related to conflicts of interest

14. CFA charterholder Spetko mentions to a friend who is considering enrolling in the CFA program that she learned a great deal from the CFA program and that many firms require their employees to be CFA charterholders. Spetko recommends the CFA program to anyone interested in a career in investment management. Did Spetko violate any Standards of Professional Conduct?

*A. No (Standard VII(B) - reference to the CFA Institute, the CFA designation, and the CFA program)

B. Yes, related to conduct as members and candidates in the CFA program

C. Yes, related to reference to the CFA Institute, the CFA designation, and the CFA program

15. CFA charterholder Shewarega manages the assets of the Ganesh Corporation Profit Sharing Plan. The president of Ganesh asks that Shewarega vote shares in the profit sharing plan in favor of the company-nominated board of directors and against the slate nominated by a dissident stockholder group. Shewarega conducts an independent investigation and concludes the dissident group's slate is better for the long-term prospects of the company than the company nominated slate, but votes based on the president's request in favor of the company-nominated board. Did Shewarega violate any Standards of Professional Conduct?

A. No

*B. Yes, related to loyalty, prudence, and care (Standard III(A) - loyalty, prudence, and care)

C. Yes, related to diligence and reasonable basis

16. CFA charterholder Palatnick completes an initial report recommending the purchase of shares of McLachlan and distributes it within his firm. Then he finds out his wife has just inherited a substantial amount of stock in McLachlan. Before he has a chance to tell his employer about the inheritance, he is asked to write a follow-up report on McLachlan. Palatnick does not mention the inheritance, and modifies the report to make it even more favorable. Did Palatnick violate any Standards of Professional Conduct?

A. No

B. Yes, related to loyalty

*C. Yes, related to disclosure of conflicts (Standard VI(A) - disclosure of conflicts)

17. Which is least appropriate relating to the standard on responsibilities of supervisors? Members with supervisory responsibilities should encourage their employers to adopt codes of ethics that are

    A. Stand-alone codes
    B. Applicable to all the firm's employees
    *C. Confidential and not shared with the firm's clients (Standard IV(C) - responsibilities of supervisors)

18. The GIPS section on private equity applies to

    A. Open-end funds
    B. Evergreen funds
    *C. Fund-of-funds investing

19. Which is closest to the growth rate if sales doubled in 10 years?

    *A. 7% = [(2 ^ (1/10)] - 1; n = 10, PV = -1, PMT = 0, FV = 2; i = 7.18 percent = 7.18%
    B. 12%
    C. 20%

20. What is the annual time-weighted rate of return for an account with a beginning value of $20, with cash inflow of $1 at the beginning of the first quarter, a value of $16 at the end of the first quarter, cash outflow of $1 at the beginning of the second quarter, a value of $14 at the end of the second quarter, cash inflow of $5 at the beginning of the third quarter, a value at the end of the third quarter of $20, cash outflow at the beginning of the fourth quarter of $5, and a value at the end of the fourth quarter of $20?

    *A. -0.2% = (16/21)(14/15)(20/19)(20/15) - 1
    B. 0.0%
    C. 0.2%

21. What measurement scale would be used for bond maturity in years?

    A. Ordinal scale
    *B. Ratio scale
    C. Nominal scale

22. Percentiles divide distributions into how many parts?

    A. 99
    *B. 100
    C. 101

23. If small caps had a mean return of 12% with a standard deviation of 20%, large caps had a mean return of 10% with a standard deviation of 16%, and the risk-free rate is 2%, which had superior risk-adjusted performance as measured by the Sharpe Ratio?

    A. Small caps
    B. Large caps
    *C.They are the same, (12% - 2%)/20% = (10% - 2%)/16%

24. What type of distribution is less peaked than the normal distribution?

    A. Leptokurtic
    B. Mesokurtic
    *C.Platykurtic

25. What are the odds of a gain on the S&P 500 if the probability of a loss is 25%?

    A. 1 to 3
    *B.3 to 1; 25% = 1 / (1 + 3)
    C. 4 to 1

26. What is the correlation between the S&P 500 and bonds for a portfolio with 75% in the S&P 500 with a variance of 2.25%, and 25% in bonds with a variance of 0.25%, given the covariance between the S&P 500 and bonds of 0.60%?

    A. -0.4
    B. 0.4
    *C.0.8 = 0.60% / [(2.25%^.5)(0.25%^.5)]

27. How many ways can 5 stocks be selected from a group of 12?

    *A. 792 = 12! / [(5!) (7!)]
    B. 19,008
    C. 95,040

28. If high yield bonds can be expected to default 20% of the time, what is the mean and standard deviation (SD) of the number of high yield bonds out of 50 that are expected to default?

    A. Mean = 10, SD =8
    *B.Mean = 10, SD = 2.8 = [50(.2)(.8)]^.5
    C. Mean = 8, SD = 10

29. Approximately what percent of normally distributed stock returns with a mean return of 10% and a standard deviation of 15% have a return that exceeds 20%?

    A. 16%
    *B.25% = (1 - 50%) / 2
    C. 32%

30. What is the probability that the return on the optimal portfolio will be less than the threshold level when a client with a portfolio of $100,000 would like to withdraw $3,000 at the year end and avoid the balance dropping below $100,000: allocation 1 with an expected return of 12% and a standard deviation of 12%, allocation 2 with an expected return of 9% and a standard deviation of 7%, or allocation 3 with an expected return of 11% and a standard deviation of 8%, given that $P(Z<=0.00) = 0.5000$; $P(Z<=0.25) = 0.5987$; $P(Z<=0.50) = 0.6915$; $P(Z<=0.75) = 0.7734$; and $P(Z<=1.00) = 0.8413$?

    *A. 16% = $P\{Z<= [-1*(11\%-3\%)/8\%)]\} = P(Z<=-1.00) = 1 - P(Z<=1.00) = 1 - 0.8413$
    B. 18%
    C. 25%

31. Which is least likely to apply to a sampling distribution of the sample mean based on the Central Limit Theorem when the sample size is large $(n>=30)$?

    *A. The distribution will be normal only if the population is normally distributed
    B. The sample mean will approximate the population mean
    C. The variance of the distribution of the sample mean will be the population variance divided by the sample size

32. What applies to a null hypothesis that the correlation coefficient is zero, given that the value of the test statistic is 1 and the critical value at the 0.05 significance level is 2?

    A. Reject the null hypothesis of the one-tailed test
    B. Reject the null hypothesis of the two-tailed test
    *C.Do not reject the null hypothesis of the two-tailed test

33. What happens to demand for a resource when the price of a close substitute resource decreases?

    *A. Large increase
    B. Small increase
    C. Decrease

34. Which is most likely to involve the free-rider problem, an obstacle to efficiency?

    A. Price and quantity regulations
    *B.Public goods
    C. Externality

35. What is total revenue minus opportunity costs?

    A. Implicit and explicit costs
    B. Normal profit
    *C.Economic profit

36. Which is least likely to be considered an advantage of a proprietorship or partnership?

    A. Easy to set up
    *B.Limited liability
    C. Profits only taxed once

37. What is the least likely result of long-run equilibrium in a market in perfect competition?

    A. Economic profit is zero
    *B.The entrepreneur makes no profit
    C. There is no entry, exit, plant expansion, or downsizing

38. What is the demand for a factor of production called?

    A. Demand for money
    B. Factor price
    *C.Derived demand

39. Which is least likely part of the total income of a factor of production?

    A. Opportunity cost
    B. Economic rent
    *C.Flow supply

40. What does an increase in potential GDP increase?

    A. Only the short run aggregate supply
    B. Only the long run aggregate supply
    *C.Both the short run and the long run aggregate supply

41. What includes currency, traveler's checks, checking deposits, times deposits, savings deposits, money market mutual funds, and other deposits?

   A. M1
   *B.M2
   C. Quantity of real money

42. How would financial innovation most likely impact the demand for money?

   A. Generally increases demand as a result of movement along the demand curve
   B. Always increases demand as a result of a shift of the demand curve
   *C.Generally decreases demand as a result of a shift of the demand curve

43. Which is most likely a generational effect of fiscal policy?

   A. Generational accounting and present values show that Social Security and Medicare obligations have been and will remain actuarially sound
   B. Budget deficits improve intergenerational equity
   *C.The international debt of the US means that in the future the US will need a surplus of exports over imports

44. Which decision rule for monetary policy sets the federal funds rate at 2% plus the inflation rate plus one-half the deviation of inflation from its target of 2% plus one-half of the output gap?

   A. McCallum rule
   *B.Taylor rule
   C. Targeting rule

45. On which would an analyst assessing a company's financial position most likely focus?

   *A. Balance sheet
   B. Statement of cash flows
   C. Statement of owners' equity

46. If assets are $500 million and liabilities are $200 million, what is owners' equity?

   *A. $300 million = $500 million - $300 million
   B. $500 million
   C. $700 million

47. What is reducing operating expense by recharacterizing certain expenses as operating activities?

    A. Judgment
    B. Creativity
    *C. Manipulation

48. What is the amount at which an asset could be exchanged or a liability settled?

    *A. Fair value
    B. Present value
    C. Historical cost

49. Which of these elements of financial statement is most closely related to the measurement of financial position?

    A. Income
    B. Expenses
    *C. Liabilities

50. Which is included in income as defined under IFRS?

    A. Increase in liabilities related to contributions from equity participants
    *B. Enhancement of assets not related to contributions from equity participants
    C. Enhancement of assets related to contributions from equity participants

51. Under IFRS, revenue from barter transactions is measured based on the fair value of revenue from

    A. Similar barter transactions with unrelated parties
    B. Similar nonbarter transactions with related parties
    *C. Similar nonbarter transactions with unrelated parties

52. Which is closest to the weighted average number of shares outstanding for calculating EPS for a calendar year if a company had $2 million in net income; paid $200,000 in preferred dividends; had 1,000,000 shares outstanding on January 1st; issued 800,000 shares on April 1st; and repurchased 200,000 shares on July 1?

    *A. $1,500,000 = 1,000,000 + (9/12)(800,000) - (6/12)(200,000)$
    B. 1,600,000
    C. 1,700,000

53. What are obligations of a company as a result of past events?

    A. Equity
    B. Assets
    *C.Liabilities

54. What type of balance sheet distinguishes between current and noncurrent items and presents a subtotal for current assets and liabilities?

    A. Report format
    B. Account format
    *C.Classified balance sheet

55. If total long-term debt is $500; total debt is $1,000; total equity is $500; and total assets are $1,500; which is closest to the total debt ratio?

    A. 1/3
    B. 1/2
    *C.2/3 = $1,000 / $1,500

56. Which permits greater discretion in classifying some cash flow items as operating, investing, or financing activities?

    *A. IFRS
    B. U.S. GAAP
    C. IFRS and U.S. GAAP are the same in this regard

57. How much cash did a company pay in wages if the wage expense was $200,000; the beginning balance of wages payable was $10,000; and the ending balance of wages payable was $30,000?

    *A. $180,000 = $200,000 - $30,000 + $10,000
    B. $220,000
    C. $240,000

58. In a period of rising prices, which is most likely greater for a company that uses LIFO compared to a company that uses FIFO?

    A. Gross margin
    B. Current ratio
    *C.Inventory turnover

59. When are research costs most likely to be expensed rather than capitalized and development costs most likely allowed to be capitalized under certain conditions?

    A. Under U.S. GAAP but not under IFRS
    *B.Under IFRS but not under U.S. GAAP
    C. Under both U.S. GAAP and IFRS

60. What would most likely be decreased in the early periods of an asset's life for a company uses accelerated depreciation rather than straight-line depreciation?

    A. Asset turnover ratios and expenses
    B. Expenses and cash flow from operations
    *C.Retained earnings and shareholders' equity

61. Which allows impairment losses to be reversed?

    A. U.S. GAAP but not IFRS
    *B.IFRS but not U.S. GAAP
    C. Both U.S. GAAP and IFRS

62. If a company has a net deferred tax asset, what would a reduction in the statutory tax rate most likely benefit?

    *A. Income statement but not the balance sheet
    B. Balance sheet but not the income statement
    C. Both the balance sheet and income statement

63. If a company issues zero-coupon bonds rather than coupon bearing bonds, what will the company's debt-to-equity ratio do as the maturity date approaches?

    *A. Rise
    B. Decline
    C. Remain constant

64. How much should an analyst increase reported liabilities to treat all leases as debt if a company has financial leases of $10 million including $2 million in interest payments and operating leases of $15 million?

    *A. $12 million = [($10 million - $2 million)/ $10 million] $15 million
    B. $15 million
    C. $25 million

65. Which is the most appropriate conclusion if ROE stayed the same, the tax burden increased, the interest burden stayed the same, the EBIT margin stayed the same, asset turnover decreased, and leverage stayed the same?

   A. Profitability and liquidity decreased
   *B. The lower tax rate offset the decrease in efficiency, leaving ROE unchanged
   C. The higher tax rate offset the increase in efficiency, leaving ROE unchanged

66. Which is least likely to increase cash flow from operations?

   A. Securitizing assets receivable
   B. Delaying payments to suppliers
   *C. Using short term debt for accounts payable

67. Which is not allowed under IFRS?

   A. FIFO
   *B. LIFO
   C. Weighted average cost

68. Which is allowed under IFRS?

   A. Revaluations of property, plant, and equipment but not intangible assets
   *B. Revaluations of property, plant, and equipment as well as intangible assets
   C. Revaluations of intangible assets but not property, plant, and equipment

69. Which is least likely to factor into a capital budgeting decision?

   *A. Sunk cost
   B. Opportunity cost
   C. Incremental cash flow

70. Which project should be chosen if mutually exclusive projects are ranked differently by the NPV and IRR?

   *A. The one with the higher NPV
   B. The one with the higher IRR
   C. The one with the lower IRR

71. What is the crossover rate for the NPV profiles for two projects?

   *A. Where the NPVs are equal
   B. Where the IRRs are equal
   C. Where the NPVs go from negative to positive

72. Which would most likely be used to discount the value a project using the net present value (NPV) method?

    A. IRR
    *B.WACC
    C. Cost of debt

73. What is an estimate of the sustainable growth rate using the dividend discount model if the dividend next year will be $2.30, the payout ratio is 30%, ROE is 15%, and the stock price is $45?

    A. 5.38%
    *B.10.50% = (1-30%)(15%)
    C. 15.61%

74. What is an estimate of the cost of equity using the bond yield plus risk premium approach if the before-tax cost of debt is 4%, the risk premium is 8%, and the tax rate is 25%?

    A. 10%
    B. 11%
    *C.12% = 4% + 8%

75. Which is graphed on the marginal cost of capital schedule?

    A. CAPM for different amounts of new capital
    *B.WACC for different amounts of new capital
    C. WACC for different amounts of new debt

76. Which is most likely to indicate greater liquidity?

    *A. Shorter operating cycle and shorter net operating cycle
    B. Shorter operating cycle and longer net operating cycle
    C. Longer operating cycle and longer net operating cycle

77. Which is closest to return on equity using DuPont analysis if net profit margin is 4.90%, operating profit margin is 7.79%, effect of non-operating items is 0.9909, the tax effect is 0.6350, total asset turnover is 2.0433, and financial leverage is 1.7184?

    A. 10.83%
    *B.17.21% = 7.79% (0.9909)(0.6350)(2.0433)(1.7184) = 4.90% (2.0433)(1.7184)
    C. 27.36%

78. Which is the system of internal controls by which companies are managed?

    A. Code of ethics
    B. Pro forma analysis
    *C.Corporate governance

79. Liquidity includes

    A. Marketability and efficiency
    B. Efficiency and price continuity
    *C.Marketability and price continuity

80. The minimum number of holders of round lots for a stock listed on the NYSE in 2004 was two

    *A. Thousand
    B. Million
    C. Billion

81. What is executed at the lowest ask price for a buy order?

    A. Short sale
    B. Limit order
    *C.Market order

82. An investor buys 100 shares at $70 using 50% margin. If the price increases 15%, the total market value of the position is

    A. $4,550 and the equity is $3,500
    B. $8,050 and the equity is $3,500
    *C.$8,050 and the equity is $4,550; $8,050 = $7,000(1.15); $4,550 = (115%)$70(100) - (100)$70(50%)

83. What is closest to the return on the unweighted index using the geometric mean for three stocks with prices at the beginning of the year for stocks A, B, and C of $11, $20, and $17, respectively, prices at the end of the year for stocks A, B, and C of $14, $25, and $15, respectively, and 3 million shares of stock A, 20 million shares of stock B, and 6 million shares of stock C?

    *A. 12.0% = [($14 / $11) ($25 / $20) ($15 / $17)]^(1/3) - 1
    B. 12.5%
    C. 13.5%

84. Event studies such as stock splits and initial public offerings (IPOs) support the

    A. Weak form of the EMH
    B. Strong form of the EMH
    *C.Semi-strong form of the EMH

85. What explains why investors fear losses more than they value gains, and would hold onto losers too long and sell winners too soon?

    A. Selection bias and confirmation bias
    B. Confirmation bias and data mining bias
    *C.Loss aversion, utility, and prospect theory

86. Which is closest to the value of common stock with an estimated dividend of $2 payable at year end and an estimated year-end sale price of $30 with a risk free rate of 4%, a market return of 10.67%, and a beta of 1.2?

    *A. $26.78
    B. $28.57 = ($2 + $30) / 112%, where 12% = 4% + 1.2(10.67% - 4%)
    C. $32.00

87. Which is closest to value of a common stock with a dividend payout ratio of 50%, a dividend growth rate of 9%, a required rate of return of 12%, and current earnings per share of $2?

    A. $32.44
    B. $33.33
    *C.$36.33 = [50% / (12% - 9%)] $2 (1.09)

88. What is the growth rate of equity earnings without any external financing if the dividend payout ratio is 75% and the ROE is 10%?

    *A. 2.5% = (1 - 75%) (10%)
    B. 5.0%
    C. 7.5%

89. What is the estimated price of a stock using the dividend discount model if the earnings retention ratio is 60%, the ROE is 20%, the current dividends are $2 per share, and the required rate of return is 15%?

    A. $30.86
    B. $44.00
    *C.$74.67 = $2 (1.12) / (15% - 12%) where 12% = 20% (60%)

90. What is the price to book (P/B) ratio for a company with $100 million in common shareholders' equity, 20 million common shares outstanding, and a closing price of $9?

    A. 0.6
    B. 0.9
    *C.1.8 = $9 / ($100 / 20)

91. Which are best described as a contingent claims?

    A. Swap agreements and convertible bonds
    *B.Convertible bonds and asset-backed securities
    C. Asset backed securities and swap agreements

92. The credit risk of a forward contract most likely be eliminated by entering into an opposite position with

    *A. The same counterparty
    B. A different counterparty
    C. The same counterparty or a different counterparty

93. What type of FRA is a contract expiring in 3 months on a 180-day LIBOR?

    A. 1 x 3
    B. 3 x 6
    *C.3 x 9

94. What are call options on interest rates?

    *A. Caps
    B. Floors
    C. Collars

95. The lower bound on a European call price the greater of zero or

    A. The price of an American put option
    B. The present value of the exercise price minus the underlying price
    *C.The underlying price minus the present value of the exercise price

96. What is the profit on a call option, where the exercise price is X and the price of the underlying security is S?

    A. Max (0, S - X)
    B. Max (0, X - S) - option cost
    *C.Max (0, S - X) - option cost

97. What is the price of a bond plus accrued interest?

    A. Price or clean price
    *B.Full price or dirty price
    C. Full price or clean price

98. Which imbedded option is an advantage to the bondholder?

    *A. Put provision
    B. Cap on a floater
    C. Accelerated sinking fund

99. Which bond has the greatest interest rate risk?

    A. Floating rate bond
    *B.Zero-coupon bond
    C. 7% fixed coupon bond

100. Which is closest to the dollar price change of a bond, with a market value of $8 million and a duration of 5, for a 50 basis point change in yield?

    A. $100,000
    *B.$200,000 = (5%/2) ($8 million)
    C. $400,000

101. What is the risk that the issuer will not make timely payments of interest and principal?

    *A. Default risk
    B. Downgrade risk
    C. Credit spread risk

102. A decrease in expected yield volatility will cause the price of

    *A. Putable bonds to decrease
    B. Callable bonds to decrease
    C. Embedded put and call options to increase

103. Which is a bank obligation used in importing and exporting that exposes an investor to credit risk and liquidity risk?

    A. Commercial paper
    *B.Bankers acceptances
    C. Index amortizing note

104. What is the shape of the yield curve when yield increases with maturity?

    A. Flat
    *B.Upward sloping
    C. Downward sloping

105. For an investor considering a taxable bond with a yield of 6.0%, and a tax-exempt
    security with a yield of 4.0%, what is the tax rate at which the investor is indifferent?

    *A. 33%; where 6.0%(1 - 33%) = 4.0%
    B. 50%
    C. 67%

106. Which is closest to the change in price due to the change in maturity of a bond
    maturing in 6 years with an 8% annual coupon, a par value of $100, a price of $95.51,
    and a yield of 9%; if the price one year earlier was $90.26 and the yield was 10%?

    *A. $1.03; where n = 6, i = 10, PMT = 8, FV = 100, resulting in PV = -91.29; $91.29
      - $90.26 = $1.03
    B. $4.22
    C. $5.25

107. Which is closest to the bond-equivalent yield if the yield to maturity on an annual
    pay bond is 6%?

    *A. 5.91% = 2 [(1 + 6%)^.5 - 1]
    B. 6.00%
    C. 6.09%

108. Which is least accurate regarding interest rate risk?

    A. Two bonds with the same duration can have different convexities
    B. The duration / convexity approach does not take into consideration how the yield
      curve can shift
    *C.If two bonds have the same duration, then the percentage change in price of the
      two bonds will be exactly the same for any given change in interest rates

109. Which is closest to the duration of a portfolio with $0.5 million in 11% coupon
    bonds with a duration of 6.2; $1.2 million in 6% coupon bonds with a duration of 5.7;
    and $0.3 million in 9% coupon bonds with a duration of 3.0?

    *A. 5.42 = ($0.5 / $2.0) 6.2 + ($1.2 / $2.0) 5.7 + ($0.3/ $2.0) 3.0
    B. 5.73
    C. 6.85

110. Which is closest to percentage price change if yields increase by 10 basis points based on duration and the convexity adjustment of a 6% coupon 20-year option-free bond selling at par of 100 to yield 6%, if the price increases to 101.1651 at a yield of 5.8%, and the price decreases to 98.8535 at a yield of 6.2%?

    A. -1.17%
    B. -1.16%
    *C.-1.15% = .1 / 100 {(101.1651 - 98.8535) / [2 (100) (0.002)]} - (.1)(.1) / 10000 {(101.1651 + 98.8535 - 2(100)) / [2 (100) (0.002)^2]}

111. Which is least accurate regarding investment styles of investment companies?

    *A. International ETFs are an insignificant segment of ETFs offered in the U.S
    B. Some ETFs track a specific investment style, such as value or growth
    C. Some ETFs track a specific index or invest in stocks from a specific industry sector

112. Which is closest to the value of a real estate investment if rents are $2,018,250, operating expenses are $1.2 million, the mortgage rate is 6%, financing is 90%, the required rate of return is 15%, the holding period is 5 years, and the tax rate is 25%?

    A. $4.000 million
    *B.$5.455 million = ($2,018,250 - $1,200,000) / 15%
    C. $6.133 million

113. Which set of characteristics is least accurate in describing venture capital investing?

    A. Illiquidity, long-term commitment period, and difficulty in determining market values
    B. Limited historical risk and return data, limited information, and entrepreneurial/management mismatches
    *C.Fund manager incentive alignment, publicly available information on competitors, stability, and only routine operations analysis and advice required

114. Which is closest to the NPV of a project with a $500,000 initial investment and an expected $15.5 million payoff at the end of 5 years if it survives, with a probability of survival for 5 years of 25%, and a required rate of return of 19%?

    A. $0.129 million
    *B.$1.124 million = 25%($15,500,000)/1.19^5 - $500,000
    C. $2.104 million

115. Which phase occurs before age 36 to 38?

    A. Gifting
    B. Spending
    *C.Accumulation

116. Which is most likely related to tax concerns?

    A. Liquidity
    B. Time horizon
    *C.Capital gains

117. Which is closest to the variance for an individual asset with a 35% probability of an 8% return, 50% probability of an 11% return, and a 15% probability of a 14% return?

    *A. $0.04\% = 35\%(8\%-10.4\%)^2 + 50\%(11\%-10.4\%)^2 + 15\%(14\%-10.4\%)^2;$
        $10.4\% = 35\%(8\%) + 50\%(11\%) + 15\%(14\%)$
    B. 2.03%
    C. 21.96%

118. Which is closest to the standard deviation of a portfolio with a 41.2% weight in a security with an expected return of 10% and a standard deviation of 7%, and a 58.8% weight in a security with an expected return of 20% and a standard deviation of 10%, if the correlation coefficient is -1.0?

    A. 0%
    *B.$3\% = [(41.2\%^2)(7\%^2) + (58.8\%^2)(10\%^2) + 2(41.2\%)(58.8\%)(-1.0)(7\%)(10\%)]^{.5}$
    C. 4%

119. Which is closest to the standard deviation of a leveraged portfolio with an investor borrowing 50% of the original wealth to buy more of a risky asset with an expected return of 8% and a standard deviation of 10%, if the risk-free asset has an expected return of 3%?

    A. 10%
    B. 11%
    *C.$15\% = 150\%(10\%)$

120. Which assumption would most likely only be made if the CAPM assumptions were relaxed?

    A. No taxes
    *B.Transaction costs exist
    C. Equal borrowing and lending rates

1. What can prompt an inquiry by the CFI Institute Professional Conduct staff?

    A. Self-disclosure or written complaints
    B. Media reports or reports from examination proctors
    C. Self-disclosure, written complaints, media reports, or reports from examination proctors

2. CFA charterholder Lindert is the investment manager of a public sector pension fund. The plan requested proposals for a bond manager. CFA charterholder Madura works for a bond manager that responded to the request for proposals. Madura met Lindert at a seminar and asked about their outstanding proposal. Lindert responded that a decision had not been made yet, then Madura told Lindert, "Since you like golf, maybe you could use this new set of golf clubs worth over $1,000 that we were going to give away as a door prize. Take the golf clubs as a gift." Lindert accepted the golf clubs as a gift, and Madura turned in a fictional expense report to his employer overstating the cost of the clubs. Who violated the Standards of Professional Conduct?

    A. Only Madura
    B. Only Lindert
    C. Both Madura and Lindert

3. CFA charterholder Hammad applies for a job and puts on his resume that he has an MBA from a top tier school in addition to the CFA designation. Hammad attended the school but did not receive a degree. Did Hammad violate any Standards of Professional Conduct?

    A. No
    B. Yes, relating to misrepresentation
    C. Yes, relating to duties to employers

4. CFA charterholder Gibaja works for Guan & Grigorov, a firm that publishes a weekly column in Securities Weekly magazine that usually affects the value of the stocks discussed. Gibaja's nephew works at the publishing company, and Gibaja has his nephew fax him a copy of the column before it is published. Gibaja then makes profitable trades based on the column. Were any Standards of Professional Conduct violated?

    A. Gibaja violated the standard relating to material nonpublic information
    B. Gibaja's nephew violated the standard relating to market manipulation
    C. Gibaja and Gibaja's nephew violated the standard relating to material nonpublic information

5. Which statement is least accurate related to the Standard of Professional Conduct on integrity of capital markets?

    A. Members and candidates must not engage in practices that distort prices or artificially inflate trading volume with the intent to mislead market participants

    B. Members and candidates must not knowingly make any misrepresentations relating to investment analysis, recommendations, actions, or other professional activities

    C. Members and candidates who possess material nonpublic information that could affect the value of an investment must not act or cause others to act on the information

6. CFA charterholder Volek gave priority to discretionary accounts over non-discretionary accounts. Volek most likely violated the Standard of Professional Conduct relating to

    A. Fair dealing

    B. Independence and objectivity

    C. Communications with clients and prospective clients

7. CFA charterholder Chang revealed confidential information about a client's illegal activities under a court order initiated by a regulatory authority. Did Chang violate any Standards of Professional Conduct?

    A. No

    B. Yes, relating to fair dealing

    C. Yes, relating to preservation of confidentiality

8. CFA charterholder Milner works as an independent contractor with access to a firm's offices and research files. Milner is preparing a study while working part-time for the firm, then gets a permanent, full-time position with another firm and uses the same study at her new employer. Did Milner violate any Standards of Professional Conduct?

    A. No

    B. Yes, relating to loyalty

    C. Yes, relating to preservation of confidentiality

9. CFA charterholder de la Cruz is an independent contractor who writes research reports for publications and always signs exclusivity contracts. Often de la Cruz makes very slight modifications to work published in one publication and submits it to another publication. Did de la Cruz violate any Standards of Professional Conduct?

    A. No

    B. Yes, relating to loyalty

    C. Yes, relating to disclosure of conflicts

10. CFA charterholder Oliver sends a memo to her staff that the firm's written compliance manual will be updated to meet industry standards, regulatory requirements, the Code and Standards, and the circumstances of the firm. Did Oliver violate any Standards of Professional Conduct?

   A. No
   B. Yes, because compliance procedures cannot be altered to meet industry standards
   C. Yes, because compliance procedures cannot be altered to meet the circumstances of the firm

11. CFA charterholder Deslandes manages funds with long investment horizons. Deslandes' employer changes his compensation package to reward short term results. Deslandes does not tell his clients about the change. Deslandes is most likely to have violated the Standard of Professional Conduct on

   A. Disclosure of conflicts
   B. Independence and objectivity
   C. Additional compensation arrangements

12. CFA charterholder Dinehart is a portfolio manager and managers the account of her parents. When an IPO becomes available, she allocates shares to her other clients first and her parents last. Which Standard of Professional Conduct did Dinehart least likely violate?

   A. Loyalty
   B. Fair dealing
   C. Priority of transactions

13. To maintain status as a CFA Institute member, members must

   A. Pay annual dues
   B. Remit a completed professional conduct statement annually
   C. Remit a completed professional conduct statement annually and pay annual dues

14. CFA charterholder Shuman infers that since he is a CFA charterholder his recommendations are correct. Did Shuman violate any Standards of Professional Conduct?

   A. No
   B. Yes, related to communication with clients and prospective clients
   C. Yes, related to reference to the CFA Institute, the CFA designation, and the CFA program

15. An investment management firm's brokerage unit has a sell recommendation on ETV Corporation. The firm has been hired by ETV to work on an initial public offering. The head of the investment banking department asks the head of the brokerage unit to change the recommendation from sell to buy. The head of the brokerage unit does not change the recommendation but places the company on a restricted list and only gives factual information about the company. Did the head of the brokerage unit violate any Standards of Professional conduct?

    A. No
    B. Yes, relating to independence and objectivity
    C. Yes, relating to diligence and reasonable basis

16. An investment-banking department of a brokerage firm often receives material nonpublic information that would have considerable value if used in advising the firm's brokerage clients. Which is the best policy for conforming with the Standards of Professional Conduct?

    A. Monitor the exchange of information between the investment-banking department and the brokerage operations
    B. Establish physical and informational barriers within the firm to prevent the exchange of information between the investment-banking and brokerage operations
    C. Prohibit purchase recommendations when the investment-banking department has access to material nonpublic information, but allow sale of current holdings

17. To comply with the GIPS, after presenting five years of compliant data, the firm must add annual performance each year going forward up to a minimum of

    A. Seven years
    B. Ten years
    C. Twelve years

18. The GIPS section on real estate applies

    A. Only if a real estate asset or investment is producing revenue
    B. Only if the firm has control of the management of the investment
    C. Irrespective of whether a real estate asset or investment is producing revenue

19. What annual contribution to a college fund for 18 years starting in one year will provide for four years of tuition at $20,000 per year starting 18 years after the first payment, if the fund earns 7% per year?

    A. $1,740
    B. $1,862
    C. $1,993

20. What is the price for a T-bill with par value of $100,000 and 90 days to maturity with a bank discount yield of 3%?

    A. $99,250
    B. $99,260
    C. $99,264

21. If a portfolio's deviation from a benchmark for five years was 28.3%, 0%, 0%, 0%, and -28.3%, what is the tracking risk?

    A. 10%
    B. 11%
    C. 20%

22. What are the 25th and 75th percentiles for funds with returns of -20%, -10%, -6%, -5%, 0%, 6%, 12%, 14%, and 20%?

    A. 25th percentile = -10%; 75th percentile = 14%
    B. 25th percentile = -8%; 75th percentile = 13%
    C. 25th percentile = -6%; 75th percentile = 12%

23. What is the Sharpe Ratio if a portfolio mean return is 8%, the standard deviation is 12%, and the risk free rate is 4%?

    A. 0.33
    B. 0.67
    C. 1.50

24. What is the skewness of a sample of 50 observations with a sum of the cubed deviation of 0.10%, a sum of the deviations to the fourth power of 2.715%, and a sample standard deviation 12%?

    A. 0.01
    B. 0.02
    C. 3.02

25. What is the probability of an event?

    A. a priori probability
    B. Conditional probability
    C. Unconditional probability

26. What is the expected return for a portfolio with 40% in the S&P 500 with an expected return of 9%, 35% in bonds with an expected return of 4%, and 25% in the EAFE with an expected return of 12%?

    A. 7%
    B. 8%
    C. 9%

27. What is the probability function for continuous random variables?

    A. Probability distribution
    B. Probability density function
    C. Continuous random variable

28. Given that P(X<=1)=0.10, P(X<=2)=0.50, P(X<=3)=0.70, and P(X<=4)=1.00, what is P(2<= X <=3)?

    A. 0.5
    B. 0.6
    C. 0.7

29. Which best describes the standard deviation of sample skewness for a sample of size "n" from a normal distribution?

    A. 6/n
    B. 8/n
    C. 24/n

30. What is the difference between the sample mean and the population mean?

    A. Sampling error
    B. Tracking error
    C. Volatility

31. Which statistic is appropriate for sampling from a normal distribution with an unknown variance for a small sample size?

    A. t-statistic
    B. z-statistic
    C. Not available

32. Which is least likely to be an assumption of technical analysis?

    A. Prices move in trends that persist over long periods of time
    B. Testing supports the efficient market hypothesis
    C. Shifts in supply and demand can be detected sooner or later in the actions of the market

33. What is the demand elasticity along a straight-line demand curve above the midpoint, where a price cut increases total revenue?

    A. Unit elastic demand
    B. Inelastic demand
    C. Elastic demand

34. Which is least likely to result in sellers paying the entire tax?

    A. Perfectly elastic supply
    B. Perfectly inelastic supply
    C. Perfectly elastic demand

35. Which is least likely to be used to cope with the principal-agent problem?

    A. Ownership
    B. Incentive pay
    C. Short-term contracts

36. What is true about average product?

    A. It decreases initially and eventually increases
    B. It increases initially and eventually diminishes
    C. It decreases initially and eventually diminishes

37. What is the least likely result of entry and plant expansion in a market in perfect competition?

    A. Increased supply
    B. Lower price
    C. Higher profit

38. What are firms acting independently in the oligopoly market structure most likely to increase?

    A. Prices but not output
    B. Output and prices
    C. Output but not prices

39. What is equivalent to the condition for profit maximization that the wage rate is equal to the marginal revenue product?

    A. Marginal profit equals marginal cost
    B. Marginal revenue equals marginal cost
    C. Marginal revenue product equals average total cost

40. What type of unemployment applies to someone who moves to an area to look for a new job?

    A. Frictional
    B. Structural
    C. Cyclical

41. The view that the economy is self regulating and always at full employment is most likely held by which school of thought?

    A. Classical
    B. Monetarist
    C. Keynesian

42. Which is least likely to be used by the Federal Reserve System to accelerate the growth of the economy?

    A. Decrease the federal funds rate
    B. Sell government securities
    C. Decrease reserve requirements

43. Which has the greatest magnification of an increase in aggregate demand?

    A. Balanced budget multiplier
    B. Government expenditure multiplier
    C. Autonomous tax multiplier

44. Which is the most likely action of the Federal Reserve System to fight inflation?

    A. Raise the target federal funds rate, sell securities, and decrease the supply of reserves in the banking system
    B. Raise the target federal funds rate, buy securities, and decrease the supply of reserves in the banking system
    C. Lower the target federal funds rate, buy securities, and increase the supply of reserves in the banking system

45. What shows revenue minus expense?

   A. Balance sheet
   B. Income statement
   C. Cash flow statement

46. Which category includes capital such as common stock par value and additional paid-in capital?

   A. Assets
   B. Liabilities
   C. Owner's equity

47. Which involves cash movement prior to accounting recognition?

   A. Unbilled revenue
   B. Unearned revenue
   C. Accrued expense

48. What values assets at the amount given to acquire them?

   A. Market value
   B. Historical cost
   C. Amortized cost

49. What type of discussion regarding new accounting standards would be most meaningful to an analyst?

   A. No material impact
   B. The standard does not apply
   C. Discussion of impact of adoption

50. Which special revenue recognition method that allows for partial recognition of revenue throughout the contract would be used under limited circumstances such as in real estate sales contracts?

   A. Installment method
   B. Completed contract method
   C. Percentage-of-completion method

51. Which is closest to the profit that will be reported in the second year under the installment method if land purchased for $20,000 was sold for $50,000 with $5,000 payable the first year and the remaining $45,000 payable the second year?

    A. $0
    B. $15,000
    C. $27,000

52. What would be the outstanding shares at the end of the year for calculating EPS if the board of a company with 1,000,000 shares outstanding on January 1st at the beginning of the year is considering either a 3 for 2 stock split or a 500,000 stock dividend on April 1st?

    A. 1,500,000 for the stock split or the stock dividend
    B. 1,375,000 for the stock split or 1,500,000 for the stock dividend
    C. 1,500,000 for the stock split or 1,375,000 for the stock dividend

53. Under U.S. GAAP, what is closest to other comprehensive income if beginning shareholders' equity is $1,100; net income is $100; cash dividends are $20; there was no issuance or repurchase of company stock; and ending shareholders' equity is $1,230?

    A. $10
    B. $30
    C. $50

54. What is a financial instrument for which the value is based on some underlying factor?

    A. Derivative
    B. Hedge fund
    C. Preferred stock

55. How is the minority interest in a consolidated subsidiary shown on the balance sheet?

    A. Asset
    B. Liability
    C. Shareholders' equity

56. Which is an appropriate method of computing free cash flow?

  A. Add operating cash flows plus after-tax interest payments and deduct capital expenditures
  B. Add operating cash flows plus capital expenditures and deduct after-tax interest payments
  C. Start with operating cash flows and deduct both capital expenditures and after-tax interest payments

57. Which is least likely to be a formula for free cash flow to the firm (FCFF)?

  A. FCFF = CFO + Int(1 - Tax rate) - FCInv
  B. FCFF = NI + NCC + Int(1 - Tax rate) - FCInv - WCInv
  C. FCFF = CFO - FCInv + Net borrowing - Net debt repayment

58. Which is the most likely to be used to measure inventory under U.S. GAAP for potential tax savings?

  A. FIFO
  B. LIFO
  C. Weighted average cost

59. Which would be most likely to provide a better assessment of a company's solvency if included in the calculation of interest coverage ratios?

  A. Goodwill
  B. Cost of goods sold
  C. Capitalized interest

60. If a company reporting under U.S. GAAP purchased equipment for $100,000 with a five-year life and a salvage value of $10,000, which would make the reported income for tax expense in the first year highest?

  A. Straight-line depreciation
  B. Accelerated depreciation
  C. Straight-line and accelerated depreciation produce the same reported income for tax purposes

61. Which is a company least likely to do when it is able to estimate the future costs it will incur when an asset is retired?

  A. Increase the carrying value of the asset
  B. Decrease the carrying value of the liability over time through an accretion charge
  C. Decrease the carrying value of the asset over time through an accretion charge

62. Which would most likely result from amortizing a capital expenditure over seven years for accounting purposes but ten years for tax purposes?

    A. Deferred tax asset
    B. Deferred tax liability
    C. No deferred tax asset or liability

63. Which does not permit the use of substantially enacted tax rates?

    A. U.S. GAAP but not IFRS
    B. IFRS but not U.S. GAAP
    C. Both U.S. GAAP and IFRS

64. For a capital lease with rental payments of $500 per year, fair value of leased equipment at inception of $3000, an implicit interest rate of 12%, with the present value of the lease equal to the present value of the equipment at inception, which is closest to the interest recorded by the lessee in the second year of the lease?

    A. $336
    B. $343
    C. $360

65. What kind of ratios measure the ability of a company to meet long-term obligations?

    A. Activity ratios
    B. Liquidity ratios
    C. Solvency ratios

66. Which would most likely explain a high fixed asset turnover ratio?

    A. Recently bought new equipment
    B. Low amortization expense
    C. Old, low cost equipment

67. What exists when companies that merge or go out of business are dropped from a database?

    A. Backtesting
    B. Look-ahead bias
    C. Survivorship bias

68. How are cash outflows for the payment of interest treated under U.S. GAAP?

    A. Operating cash flows
    B. Financing or investing cash flows
    C. Operating or financing cash flows

69. Which step of the capital budgeting process involves gathering information to forecast cash flows?

    A. Generating ideas
    B. Planning the capital budget
    C. Analyzing individual proposals

70. What is the discounted payback period closest to if the initial investment is $40 million, the cash flows are $15 million per year at the end of the each of 4 years, and the required rate of return is 10%?

    A. 3.00 years
    B. 3.26 years
    C. 3.75 years

71. Which capital budgeting method is most likely to have problems with negative cash flows after the initial investment?

    A. NPV
    B. IRR
    C. Discounted payback period

72. Which method is least likely to be used to estimate the before-tax cost of debt?

    A. WACC
    B. Bond rating
    C. Yield to maturity

73. What is the best estimate for the value of preferred stock with a $1.75 dividend previously issued for $25, if the coupon rate on preferred stock issued today would be 6.5%?

    A. $25.00
    B. $26.92
    C. $37.31

74. What is an estimate of the equity risk premium if the expected dividends are $5, the market price is $100, EPS is $15, ROE is 6%, and the risk-free rate is 3%?

    A. 4%
    B. 5%
    C. 6%

75. Which company had the lowest accounts receivable turnover if company A had credit sales of $50 million and an average receivables balance of $10 million, company B had credit sales of $30 million and an average receivables balance of $12 million, and company C had credit sales of $25 million and an average receivables balance of $8 million?

    A. Company A
    B. Company B
    C. Company C

76. What equals [(face value - purchase price) / purchase price] (365/ number of days to maturity)?

    A. Money market yield
    B. Bond equivalent yield
    C. Discount-basis yield

77. Which is closest to the total asset turnover if financial leverage is 1.33, the net profit margin is 4%, and the return on equity is 8%?

    A. 0.4
    B. 1.5
    C. 2.7

78. Which is the third step in pro forma analysis, following estimating fixed burdens such as interest and taxes?

    A. Forecast revenues
    B. Construct future period income statement and balance sheet
    C. Estimate typical relation between revenues and sales-driven accounts

79. What are auctions of U.S. Treasury securities and new issues of common stock?

    A. Primary markets
    B. Secondary markets
    C. Over-the-counter markets

80. What is the least accurate way to describe a pure auction market?

   A. Price-driven
   B. Order-driven
   C. Quote-driven

81. For a margin account used to purchase 200 shares of stock at $50, what is minimum initial deposit if the margin is 50%?

   A. $2,500
   B. $5,000
   C. $10,000

82. What type of security market index is based on capitalization?

   A. Unweighted
   B. Price-weighted
   C. Value-weighted

83. Which is closest to the return on the price-weighted index for three stocks with prices at the beginning of the year for stocks A, B, and C of $100, $50, and $30, respectively, and prices at the end of the year for stocks A, B, and C of $110, $50, and $30, respectively?

   A. 3.2%
   B. 3.3%
   C. 5.5%

84. Which form of the efficient market hypothesis (EMH) states that current stock prices reflect all information about P/E ratios, dividend yield ratios, price to book value ratios, and stock splits?

   A. Weak form
   B. Strong form
   C. Semi-strong form

85. Which is least likely to be considered a limitation to market efficiency?

   A. Escalation bias
   B. Cost of trading
   C. Limits of arbitrage

86. Which is closest to the value of preferred stock with an annual dividend of $5 and a yield on preferred 50 basis points below the bond yield of 7%?

    A. $71
    B. $77
    C. $83

87. Which is closest to the value of common stock with no dividends expected for the next two years, an expected dividend of $2 in the third year, a dividend growth rate of 9% after year 3, and a required rate of return of 12%?

    A. $53
    B. $60
    C. $67

88. Which is closest to the growth rate of equity earnings without any external financing if the retention rate is 40%, earnings per share are $1, and the stock price is $9.26?

    A. 3.6%
    B. 4.3%
    C. 6.5%

89. What best describes an overpriced stock with a P/E value substantially higher than the industry average?

    A. Cyclical stock
    B. Defensive stock
    C. Speculative stock

90. Which is least likely to be considered a rationale for using price to cash flow (P / CF) ratios?

    A. More stable than P/E
    B. Cash flow cannot be negative
    C. Cash flow less subject to manipulation than earnings

91. What is an agreement between two parties in which one party agrees to buy and the other party agrees to sell an asset at a future date at a price agreed on today?

    A. Option
    B. Contingent claim
    C. Forward commitment

92. Which statement is least accurate regarding forward commitments?

    A. Forward contracts are market to market daily
    B. Forward contracts have more default risk than futures contracts
    C. Forward contracts require that both parties to the transaction have a high degree of creditworthiness

93. What is the balance initially and at the end of day 3 for a holder of a short position of 20 futures contracts if the initial futures price on day 0 is $85, the initial margin requirement is $7.5, the maintenance margin requirement is $7, the settlement price on day 1 is $86, the settlement price on day 2 is $84.25, and the settlement price on day 3 is $85.50?

    A. $140 initially and $150 at the end of day 3
    B. $150 initially and $140 at the end of day 3
    C. $150 initially and $160 at the end of day 3

94. An investor buys a call at $95 for $2 when the price of the stock was $95. What is the intrinsic value of the call if the new price of the stock is $96?

    A. -$1.00
    B. $0.00
    C. $1.00 = $96 - $95

95. An asset manager enters into a $100 million equity swap and agrees to pay a dealer the return on a large-cap index and the dealer agrees to pay the return on a small-cap index. Payments are made semi-annually. The value of the small-cap index starts at 689.40 and the large-cap index starts at 1130.20. In six months, the small cap index is at 625.60 and the large cap index is at 1251.83. Which party pays what amount after the payments are netted?

    A. The asset manager pays the dealer $20,016,236
    B. The dealer pays the asset manager $10,761,812
    C. The dealer pays the asset manager $20,016,236

96. What is the maximum gain to the seller of a put option (short position), where the exercise price is X?

    A. Unlimited
    B. Option cost
    C. X - option cost

97. What are attractive features for issuers of floating-rate securities?

    A. Caps
    B. Floors
    C. Both caps and floors

98. Which imbedded option is least likely to be considered an advantage to the issuer?

    A. Put provision
    B. Cap on a floater
    C. Prepayment rights

99. When interest rates rise, the price of a callable bond

    A. Will fall more than an option-free bond
    B. Will not fall as much as an option-free bond because the price decline is offset by a decrease in the value of the call option
    C. Will not fall as much as an option-free bond because the price decline is offset by an increase in the value of the call option

100. What is rate duration?

    A. A measure of the price sensitivity of a bond to a change in yield
    B. The approximate dollar price change for a 100 basis point change in yield
    C. The percentage change in the value of a portfolio if only one maturity's yield changes

101. For amortizing bonds, the reinvestment risk for an investor holding bonds to maturity is greatest for bonds selling

    A. At par
    B. At a discount
    C. At a premium

102. What is the external bond market of a country?

    A. Eurobond market or the Bulldog bond market
    B. National bond market, international bond market, or the offshore bond market
    C. International bond market, the offshore bond market, or the Eurobond market

103. What are corporate debt obligations offered on a continuous basis and are offered through agents with maturities from 9 month to 30 years, and are most likely to use shelf registration?

    A. Commercial paper
    B. Bankers acceptances
    C. Medium-term notes (MTNs)

104. Under the market expectations theory, what is the most likely explanation for an upwardly sloping yield curve?

    A. Increasing yield premium required
    B. Expectations that short term rates will rise
    C. Different levels of supply and demand for short and long term funds

105. What is the yield spread between a non-Treasury security and a similar Treasury security?

    A. Yield ratio
    B. Credit spread
    C. Relative yield spread

106. Which is closest to the percentage change in price due to the change in yield of a bond maturing in 6 years with an 8% annual coupon, a par value of $100, and a yield of 8%; if the yield changes to 7%?

    A. 4.76%; where n = 6, i = 7, PMT = 8, FV = 100, resulting in PV = -104.76; ($104.76 - $100) / $100 = 4.76%
    B. 5.38%
    C. 6.00%

107. When are the Z-spread and the OAS equal?

    A. If the bond is option free
    B. When the yield curve is flat
    C. When the yield curve is upwardly sloping

108. Which is least accurate regarding methods to measure interest rate risk?

    A. Yield curve scenarios are part of the full valuation method
    B. An advantage of the full valuation approach is it requires revaluing all the bonds in the portfolio
    C. The duration / convexity approach does not take into consideration how the yield curve can shift

109. Which is closest to the duration of a 6% coupon 20-year option-free bond selling at par, if the price increases to 101.17 to yield 5.9%, and the price decreases to 98.85 to yield 6.1%?

    A. 10.5
    B. 10.6
    C. 11.6

110. Which is closest to percentage price change for a bond with modified duration of 6.5 and convexity of 42.4 if yields increase by 100 basis points ?

    A. -6.92%
    B. -6.08%
    C. 6.92%

111. An investor is considering 3 classes of mutual funds: class A has a 3% sales load on purchases, no deferred sales charge on redemptions, and 1.25% in annual expenses; class B has no sales load on purchases, a deferred sales charge on redemptions of 5% in the first year declining by 1 percentage point each year thereafter, and 1.50% in annual expenses for the first 6 years then 1.25% per year thereafter; and class C has no sales load on purchases, a deferred sales charge on redemptions of 1% per year for the initial two years, and 1.50% in annual expenses. Which class would provide the greatest net return for an investor who redeems after 10 years with gross returns of 8% per year?

    A. Class A ($1.8566), followed by class C ($1.8561), and class B ($1.8550)
    B. Class B ($1.8750), followed by class C ($1.8561), and class A ($1.8466)
    C. Class C ($1.8761), followed by class B ($1.8750), and class A ($1.8466)

112. Which real estate valuation approach is most likely to use a hedonic price model and regression analysis with the transaction price as a dependent variable and the ratings for characteristics as independent variables to evaluate a property?

    A. Cost approach
    B. Income approach
    C. Sales comparison approach

113. Which is least accurate regarding real estate appraisals?

    A. Real estate appraisals are done infrequently
    B. Real estate appraisal values are a series with more significant peaks and valleys than market values
    C. Real estate appraisal-based indexes should not be used in a global portfolio optimization

114. What are least likely to be considered benefits of a fund of funds?

    A. Retailing, access, and diversification
    B. Expertise and due diligence process
    C. Fees, performance, and lower return from diversification

115. Which investment strategy is most appropriate for investors using portfolio earnings for living expenses?

    A. Total return
    B. Current income
    C. Capital appreciation

116. Which is associated with higher equity allocation in different countries?

    A. Low inflation
    B. High inflation
    C. Higher average age of the population

117. If an investor has a portfolio with equal weights of four securities with returns of 10%, 12%, 16%, and 26%, what will happen to the expected return for the portfolio if the security with the 16% return is replaced with a security with a return equal to the original portfolio?

    A. Increases
    B. Decreases
    C. Remains the same

118. Which is closest to the standard deviation of a portfolio with a 50% weight in each of two securities, both of which have an expected return of 20% and a standard deviation of 10%, if the correlation coefficient is 0.0?

    A. 5%
    B. 7%
    C. 9%

119. Under capital market theory, what is diversifiable risk?

    A. Systematic risk
    B. Market portfolio
    C. Unsystematic risk

120. If the risk free rate is 3%, the expected return on the market portfolio is 12%, the estimated rate of return for the stock is 10%, and the covariance of the returns on the stock with the returns on the market is equal to the variance of the returns on the market portfolio, the stock is

    A. Overvalued
    B. Undervalued
    C. Properly valued

1. C	41. A	81. B
2. C	42. B	82. C
3. B	43. B	83. C
4. C	44. A	84. C
5. B	45. B	85. A
6. A	46. C	86. B
7. A	47. B	87. A
8. B	48. B	88. B
9. B	49. C	89. C
10. A	50. A	90. B
11. A	51. C	91. C
12. A	52. A	92. A
13. C	53. C	93. C
14. C	54. A	94. C
15. A	55. C	95. A
16. B	56. A	96. B
17. B	57. C	97. A
18. C	58. B	98. A
19. C	59. C	99. B
20. A	60. A	100. C
21. C	61. B	101. C
22. B	62. A	102. C
23. A	63. A	103. C
24. A	64. B	104. C
25. C	65. C	105. B
26. B	66. C	106. A
27. B	67. C	107. A
28. B	68. A	108. B
29. A	69. C	109. C
30. A	70. B	110. B
31. A	71. C	111. B
32. B	72. A	112. C
33. C	73. B	113. B
34. A	74. C	114. C
35. C	75. B	115. B
36. B	76. B	116. B
37. C	77. B	117. C
38. C	78. A	118. B
39. B	79. A	119. C
40. A	80. C	120. A

1. What can prompt an inquiry by the CFI Institute Professional Conduct staff?

   A. Self-disclosure or written complaints
   B. Media reports or reports from examination proctors
   *C. Self-disclosure, written complaints, media reports, or reports from examination proctors

2. CFA charterholder Lindert is the investment manager of a public sector pension fund. The plan requested proposals for a bond manager. CFA charterholder Madura works for a bond manager that responded to the request for proposals. Madura met Lindert at a seminar and asked about their outstanding proposal. Lindert responded that a decision had not been made yet, then Madura told Lindert, "Since you like golf, maybe you could use this new set of golf clubs worth over $1,000 that we were going to give away as a door prize. Take the golf clubs as a gift." Lindert accepted the golf clubs as a gift, and Madura turned in a fictional expense report to his employer overstating the cost of the clubs. Who violated the Standards of Professional Conduct?

   A. Only Madura
   B. Only Lindert
   *C. Both Madura and Lindert (Standard I(B) - independence and objectivity and Standard I(D) - misconduct)

3. CFA charterholder Hammad applies for a job and puts on his resume that he has an MBA from a top tier school in addition to the CFA designation. Hammad attended the school but did not receive a degree. Did Hammad violate any Standards of Professional Conduct?

   A. No
   *B. Yes, relating to misrepresentation (Standard I(C) - misrepresentation)
   C. Yes, relating to duties to employers

4. CFA charterholder Gibaja works for Guan & Grigorov, a firm that publishes a weekly column in Securities Weekly magazine that usually affects the value of the stocks discussed. Gibaja's nephew works at the publishing company, and Gibaja has his nephew fax him a copy of the column before it is published. Gibaja then makes profitable trades based on the column. Were any Standards of Professional Conduct violated?

   A. Gibaja violated the standard relating to material nonpublic information
   B. Gibaja's nephew violated the standard relating to market manipulation
   *C. Gibaja and Gibaja's nephew violated the standard relating to material nonpublic information (Standard II(A) - material nonpublic information)

5. Which statement is least accurate related to the Standard of Professional Conduct on integrity of capital markets?

    A. Members and candidates must not engage in practices that distort prices or artificially inflate trading volume with the intent to mislead market participants

    *B. Members and candidates must not knowingly make any misrepresentations relating to investment analysis, recommendations, actions, or other professional activities

    C. Members and candidates who possess material nonpublic information that could affect the value of an investment must not act or cause others to act on the information

6. CFA charterholder Volek gave priority to discretionary accounts over non-discretionary accounts. Volek most likely violated the Standard of Professional Conduct relating to

    *A. Fair dealing (Standard III(B) - fair dealing)
    B. Independence and objectivity
    C. Communications with clients and prospective clients

7. CFA charterholder Chang revealed confidential information about a client's illegal activities under a court order initiated by a regulatory authority. Did Chang violate any Standards of Professional Conduct?

    *A. No (Standard III(E) - preservation of confidentiality)
    B. Yes, relating to fair dealing
    C. Yes, relating to preservation of confidentiality

8. CFA charterholder Milner works as an independent contractor with access to a firm's offices and research files. Milner is preparing a study while working part-time for the firm, then gets a permanent, full-time position with another firm and uses the same study at her new employer. Did Milner violate any Standards of Professional Conduct?

    A. No
    *B. Yes, relating to loyalty (Standard IV(A) - loyalty)
    C. Yes, relating to preservation of confidentiality

9. CFA charterholder de la Cruz is an independent contractor who writes research reports for publications and always signs exclusivity contracts. Often de la Cruz makes very slight modifications to work published in one publication and submits it to another publication. Did de la Cruz violate any Standards of Professional Conduct?

    A. No
    *B. Yes, relating to loyalty (Standard IV(A) - loyalty)
    C. Yes, relating to disclosure of conflicts

10. CFA charterholder Oliver sends a memo to her staff that the firm's written compliance manual will be updated to meet industry standards, regulatory requirements, the Code and Standards, and the circumstances of the firm. Did Oliver violate any Standards of Professional Conduct?

   *A. No (Standard IV(C) - responsibilities of supervisors)
   B. Yes, because compliance procedures cannot be altered to meet industry standards
   C. Yes, because compliance procedures cannot be altered to meet the circumstances of the firm

11. CFA charterholder Deslandes manages funds with long investment horizons. Deslandes' employer changes his compensation package to reward short term results. Deslandes does not tell his clients about the change. Deslandes is most likely to have violated the Standard of Professional Conduct on

   *A. Disclosure of conflicts (Standard VI(A) - disclosure of conflicts)
   B. Independence and objectivity
   C. Additional compensation arrangements

12. CFA charterholder Dinehart is a portfolio manager and managers the account of her parents. When an IPO becomes available, she allocates shares to her other clients first and her parents last. Which Standard of Professional Conduct did Dinehart least likely violate?

   *A. Loyalty (Standard VI(B) - priority of transactions and Standard III(B) - fair dealing)
   B. Fair dealing
   C. Priority of transactions

13. To maintain status as a CFA Institute member, members must

   A. Pay annual dues
   B. Remit a completed professional conduct statement annually
   *C. Remit a completed professional conduct statement annually and pay annual dues (Standard VII(B) - reference to the CFA Institute, the CFA designation, and the CFA program)

14. CFA charterholder Shuman infers that since he is a CFA charterholder his recommendations are correct. Did Shuman violate any Standards of Professional Conduct?

  A. No
  B. Yes, related to communication with clients and prospective clients
  *C.Yes, related to reference to the CFA Institute, the CFA designation, and the CFA program (Standard VII(B) - reference to the CFA Institute, the CFA designation, and the CFA program)

15. An investment management firm's brokerage unit has a sell recommendation on ETV Corporation. The firm has been hired by ETV to work on an initial public offering. The head of the investment banking department asks the head of the brokerage unit to change the recommendation from sell to buy. The head of the brokerage unit does not change the recommendation but places the company on a restricted list and only gives factual information about the company. Did the head of the brokerage unit violate any Standards of Professional conduct?

  *A. No (Standard I(B) - independence and objectivity)
  B. Yes, relating to independence and objectivity
  C. Yes, relating to diligence and reasonable basis

16. An investment-banking department of a brokerage firm often receives material nonpublic information that would have considerable value if used in advising the firm's brokerage clients. Which is the best policy for conforming with the Standards of Professional Conduct?

  A. Monitor the exchange of information between the investment-banking department and the brokerage operations
  *B.Establish physical and informational barriers within the firm to prevent the exchange of information between the investment-banking and brokerage operations (Standard II(A) - material nonpublic information)
  C. Prohibit purchase recommendations when the investment-banking department has access to material nonpublic information, but allow sale of current holdings

17. To comply with the GIPS, after presenting five years of compliant data, the firm must add annual performance each year going forward up to a minimum of

  A. Seven years
  *B.Ten years
  C. Twelve years

18. The GIPS section on real estate applies

    A. Only if a real estate asset or investment is producing revenue
    B. Only if the firm has control of the management of the investment
    *C.Irrespective of whether a real estate asset or investment is producing revenue

19. What annual contribution to a college fund for 18 years starting in one year will provide for four years of tuition at $20,000 per year starting 18 years after the first payment, if the fund earns 7% per year?

    A. $1,740
    B. $1,862
    *C.$1,993 ={ $20,000 [1 - (1/1.07)^4)] / .07] / (1.07)^18 } / [1 - (1/1.07)^18)] / .07]; n = 4, i = 7, PMT = 20,000, FV = 0; PV = $67,744; n = 18, i = 7, PV = 0, FV = 67,744; PMT = $1,993

20. What is the price for a T-bill with par value of $100,000 and 90 days to maturity with a bank discount yield of 3%?

    *A. $99,250 = $100,000 - 3% (90/360) ($100,000); BDY = (D / F) (360 / t); D = $750; $100,000 - $750 = $99,250
    B. $99,260
    C. $99,264

21. If a portfolio's deviation from a benchmark for five years was 28.3%, 0%, 0%, 0%, and -28.3%, what is the tracking risk?

    A. 10%
    B. 11%
    *C.20% = {[(28.3%-0%)^2+3(28.3%-0%)^2+(28.3%-0%)^2]/(5-1)}^.5

22. What are the 25th and 75th percentiles for funds with returns of -20%, -10%, -6%, -5%, 0%, 6%, 12%, 14%, and 20%?

    A. 25th percentile = -10%; 75th percentile = 14%
    *B.25th percentile = -8%; 75th percentile = 13%
    C. 25th percentile = -6%; 75th percentile = 12%

23. What is the Sharpe Ratio if a portfolio mean return is 8%, the standard deviation is 12%, and the risk free rate is 4%?

    *A. 0.33 = (8% - 4%) / 12%
    B. 0.67
    C. 1.50

24. What is the skewness of a sample of 50 observations with a sum of the cubed deviation of 0.10%, a sum of the deviations to the fourth power of 2.715%, and a sample standard deviation 12%?

    *A. 0.01 = [50/(49)(48)] 0.0010 / (0.12^3)
    B. 0.02
    C. 3.02

25. What is the probability of an event?

    A. a priori probability
    B. Conditional probability
    *C. Unconditional probability

26. What is the expected return for a portfolio with 40% in the S&P 500 with an expected return of 9%, 35% in bonds with an expected return of 4%, and 25% in the EAFE with an expected return of 12%?

    A. 7%
    *B. 8% = .40 (9%) + .35 (4%) + .25 (12%)
    C. 9%

27. What is the probability function for continuous random variables?

    A. Probability distribution
    *B. Probability density function
    C. Continuous random variable

28. Given that P(X<=1)=0.10, P(X<=2)=0.50, P(X<=3)=0.70, and P(X<=4)=1.00, what is P(2<= X <=3)?

    A. 0.5
    *B. 0.6 = 0.4 + 0.2
    C. 0.7

29. Which best describes the standard deviation of sample skewness for a sample of size "n" from a normal distribution?

    *A. 6/n
    B. 8/n
    C. 24/n

30. What is the difference between the sample mean and the population mean?

    *A. Sampling error
    B. Tracking error
    C. Volatility

31. Which statistic is appropriate for sampling from a normal distribution with an unknown variance for a small sample size?

    *A. t-statistic
    B. z-statistic
    C. Not available

32. Which is least likely to be an assumption of technical analysis?

    A. Prices move in trends that persist over long periods of time
    *B.Testing supports the efficient market hypothesis
    C. Shifts in supply and demand can be detected sooner or later in the actions of the market

33. What is the demand elasticity along a straight-line demand curve above the midpoint, where a price cut increases total revenue?

    A. Unit elastic demand
    B. Inelastic demand
    *C.Elastic demand

34. Which is least likely to result in sellers paying the entire tax?

    *A. Perfectly elastic supply
    B. Perfectly inelastic supply
    C. Perfectly elastic demand

35. Which is least likely to be used to cope with the principal-agent problem?

    A. Ownership
    B. Incentive pay
    *C.Short-term contracts

36. What is true about average product?

    A. It decreases initially and eventually increases
    *B.It increases initially and eventually diminishes
    C. It decreases initially and eventually diminishes

37. What is the least likely result of entry and plant expansion in a market in perfect competition?

    A. Increased supply
    B. Lower price
    *C.Higher profit

38. What are firms acting independently in the oligopoly market structure most likely to increase?

    A. Prices but not output
    B. Output and prices
    *C.Output but not prices

39. What is equivalent to the condition for profit maximization that the wage rate is equal to the marginal revenue product?

    A. Marginal profit equals marginal cost
    *B.Marginal revenue equals marginal cost
    C. Marginal revenue product equals average total cost

40. What type of unemployment applies to someone who moves to an area to look for a new job?

    *A. Frictional
    B. Structural
    C. Cyclical

41. The view that the economy is self regulating and always at full employment is most likely held by which school of thought?

    *A. Classical
    B. Monetarist
    C. Keynesian

42. Which is least likely to be used by the Federal Reserve System to accelerate the growth of the economy?

    A. Decrease the federal funds rate
    *B.Sell government securities
    C. Decrease reserve requirements

43. Which has the greatest magnification of an increase in aggregate demand?

    A. Balanced budget multiplier
    *B.Government expenditure multiplier
    C. Autonomous tax multiplier

44. Which is the most likely action of the Federal Reserve System to fight inflation?

    *A. Raise the target federal funds rate, sell securities, and decrease the supply of reserves in the banking system
    B. Raise the target federal funds rate, buy securities, and decrease the supply of reserves in the banking system
    C. Lower the target federal funds rate, buy securities, and increase the supply of reserves in the banking system

45. What shows revenue minus expense?

    A. Balance sheet
    *B.Income statement
    C. Cash flow statement

46. Which category includes capital such as common stock par value and additional paid-in capital?

    A. Assets
    B. Liabilities
    *C.Owner's equity

47. Which involves cash movement prior to accounting recognition?

    A. Unbilled revenue
    *B.Unearned revenue
    C. Accrued expense

48. What values assets at the amount given to acquire them?

    A. Market value
    *B.Historical cost
    C. Amortized cost

49. What type of discussion regarding new accounting standards would be most meaningful to an analyst?

    A. No material impact
    B. The standard does not apply
    *C.Discussion of impact of adoption

50. Which special revenue recognition method that allows for partial recognition of revenue throughout the contract would be used under limited circumstances such as in real estate sales contracts?

    *A. Installment method
    B. Completed contract method
    C. Percentage-of-completion method

51. Which is closest to the profit that will be reported in the second year under the installment method if land purchased for $20,000 was sold for $50,000 with $5,000 payable the first year and the remaining $45,000 payable the second year?

    A. $0
    B. $15,000
    *C.$27,000 = ($45,000/$50,000) ($50,000 - $20,000)

52. What would be the outstanding shares at the end of the year for calculating EPS if the board of a company with 1,000,000 shares outstanding on January 1st at the beginning of the year is considering either a 3 for 2 stock split or a 500,000 stock dividend on April 1st?

    *A. 1,500,000 for the stock split or the stock dividend
    B. 1,375,000 for the stock split or 1,500,000 for the stock dividend
    C. 1,500,000 for the stock split or 1,375,000 for the stock dividend

53. Under U.S. GAAP, what is closest to other comprehensive income if beginning shareholders' equity is $1,100; net income is $100; cash dividends are $20; there was no issuance or repurchase of company stock; and ending shareholders' equity is $1,230?

    A. $10
    B. $30
    *C.$50 = $1,230 - ($1,100 + $100 - $20)

54. What is a financial instrument for which the value is based on some underlying factor?

   *A. Derivative
   B. Hedge fund
   C. Preferred stock

55. How is the minority interest in a consolidated subsidiary shown on the balance sheet?

   A. Asset
   B. Liability
   *C.Shareholders' equity

56. Which is an appropriate method of computing free cash flow?

   *A. Add operating cash flows plus after-tax interest payments and deduct capital expenditures
   B. Add operating cash flows plus capital expenditures and deduct after-tax interest payments
   C. Start with operating cash flows and deduct both capital expenditures and after-tax interest payments

57. Which is least likely to be a formula for free cash flow to the firm (FCFF)?

   A. FCFF = CFO + Int(1 - Tax rate) - FCInv
   B. FCFF = NI + NCC + Int(1 - Tax rate) - FCInv - WCInv
   *C.FCFF = CFO - FCInv + Net borrowing - Net debt repayment

58. Which is the most likely to be used to measure inventory under U.S. GAAP for potential tax savings?

   A. FIFO
   *B.LIFO
   C. Weighted average cost

59. Which would be most likely to provide a better assessment of a company's solvency if included in the calculation of interest coverage ratios?

   A. Goodwill
   B. Cost of goods sold
   *C.Capitalized interest

60. If a company reporting under U.S. GAAP purchased equipment for $100,000 with a five-year life and a salvage value of $10,000, which would make the reported income for tax expense in the first year highest?

   *A. Straight-line depreciation
   B. Accelerated depreciation
   C. Straight-line and accelerated depreciation produce the same reported income for tax purposes

61. Which is a company least likely to do when it is able to estimate the future costs it will incur when an asset is retired?

   A. Increase the carrying value of the asset
   *B.Decrease the carrying value of the liability over time through an accretion charge
   C. Decrease the carrying value of the asset over time through an accretion charge

62. Which would most likely result from amortizing a capital expenditure over seven years for accounting purposes but ten years for tax purposes?

   *A. Deferred tax asset
   B. Deferred tax liability
   C. No deferred tax asset or liability

63. Which does not permit the use of substantially enacted tax rates?

   *A. U.S. GAAP but not IFRS
   B. IFRS but not U.S. GAAP
   C. Both U.S. GAAP and IFRS

64. For a capital lease with rental payments of $500 per year, fair value of leased equipment at inception of $3000, an implicit interest rate of 12%, with the present value of the lease equal to the present value of the equipment at inception, which is closest to the interest recorded by the lessee in the second year of the lease?

   A. $336
   *B.$343 = 12% [$3,000 - ($500 - 12%($3,000))]
   C. $360

65. What kind of ratios measure the ability of a company to meet long-term obligations?

   A. Activity ratios
   B. Liquidity ratios
   *C.Solvency ratios

66. Which would most likely explain a high fixed asset turnover ratio?

    A. Recently bought new equipment
    B. Low amortization expense
    *C.Old, low cost equipment

67. What exists when companies that merge or go out of business are dropped from a database?

    A. Backtesting
    B. Look-ahead bias
    *C.Survivorship bias

68. How are cash outflows for the payment of interest treated under U.S. GAAP?

    *A. Operating cash flows
    B. Financing or investing cash flows
    C. Operating or financing cash flows

69. Which step of the capital budgeting process involves gathering information to forecast cash flows?

    A. Generating ideas
    B. Planning the capital budget
    *C.Analyzing individual proposals

70. What is the discounted payback period closest to if the initial investment is $40 million, the cash flows are $15 million per year at the end of the each of 4 years, and the required rate of return is 10%?

    A. 3.00 years
    *B.3.26 years = 3 + ($40 - $13.63 - $12.40 -$11.27) / $10.25
    C. 3.75 years

71. Which capital budgeting method is most likely to have problems with negative cash flows after the initial investment?

    A. NPV
    B. IRR
    *C.Discounted payback period

72. Which method is least likely to be used to estimate the before-tax cost of debt?

    *A. WACC
    B. Bond rating
    C. Yield to maturity

73. What is the best estimate for the value of preferred stock with a $1.75 dividend previously issued for $25, if the coupon rate on preferred stock issued today would be 6.5%?

    A. $25.00
    *B.$26.92 = $1.75 / 6.5%
    C. $37.31

74. What is an estimate of the equity risk premium if the expected dividends are $5, the market price is $100, EPS is $15, ROE is 6%, and the risk-free rate is 3%?

    A. 4%
    B. 5%
    *C.6% = ($5/$100) + [(1 - $5/$15)(6%)] - 3%

75. Which company had the lowest accounts receivable turnover if company A had credit sales of $50 million and an average receivables balance of $10 million, company B had credit sales of $30 million and an average receivables balance of $12 million, and company C had credit sales of $25 million and an average receivables balance of $8 million?

    A. Company A
    *B.Company B; $30 / $12 = 2.5 < $25 / $8 = 3.1 < $50 / $10 = 5
    C. Company C

76. What equals [(face value - purchase price) / purchase price] (365/ number of days to maturity)?

    A. Money market yield
    *B.Bond equivalent yield
    C. Discount-basis yield

77. Which is closest to the total asset turnover if financial leverage is 1.33, the net profit margin is 4%, and the return on equity is 8%?

    A. 0.4
    *B.1.5 = 8% / [4% (1.33)]
    C. 2.7

78. Which is the third step in pro forma analysis, following estimating fixed burdens such as interest and taxes?

   *A. Forecast revenues
   B. Construct future period income statement and balance sheet
   C. Estimate typical relation between revenues and sales-driven accounts

79. What are auctions of U.S. Treasury securities and new issues of common stock?

   *A. Primary markets
   B. Secondary markets
   C. Over-the-counter markets

80. What is the least accurate way to describe a pure auction market?

   A. Price-driven
   B. Order-driven
   *C.Quote-driven

81. For a margin account used to purchase 200 shares of stock at $50, what is minimum initial deposit if the margin is 50%?

   A. $2,500
   *B.$5,000 = ($50)(200)(50%)
   C. $10,000

82. What type of security market index is based on capitalization?

   A. Unweighted
   B. Price-weighted
   *C.Value-weighted

83. Which is closest to the return on the price-weighted index for three stocks with prices at the beginning of the year for stocks A, B, and C of $100, $50, and $30, respectively, and prices at the end of the year for stocks A, B, and C of $110, $50, and $30, respectively?

   A. 3.2%
   B. 3.3%
   *C.5.5% = [($190 / 3) / ($180 / 3)] - 1

84. Which form of the efficient market hypothesis (EMH) states that current stock prices reflect all information about P/E ratios, dividend yield ratios, price to book value ratios, and stock splits?

    A. Weak form
    B. Strong form
    *C.Semi-strong form

85. Which is least likely to be considered a limitation to market efficiency?

    *A. Escalation bias
    B. Cost of trading
    C. Limits of arbitrage

86. Which is closest to the value of preferred stock with an annual dividend of $5 and a yield on preferred 50 basis points below the bond yield of 7%?

    A. $71
    *B.$77 = $5 / 6.5%
    C. $83

87. Which is closest to the value of common stock with no dividends expected for the next two years, an expected dividend of $2 in the third year, a dividend growth rate of 9% after year 3, and a required rate of return of 12%?

    *A. $53 = [$2 / (12% - 9%)] / 1.12^2
    B. $60
    C. $67

88. Which is closest to the growth rate of equity earnings without any external financing if the retention rate is 40%, earnings per share are $1, and the stock price is $9.26?

    A. 3.6%
    *B.4.3% = 40% ($1 / $9.26)
    C. 6.5%

89. What best describes an overpriced stock with a P/E value substantially higher than the industry average?

    A. Cyclical stock
    B. Defensive stock
    *C.Speculative stock

90. Which is least likely to be considered a rationale for using price to cash flow (P / CF) ratios?

   A. More stable than P/E
   *B.Cash flow cannot be negative
   C. Cash flow less subject to manipulation than earnings

91. What is an agreement between two parties in which one party agrees to buy and the other party agrees to sell an asset at a future date at a price agreed on today?

   A. Option
   B. Contingent claim
   *C.Forward commitment

92. Which statement is least accurate regarding forward commitments?

   *A. Forward contracts are market to market daily
   B. Forward contracts have more default risk than futures contracts
   C. Forward contracts require that both parties to the transaction have a high degree of creditworthiness

93. What is the balance initially and at the end of day 3 for a holder of a short position of 20 futures contracts if the initial futures price on day 0 is $85, the initial margin requirement is $7.5, the maintenance margin requirement is $7, the settlement price on day 1 is $86, the settlement price on day 2 is $84.25, and the settlement price on day 3 is $85.50?

   A. $140 initially and $150 at the end of day 3
   B. $150 initially and $140 at the end of day 3
   *C.$150 initially and $160 at the end of day 3; $160 = $150 - $20 + $20 + $35 - $25; where $150 is the initial deposit, $20 is the loss on day 1, triggering a maintenance call, $20 is the deposit on day 2 to bring the balance to $150, $35 is the gain on day 2, and $25 is the loss on day 3; the ending balances days 0 through 3 are $150, $130, $185, and $160

94. An investor buys a call at $95 for $2 when the price of the stock was $95. What is the intrinsic value of the call if the new price of the stock is $96?

   A. -$1.00
   B. $0.00
   *C.$1.00 = $96 - $95

95. An asset manager enters into a $100 million equity swap and agrees to pay a dealer the return on a large-cap index and the dealer agrees to pay the return on a small-cap index. Payments are made semi-annually. The value of the small-cap index starts at 689.40 and the large-cap index starts at 1130.20. In six months, the small cap index is at 625.60 and the large cap index is at 1251.83. Which party pays what amount after the payments are netted?

    *A. The asset manager pays the dealer $20,016,236 = (-1)$100,000,000(625.60/689.40 - 1) + $100,000,000(1251.83/1130.20 - 1)
    B. The dealer pays the asset manager $10,761,812
    C. The dealer pays the asset manager $20,016,236

96. What is the maximum gain to the seller of a put option (short position), where the exercise price is X?

    A. Unlimited
    *B. Option cost
    C. X - option cost

97. What are attractive features for issuers of floating-rate securities?

    *A. Caps
    B. Floors
    C. Both caps and floors

98. Which imbedded option is least likely to be considered an advantage to the issuer?

    *A. Put provision
    B. Cap on a floater
    C. Prepayment rights

99. When interest rates rise, the price of a callable bond

    A. Will fall more than an option-free bond
    *B. Will not fall as much as an option-free bond because the price decline is offset by a decrease in the value of the call option
    C. Will not fall as much as an option-free bond because the price decline is offset by an increase in the value of the call option

100. What is rate duration?

    A. A measure of the price sensitivity of a bond to a change in yield
    B. The approximate dollar price change for a 100 basis point change in yield
    *C. The percentage change in the value of a portfolio if only one maturity's yield changes

101. For amortizing bonds, the reinvestment risk for an investor holding bonds to maturity is greatest for bonds selling

    A. At par
    B. At a discount
    *C.At a premium

102. What is the external bond market of a country?

    A. Eurobond market or the Bulldog bond market
    B. National bond market, international bond market, or the offshore bond market
    *C.International bond market, the offshore bond market, or the Eurobond market

103. What are corporate debt obligations offered on a continuous basis and are offered through agents with maturities from 9 month to 30 years, and are most likely to use shelf registration?

    A. Commercial paper
    B. Bankers acceptances
    *C.Medium-term notes (MTNs)

104. Under the market expectations theory, what is the most likely explanation for an upwardly sloping yield curve?

    A. Increasing yield premium required
    B. Expectations that short term rates will rise
    *C.Different levels of supply and demand for short and long term funds

105. What is the yield spread between a non-Treasury security and a similar Treasury security?

    A. Yield ratio
    *B.Credit spread
    C. Relative yield spread

106. Which is closest to the percentage change in price due to the change in yield of a bond maturing in 6 years with an 8% annual coupon, a par value of $100, and a yield of 8%; if the yield changes to 7%?

    *A. 4.76%; where n = 6, i = 7, PMT = 8, FV = 100, resulting in PV = -104.76; ($104.76 - $100) / $100 = 4.76%
    B. 5.38%
    C. 6.00%

107. When are the Z-spread and the OAS equal?

   *A. If the bond is option free
   B. When the yield curve is flat
   C. When the yield curve is upwardly sloping

108. Which is least accurate regarding methods to measure interest rate risk?

   A. Yield curve scenarios are part of the full valuation method
   *B.An advantage of the full valuation approach is it requires revaluing all the bonds in the portfolio
   C. The duration / convexity approach does not take into consideration how the yield curve can shift

109. Which is closest to the duration of a 6% coupon 20-year option-free bond selling at par, if the price increases to 101.17 to yield 5.9%, and the price decreases to 98.85 to yield 6.1%?

   A. 10.5
   B. 10.6
   *C.11.6 = (101.17 - 98.85) / [2 (100) (0.001)]

110. Which is closest to percentage price change for a bond with modified duration of 6.5 and convexity of 42.4 if yields increase by 100 basis points ?

   A. -6.92%
   *B.-6.08% = -6.5 (.01) + 42.4 (.01)^2
   C. 6.92%

111. An investor is considering 3 classes of mutual funds: class A has a 3% sales load on purchases, no deferred sales charge on redemptions, and 1.25% in annual expenses; class B has no sales load on purchases, a deferred sales charge on redemptions of 5% in the first year declining by 1 percentage point each year thereafter, and 1.50% in annual expenses for the first 6 years then 1.25% per year thereafter; and class C has no sales load on purchases, a deferred sales charge on redemptions of 1% per year for the initial two years, and 1.50% in annual expenses. Which class would provide the greatest net return for an investor who redeems after 10 years with gross returns of 8% per year?

   A. Class A ($1.8566), followed by class C ($1.8561), and class B ($1.8550)
   *B.Class B ($1.8750), followed by class C ($1.8561), and class A ($1.8466);
      $0.97(1.08)^10(1-.0125)^10=$1.8466; $1(1.08)^10(1-.015)^6(1-
      0.0125)^4=$1.8750; $1(1.08)^10(1-0.015)^10=$1.8561
   C. Class C ($1.8761), followed by class B ($1.8750), and class A ($1.8466)

112. Which real estate valuation approach is most likely to use a hedonic price model and regression analysis with the transaction price as a dependent variable and the ratings for characteristics as independent variables to evaluate a property?

    A. Cost approach
    B. Income approach
    *C.Sales comparison approach

113. Which is least accurate regarding real estate appraisals?

    A. Real estate appraisals are done infrequently
    *B.Real estate appraisal values are a series with more significant peaks and valleys than market values
    C. Real estate appraisal-based indexes should not be used in a global portfolio optimization

114. What are least likely to be considered benefits of a fund of funds?

    A. Retailing, access, and diversification
    B. Expertise and due diligence process
    *C.Fees, performance, and lower return from diversification

115. Which investment strategy is most appropriate for investors using portfolio earnings for living expenses?

    A. Total return
    *B.Current income
    C. Capital appreciation

116. Which is associated with higher equity allocation in different countries?

    A. Low inflation
    *B.High inflation
    C. Higher average age of the population

117. If an investor has a portfolio with equal weights of four securities with returns of 10%, 12%, 16%, and 26%, what will happen to the expected return for the portfolio if the security with the 16% return is replaced with a security with a return equal to the original portfolio?

    A. Increases
    B. Decreases
    *C.Remains the same; $(10\% + 12\% + 16\% + 26\%) / 4 = 16\% = (10\% + 12\% + 16\% + 22\%) / 4 = 16\%$

118. Which is closest to the standard deviation of a portfolio with a 50% weight in each of two securities, both of which have an expected return of 20% and a standard deviation of 10%, if the correlation coefficient is 0.0?

    A. 5%
    *B.7% = [(50%^2)(10%^2) + (50%^2)(10%^2) + 2(50%)(50%)(0.0)(10%)(10%)]^.5
    C. 9%

119. Under capital market theory, what is diversifiable risk?

    A. Systematic risk
    B. Market portfolio
    *C.Unsystematic risk

120. If the risk free rate is 3%, the expected return on the market portfolio is 12%, the estimated rate of return for the stock is 10%, and the covariance of the returns on the stock with the returns on the market is equal to the variance of the returns on the market portfolio, the stock is

    *A. Overvalued; beta = 1.0; 10% < 3% + 1.0 (12% - 3%) = 12%
    B. Undervalued
    C. Properly valued

1. Which topic of the CFA Institute's Standards of Professional Conduct includes conduct as members and candidates in the CFA program and reference to CFA Institute, the CFA designation, and the CFA program?

    A. Conflicts of interest
    B. Titles and designations
    C. Responsibilities as CFA institute as CFA member of CFA candidate

2. CFA charterholder Stroup directs a large amount of commission business to a New York-based brokerage house. The brokerage house gives Stroup two tickets to the World Cup plus all travel expenses. Stroup fails to disclose the package to his supervisor. Stroup is least likely to have violated which Standard of Professional Conduct?

    A. Misrepresentation
    B. Independence and objectivity
    C. Additional compensation arrangements

3. CFA charterholder Patel works for a small firm offering investment advice. The firm is qualified to provide investment advice but does not offer a full array of financial and investment services. She tells a potential client who just inherited a large sum of money that her firm can provide investment advice and could help find financial and investment services that they do not provide. Did Patel violate any Standards of Professional Conduct?

    A. No
    B. Yes, relating to misrepresentation
    C. Yes, relating to independence and objectivity

4. CFA charterholder Ding is a portfolio manager for Dahl Aggressive Growth Fund. The fund is preparing to liquidate its holdings of Colmet Industries. Ding contacts several family members to advise them that the fund is about to liquidate its holdings in the company. Did Ding violate any Standards of Professional Conduct?

    A. No
    B. Yes, relating to material nonpublic information
    C. Yes, relating to diligence and reasonable basis

5. The owner of Chong Services agrees to promote the stock of companies in exchange for stock and compensation. The owner sends e-mails and newsletters and creates web sites containing inaccurate information to promote the stock which leads to higher stock prices. The owner least likely violated the Standards of Professional Conduct relating to

    A. Market manipulation
    B. Disclosure of conflicts
    C. Performance presentation

6. According to the Standards of Professional Conduct related to suitability, when members and candidates are in an advisory relationship with a client, they must judge the suitability of

    A. Investments in the context of the client's total portfolio
    B. The client's total portfolio in the context of the investments
    C. Taking investment action and must reassess and update this information regularly

7. CFA charterholder Rao circulates marketing material showing simulated performance and disclosing that the results were simulated by retroactively applying a model to a time period. Did Rao violate and Standards of Professional Conduct?

    A. No
    B. Yes, relating to misrepresentation
    C. Yes, relating to performance presentation

8. CFA charterholder Kadam leads an employee-led buyout of his employer's equity management business. Did Kadam violate any Standards of Professional Conduct?

    A. No (Standard IV(A) - loyalty)
    B. Yes, relating to loyalty
    C. Yes, relating to preservation of confidentiality

9. Which is least likely to violate the Standard of Professional Conduct on loyalty?

    A. Taking client lists
    B. Starting a competing business while under a non-compete agreement
    C. Contacting former clients after obtaining their phone numbers through public records

10. CFA charterholder Lamich plans to issue a newsletter that only lists the top five buy and sell recommendations because describing the investment system would be too complex. No details on the basic process or logic would be disclosed. Do Lamich's plans for the newsletter violate any Standards of Professional Conduct?

    A. No
    B. Yes, relating to diligence and reasonable basis
    C. Yes, relating to communications with clients and prospective clients

11. Which is least likely to require disclosure to clients and prospective clients?

    A. Service as a director
    B. Underwriting relationships
    C. Compliance with the CFA Code of Ethics and Standards of Practice

12. CFA candidate Banerjee makes substantial investment gains by purchasing stocks just before they were put on his employer's recommended purchase list. Banerjee was regularly given the firm's quarterly personal transaction form but declined to complete it. Which Standard of Professional Conduct did Banerjee least likely violate?

    A. Market manipulation
    B. Priority of transactions
    C. Material nonpublic information

13. CFA charterholder Carson receives a bonus from his employer for assisting to bring in new clients. Carson discloses to clients that he is compensated for referring clients to firm products. Did Carson violate any Standards of Professional Conduct?

    A. No
    B. Yes, related to referral fees
    C. Yes, related to additional compensation arrangements

14. Malone signed up for a CFA exam but did not sit for it and signed up for the next sitting. Malone told his employer that he passed the exam. Did Malone violate any Standards of Professional Conduct?

    A. No
    B. Yes, related to misconduct
    C. Yes, related to disclosure of conflicts

15. Which is least likely to ensure fair treatment of clients when a new investment recommendation is made?

    A. Distribute recommendations to institutional clients before individual clients
    B. Minimize the elapsed time between the decision and the dissemination of a recommendation
    C. Limit the number of people in the firm who are aware in advance that a recommendation is to be disseminated

16. CFA charterholder Chauhan is a portfolio manager. Chauhan uses the same broker exclusively for all portfolio transactions because the broker that gives Chauhan lower prices for personal sales than to Chauhan's portfolio accounts and other investors. Chauhan's employer requires monthly reports of personal stock transactions. Chauhan only files reports for months in which she has no transactions, about every fourth month. Which Standards of Professional Conduct did Chauhan least likely violate?

    A. Misconduct
    B. Misrepresentation
    C. Loyalty, prudence, and care

17. According to GIPS,

    A. Terminated portfolios must be excluded in historical returns of appropriate composites
    B. Firms may not set minimum asset levels for portfolios to be included in a composite
    C. Firms may set minimum asset levels for portfolios to be included in a composite, but the changes to a composite-specific minimum asset level are not permitted retroactively

18. Which asset classes have their own sections in the GIPS?

    A. Alternatives and real estate
    B. Private equity and real estate
    C. Private placements and venture capital

19. What is the value of 9 years of $1,000 payments beginning in one year plus a payment of $2,000 in 10 years using a discount rate of 8% per year?

    A. $6,710
    B. $7,139
    C. $7,173

20. What is any descriptive measure of a population characteristic?

    A. Parameter
    B. Sample statistic
    C. Frequency distribution

21. What are the cumulative frequencies for the return intervals for a frequency distribution with three equally spaced intervals for a range of returns for funds with returns of -20%, -10%, -6%, -5%, 0%, 6%, 12%, 14%, and 20%?

    A. 3, 2, and 4
    B. 3, 5, and 9
    C. 2, 6, and 9

22. Which is closest to the sample variance for a fund with annual returns of 6%, -10%, -5%, and 29%?

    A. 3%
    B. 15%
    C. 17%

23. What percent of a normal distribution's observations lie between plus and minus one standard deviation from the mean?

    A. 68.3%
    B. 95.5%
    C. 99.7%

24. What means that the events cover all possible outcomes?

    A. Probability
    B. Exhaustive
    C. Mutually exclusive

25. If a buy order at $20 has a 75% probability of being executed and a buy order on an uncorrelated different stock at $15 has a 60% probability of being executed, what is the probability that at least one of the orders will execute?

    A. 75%
    B. 90%
    C. 95%

26. If there is a 20% probability of EPS of $1.50, a 30% probability of an EPS of $9.00, and a 50% probability of an EPS of $10.00, what is the variance of the expected EPS?

    A. $2.78
    B. $7.73
    C. $10.75

27. What is the covariance between fund A and fund B, if there is an 80% probability that fund A will return 5% and fund B will return 10%, and a 20% probability that fund A will return 15% and fund B will return -5%?

    A. -0.24%
    B. -0.12%
    C. 0.12%

28. If an investment manager has a 50% probability of beating a benchmark each year, what is the probability of beating the benchmark in 4 out of 4 years?

    A. 0.03125
    B. 0.06250
    C. 0.25000

29. What do safety-first rules focus on?

    A. Utility function
    B. Mismatch risk
    C. Shortfall risk

30. Which is the closest to the continuous compounding rate of return for an asset that increases from $30 to $34.50 during the holding period?

    A. 13%
    B. 14%
    C. 15%

31. What is the year-end book value of NYSE-listed companies an example of?

    A. Time series
    B. Sampling distribution
    C. Cross-sectional data

32. What is accepted if the hypothesis to be tested is rejected?

    A. Test statistic
    B. Null hypothesis
    C. Alternative hypothesis

33. Which is least likely to impact the magnitude of the elasticity of demand?

    A. The closeness of substitutes
    B. The proportion of income spent on the good
    C. The elasticity of supply

34. What strives to achieve the greatest happiness for the greatest number?

    A. Utilitarianism
    B. Symmetry principle
    C. The big tradeoff

35. Which best describes the demand for most farm products?

    A. Elastic
    B. Inelastic
    C. Neither elastic nor inelastic

36. What arises when one firm produces an item that has no close substitutes and the firm is protected by a barrier to entry that prevents the entry of competitors?

    A. Monopoly
    B. Monopolistic competition
    C. Oligopoly

37. What induces entry into a market in perfect competition?

    A. Normal profit
    B. Accounting profit
    C. Economic profit

38. Which is least likely a characteristic of a monopoly with perfect price discrimination?

    A. Produces the same output than a perfectly competitive industry
    B. Obtains the maximum price that each consumer is willing to pay
    C. Extracts one-half of the consumer surplus

39. What determines the real interest rate?

    A. Capital market equilibrium
    B. Demand of physical capital
    C. Marginal revenue product

40. What is an indicator of the willingness of people of working age to take jobs, based on the labor force divided by the working-age population?

    A. Unemployment rate
    B. Labor force participation rate
    C. Employment-to-population ratio

41. Which is most likely to change aggregate demand?

    A. Stability in expected future income, inflation, and profits
    B. World economy and exchange rates
    C. Fluctuations in aggregate supply

42. What is least likely to trigger demand-pull inflation?

    A. Increase in exports
    B. Increase in investment stimulated by an increase in expected future profits
    C. Increase in the interest rate

43. Which is least likely to apply to the goal of stable prices?

    A. Expansionary fiscal policy
    B. Can conflict with other goals in the short run
    C. Maximum employment and low interest rates in the long run

44. Which is least likely to result from the Federal Reserve System buying securities in the open market?

    A. Fed assets and liabilities decrease
    B. Selling bank exchanges securities for reserves
    C. Creates bank reserves

45. What would be best to evaluate to determine a company's profitability?

    A. Balance sheet
    B. Income statement
    C. Cash flow statement

46. Which is an investment activity?

    A. Issuing debt
    B. Paying taxes
    C. Buying equities of a supplier

47. Which is the most likely net result after $10,000 in products are sold with the payment due in 30 days if the products cost $8,000?

    A. Assets increase by $2,000
    B. Assets increase by $10,000
    C. There is no change in assets

48. Which is least likely to contribute to the qualitative characteristic of reliability?

    A. Neutrality
    B. Consistency
    C. Completeness

49. What are conflicting approaches under different financial reporting frameworks?

    A. Cash basis versus and accrual basis
    B. Transparency versus comprehensiveness
    C. Balance sheet focus versus income statement focus

50. What is net income if revenue is $5,000; cost of goods sold equals $4,000; other operating expenses are $400; interest expense is $100; and tax expense is $100?

    A. $400
    B. $600
    C. $1,000

51. Which inventory costing method produces the highest cost of goods sold when prices are rising?

    A. LIFO
    B. FIFO
    C. Weighted average cost

52. Which is closest to the basic EPS for a calendar year if a company had $2 million in net income; paid $200,000 in preferred dividends; had 1,000,000 shares outstanding on January 1st; issued 800,000 shares on April 1st; repurchased 200,000 shares on July 1; and had a 2 for 1 stock split on October 1st?

    A. $0.58
    B. $0.60
    C. $0.67

53. What is net income divided by revenue?

    A. Pretax margin
    B. Net profit margin
    C. Gross profit margin

54. What best describes long-term assets with physical substance that are used in company operations?

    A. Tangible assets
    B. Current assets
    C. Nontangible assets

55. What is the most stringent test of liquidity?

    A. Cash ratio
    B. Quick ratio
    C. Current ratio

56. How are dividends received classified on a cash flow statement?

    A. Operating under IFRS; financing or operating under U.S. GAAP
    B. Operating or financing under IFRS; financing under U.S. GAAP
    C. Operating or investing under IFRS; operating under U.S. GAAP

57. Which is closest to the financing cash flow for issuing common stock if net income was $50 million; the balance sheet for the prior year showed common stock of $100 million; additional paid in capital of $100 million; retained earnings of $100 million; and total stockholder's equity of $300 million; and the balance sheet for the current year showed common stock of $105 million; additional paid in capital of $135 million; retained earnings of $125 million; and total stockholder's equity of $365 million?

    A. $25 million
    B. $30 million
    C. $40 million

58. If a company started in 2008; and in 2008 purchased 10,000 units of inventory at $12 each; and sold 5,000 units at $15 each; then in 2009 purchased 20,000 units of inventory at $18 each; and sold 22,000 units at $20 each; which is closest to the 2009 ending inventory balance under the FIFO inventory method?

    A. $36,000
    B. $50,400
    C. $54,000

59. What impact does capitalizing expenses rather than expensing and continuing to purchase similar or increasing amounts of assets each year have on profitability?

    A. Lower profitability initially and higher profitability in subsequent years
    B. Higher profitability initially and lower profitability in subsequent years
    C. The profitability enhancing effect of capitalization continues

60. Which estimate regarding an asset has the lowest amortization expense?

    A. Six-year useful life and no salvage value
    B. Six-year useful life and positive salvage value
    C. Seven-year useful life and positive salvage value

61. If company A has accumulated depreciation of $4 million and annual depreciation expense of $1 million; company B has accumulated depreciation of $10 million and annual depreciation expense of $2 million; and company C has accumulated depreciation of $9 million and annual depreciation expense of $3 million; which company is least likely to require capital expenditures in the near future if all companies have the same growth rate, use the same equipment, and use the same depreciation method?

    A. Company A
    B. Company B
    C. Company C

62. Which would most likely explain a decrease in the valuation allowance for deferred tax assets?

    A. Decreased prospects for profitability
    B. Increased prospects for profitability
    C. Expectation of no taxable income prior to expiration of deferred tax asset

63. How are expenses incurred when issuing bonds recorded under U.S. GAAP?

    A. Asset
    B. Liability
    C. Equity

64. What ratios measure the efficiency of a company's operations, such as collection of receivables or management of inventory?

    A. Activity ratios
    B. Liquidity ratios
    C. Solvency ratios

65. Which is closest to ROE if the tax burden is 0.84, the interest burden is 0.88, the EBIT margin is 4.5%, asset turnover is 1.8, and leverage is 2.2?

    A. 12%
    B. 13%
    C. 14%

66. If ROE is 10% for both companies, what is true about company A compared to company B if company A has sales of $300 million, assets of $100 million, and liabilities of $50 million; and company B has sales of $150 million, assets of $75 million, and liabilities of $45 million?

    A. Higher profit margin
    B. Higher total assets turnover
    C. Higher financial leverage

67. What are the broad elements for grouping the effects of transactions and other events on financial statements?

    A. Assets, liabilities, equity, income, and expenses
    B. Assets, liabilities, equity, statement of cash flows, and statement of changes in equity
    C. Balance sheet, income statement, statement of cash flows, and statement of changes in equity

68. How do international standards allow companies to report cash inflows from interest and dividends?

    A. Operating or financing activities
    B. Operating or investing activities
    C. Financing or investing activities

69. Which is the cash flow realized because of a decision?

    A. Sunk cost
    B. Opportunity cost
    C. Incremental cash flow

70. Which is least likely to be a decision rule for capital budgeting?

    A. NPV > 0
    B. Profitability index < 1
    C. IRR $>$ required rate of return

71. What happens to the NPV profile for a project with an initial investment of $100 and cash flows at the end of years 1 and 2 of $60; if the project is enhanced so that $20 is added to the initial investment and $20 is added to each of the cash flows at years 1 and 2?

    A. The vertical intercept shifts up and the horizontal intercept shifts left
    B. The vertical intercept shifts up and the horizontal intercept shifts right
    C. The vertical intercept shifts down and the horizontal intercept shifts right

72. Which is closest to the cost of debt if a company sells a $1,000 face value 10-year 6% semi-annual coupon bond for $864 and the marginal tax rate is 35%?

    A. 2.6%
    B. 5.2%
    C. 8.0%

73. Which is closest to the cost of equity if the risk-free rate is 5%, the equity risk premium is 4%, and beta is 1.3?

    A. 8.1%
    B. 10.2%
    C. 10.5%

74. What is the relationship between the asset beta and the equity beta if a company has no debt financing?

    A. Asset beta $<$ equity beta
    B. Asset beta $=$ equity beta
    C. Asset beta $>$ equity beta

75. Which is closest to the country risk premium if the bond yield for a 10-year government bond in the country is 9% compared to 5% for a similar U.S. Treasury bond, the annualized standard deviation of the equity index in the country is 25%, and the standard deviation of the country's bond market in terms of the U.S. dollar is 15%?

   A. 2.4%
   B. 6.7%
   C. 9.1%

76. What is the company's operating cycle and cash conversion cycle compared to the industry if the company's accounts receivables turnover is 5.6 times, inventory turnover is 4.2 times, and number of days of payables is 34 days; and for the industry, accounts receivables turnover is 5.7 times, inventory turnover is 4.0 times, and number of days of payables is 26 days?

   A. The company's operating cycle and cash conversion cycle are both shorter
   B. The company's operating cycle is longer and cash conversion cycle is shorter
   C. The company's operating cycle and cash conversion cycle are both longer

77. DuPont analysis breaks net profit margin into

   A. Financial leverage times total asset turnover
   B. Operating profit margin times effect of non-operating items times tax effect
   C. Operating profit margin times effect of non-operating items times tax effect times total asset turnover times financial leverage

78. Which is least likely to be supportive of shareowner protection?

   A. Code of ethics
   B. Transparency
   C. Takeover defense

79. What type of municipal bond sales involve contractual arrangements between underwriters and issuers?

   A. Competitive bid
   B. Negotiated sales
   C. Private placements

80. What are NASDAQ and the National Quotation Bureau (NQB) pink sheets?

   A. Regional markets
   B. Primary listing markets
   C. Alternate trading systems

81. What is a leveraged transaction?

    A. Short sale
    B. Stop order
    C. Buying on margin

82. For a margin account with an initial deposit of $5,000, a purchase of 300 shares at $30, and a maintenance margin of 30%, what is the margin call closest to if the stock declines to $18?

    A. $0
    B. $220
    C. $1,080

83. Which bond indexes include bonds rated Bbb or higher?

    A. High-yield bond indexes
    B. U.S. investment-grade bond indexes
    C. Morgan Stanley Capital International (MCSI) Indexes

84. Which form of the efficient market hypothesis (EMH) has had the most mixed results from testing and is mostly supported by empirical evidence?

    A. Weak form
    B. Strong form
    C. Semi-strong form

85. Which is least likely to be considered a problem that may prevent arbitrageurs from correcting anomalies?

    A. It is obvious when mispricing will disappear
    B. Arbitrageurs have a limited amount of capital
    C. It is rare to find two assets with exactly the same risk

86. Forms of investment return include

    A. Earnings, cash flows, dividends, interest payments, or capital gains
    B. Earnings, cash flows, dividends, or interest payments, but not capital gains
    C. Capital gains but not earnings, cash flows, dividends, or interest payments

87. Which is closest to the value of common stock with a current dividend of $1, a dividend growth rate of 25% for two years, a dividend growth rate of 6% from year 3 on, and a required rate of return of 10%?

    A. $34
    B. $36
    C. $37

88. Which component of a country's risk premium varies based on leverage within a country?

    A. Financial risk
    B. Liquidity risk
    C. Exchange rate risk

89. What best describes steel and machinery companies?

    A. Cyclical companies
    B. Defensive companies
    C. Speculative companies

90. If the market price is $20, the EPS over the previous 12 months is $2, and the forecast EPS over the next 12 months is $3, which is closest to the trailing P/E?

    A. 7
    B. 9
    C. 10

91. What is a swap with a single payment most likely similar to?

    A. Option
    B. Futures contract
    C. Forward contract

92. For derivative contracts, the notional principal is best described as

    A. A stock index
    B. The amount of the underlying asset
    C. A measure of payments made under the contract

93. For a $10 million FRA with a contract rate of 5% on 180-day LIBOR, if 180-day LIBOR is 4% at settlement, the short will

   A. Pay $49,020
   B. Receive $49,020
   C. Receive $49,260

94. Which is least accurate regarding futures contracts?

   A. Treasury bill futures have an underlying asset of $1 million in 90-day T-bills
   B. Eurodollar futures have an underlying asset is $1 million of a 90-day Eurodollar time deposit
   C. Treasury bond futures have an underlying asset of a $10 million Treasury bond with a minimum 5-year maturity

95. Which way to terminate a swap is most common, could involve a swaption, and exposes the company to potential default risk if entered into with a third party?

   A. Selling the swap
   B. Agreeing to terminate
   C. Entering into an offsetting swap

96. What is the breakeven point of a covered call option, where the exercise price is X and the price of the underlying security is S?

   A. S_0 - option cost
   B. S_0 + option cost
   C. S_0 - Max $(0, X - S_t)$ + option cost

97. What is an advantage to the issuer and disadvantage to the bondholder?

   A. Sinking fund
   B. Put provision
   C. Call provision

98. Which is a collateralized borrowing arrangement used by investors with a commitment to buy the security back?

   A. Sinking fund
   B. Make-whole premium
   C. Repurchase agreement

99. Which feature decreases interest rate risk?

    A. High yield
    B. Low coupon
    C. Long maturity

100. Which is closest to the duration of a bond if the current price is 102, and the price changes by 2.5 if the yield changes by 0.50%?

    A. 2.5
    B. 4.9
    C. 5.0

101. Which has the greatest credit risk?

    A. 10-year Treasury security
    B. 30-year Treasury security
    C. AAA 10-year corporate bond

102. Under what system does a government issue additional bonds of a previously outstanding bond issue via an auction?

    A. Tap system
    B. Ad hoc auction system
    C. Regular auction system

103. What are bonds secured by receipts from projects such as utilities, bridges, or toll roads?

    A. Insured bonds
    B. Revenue bonds
    C. Tax-backed debt

104. What is the yield on bond X divided by the yield of an on-the-run Treasury?

    A. Yield ratio
    B. Yield spread
    C. Relative yield spread

105. What bond features are most likely to make estimating cash flows a challenge?

    A. Zero-coupon and sinking funds
    B. High coupon and sinking funds
    C. Put and call options, resets, and conversion options

106. Which is the arbitrage opportunity if the market value of a Treasury bond maturing in 2 years with a face value of $1,000 and a 5% annual coupon is selling for $1,035, if the Treasury spot rate is 3.0% for year 1, and 3.5% for year 2?

    A. Sell the bond and buy the pieces for a profit of $6.28
    B. Buy the bond and sell the pieces for a profit of $6.28
    C. Buy the bond and sell the pieces for a profit of $9.42

107. An investor buys a CD with 8 years to maturity at a price of $94.17, a par value of $100, interest of 4% payable every six months, and a bond-equivalent yield of 8%. Which is closest to the percentage of the dollar return that must be generated from reinvestment income in order to generate a yield of 8%?

    A. 25%
    B. 50%
    C. 75%

108. Which is a characteristic of an option free bond for large increases in yield?

    A. The price decreases at a decreasing rate
    B. The price increases at a decreasing rate
    C. The price increases at an increasing rate

109. What statement about duration and the pricing curve is least accurate?

    A. Duration is the tangent line to the actual pricing curve for a given interest rate
    B. The actual pricing curve for an option-free bond is concave
    C. Actual prices will always be at or above the tangent line for bonds with positive convexity

110. What approximates bond price changes not explained by duration?

    A. Kurtosis
    B. Skewness
    C. Convexity

111. Which types of risk are most likely to affect all ETFs?

    A. Market risk, trading risk, and tracking error risk
    B. Derivatives risk, sector risk, and tracking error risk
    C. Country and currency risk, trading risk, and sector risk

112. Which real estate valuation approach values property is least likely to be accurate for longer lease terms that delay the pass-through of inflation, and performs all calculations before tax?

    A. Income approach
    B. Sales comparison approach
    C. Discounted cash flow approach

113. A real estate investment project has a first-year NOI of $170,000 that is expected to grow by 4% per year. The purchase price is $1.5 million which is financed 20% by equity and 80% by a mortgage loan at 9% pre-tax interest and level annual payments of $120,000. Which is closest to the second-year after-tax cash flow if depreciation is $37,500 per year , the marginal tax rate is 30%, and the second year mortgage interest is $106,920?

    A. $42,650
    B. $47,086
    C. $51,683

114. Which statement is least accurate regarding hedge funds?

    A. Hedge funds have fixed fees
    B. Hedge funds search for absolute returns
    C. Hedge funds have a legal structure that avoids some government regulations

115. Which portfolio is most appropriate for a very short-term investor with low risk tolerance?

    A. 100% cash
    B. 20% bonds, 80% stocks
    C. 30% cash, 50% bonds, 20% stocks

116. Across all funds, an average of what percent of the variation in fund returns is explained by the asset allocation decision?

    A. 20%
    B. 30%
    C. 40%

117. What is the correlation coefficient closest to if the variance of security A is 4%, the variance of security B is 2.25%, and the covariance is 1.5%?

    A. 0.4
    B. 0.5
    C. 0.6

118. Which is closest to the standard deviation of a portfolio with a 50% weight in each of two securities, one with an expected return of 10% and a standard deviation of 7%, and the other with an expected return of 20% and a standard deviation of 10%, if the correlation coefficient is -0.5?

    A. 4.4%
    B. 6.1%
    C. 7.4%

119. What is the shape of the set of portfolio possibilities from combining the risk-free rate with any risky asset on the efficient frontier?

    A. Convex
    B. Concave
    C. Straight line

120. What could most likely make additional diversification costs exceed its benefits after a portfolio reaches 90% of complete diversification?

    A. Taxes
    B. Transaction costs
    C. Different borrowing and lending rates

1. C	41. B	81. C
2. A	42. C	82. B
3. A	43. A	83. B
4. B	44. A	84. C
5. C	45. B	85. A
6. A	46. C	86. A
7. A	47. A	87. C
8. A	48. B	88. A
9. C	49. C	89. A
10. C	50. A	90. C
11. C	51. A	91. C
12. A	52. B	92. B
13. A	53. B	93. B
14. B	54. A	94. C
15. A	55. A	95. C
16. B	56. C	96. A
17. C	57. C	97. C
18. B	58. C	98. C
19. C	59. C	99. A
20. A	60. C	100. B
21. C	61. C	101. C
22. A	62. B	102. A
23. A	63. A	103. B
24. B	64. A	104. A
25. B	65. B	105. C
26. C	66. B	106. A
27. A	67. A	107. A
28. B	68. B	108. A
29. C	69. C	109. B
30. B	70. B	110. C
31. C	71. B	111. A
32. C	72. B	112. A
33. C	73. B	113. B
34. A	74. B	114. A
35. B	75. B	115. A
36. A	76. A	116. C
37. C	77. B	117. B
38. C	78. C	118. A
39. A	79. B	119. C
40. B	80. B	120. B

1. Which topic of the CFA Institute's Standards of Professional Conduct includes conduct as members and candidates in the CFA program and reference to CFA Institute, the CFA designation, and the CFA program?

    A. Conflicts of interest
    B. Titles and designations
    *C. Responsibilities as CFA institute as CFA member of CFA candidate

2. CFA charterholder Stroup directs a large amount of commission business to a New York-based brokerage house. The brokerage house gives Stroup two tickets to the World Cup plus all travel expenses. Stroup fails to disclose the package to his supervisor. Stroup is least likely to have violated which Standard of Professional Conduct?

    *A. Misrepresentation (Standard I(B) - independence and objectivity)
    B. Independence and objectivity
    C. Additional compensation arrangements

3. CFA charterholder Patel works for a small firm offering investment advice. The firm is qualified to provide investment advice but does not offer a full array of financial and investment services. She tells a potential client who just inherited a large sum of money that her firm can provide investment advice and could help find financial and investment services that they do not provide. Did Patel violate any Standards of Professional Conduct?

    *A. No (Standard I(C) - misrepresentation)
    B. Yes, relating to misrepresentation
    C. Yes, relating to independence and objectivity

4. CFA charterholder Ding is a portfolio manager for Dahl Aggressive Growth Fund. The fund is preparing to liquidate its holdings of Colmet Industries. Ding contacts several family members to advise them that the fund is about to liquidate its holdings in the company. Did Ding violate any Standards of Professional Conduct?

    A. No
    *B. Yes, relating to material nonpublic information (Standard II(A) - material nonpublic information)
    C. Yes, relating to diligence and reasonable basis

5. The owner of Chong Services agrees to promote the stock of companies in exchange for stock and compensation. The owner sends e-mails and newsletters and creates web sites containing inaccurate information to promote the stock which leads to higher stock prices. The owner least likely violated the Standards of Professional Conduct relating to

    A. Market manipulation
    B. Disclosure of conflicts
    *C. Performance presentation (Standard II(B) - market manipulation, Standard V(A) - diligence and reasonable basis, and Standard VI(A) - disclosure of conflicts)

6. According to the Standards of Professional Conduct related to suitability, when members and candidates are in an advisory relationship with a client, they must judge the suitability of

    *A. Investments in the context of the client's total portfolio
    B. The client's total portfolio in the context of the investments
    C. Taking investment action and must reassess and update this information regularly

7. CFA charterholder Rao circulates marketing material showing simulated performance and disclosing that the results were simulated by retroactively applying a model to a time period. Did Rao violate and Standards of Professional Conduct?

    *A. No (Standard III(D) - performance presentation)
    B. Yes, relating to misrepresentation
    C. Yes, relating to performance presentation

8. CFA charterholder Kadam leads an employee-led buyout of his employer's equity management business. Did Kadam violate any Standards of Professional Conduct?

    *A. No (Standard IV(A) - loyalty)
    B. Yes, relating to loyalty
    C. Yes, relating to preservation of confidentiality

9. Which is least likely to violate the Standard of Professional Conduct on loyalty?

    A. Taking client lists
    B. Starting a competing business while under a non-compete agreement
    *C. Contacting former clients after obtaining their phone numbers through public records (Standard IV(A) - loyalty)

10. CFA charterholder Lamich plans to issue a newsletter that only lists the top five buy and sell recommendations because describing the investment system would be too complex. No details on the basic process or logic would be disclosed. Do Lamich's plans for the newsletter violate any Standards of Professional Conduct?

    A. No
    B. Yes, relating to diligence and reasonable basis
    *C.Yes, relating to communications with clients and prospective clients (Standard V(B) - communications with clients and prospective clients)

11. Which is least likely to require disclosure to clients and prospective clients?

    A. Service as a director
    B. Underwriting relationships
    *C.Compliance with the CFA Code of Ethics and Standards of Practice (Standard VI(A) - disclosure of conflicts)

12. CFA candidate Banerjee makes substantial investment gains by purchasing stocks just before they were put on his employer's recommended purchase list. Banerjee was regularly given the firm's quarterly personal transaction form but declined to complete it. Which Standard of Professional Conduct did Banerjee least likely violate?

    *A. Market manipulation (Standard VI(B) - priority of transactions and Standard II(A) - material nonpublic information)
    B. Priority of transactions
    C. Material nonpublic information

13. CFA charterholder Carson receives a bonus from his employer for assisting to bring in new clients. Carson discloses to clients that he is compensated for referring clients to firm products. Did Carson violate any Standards of Professional Conduct?

    *A. No (Standard VI(C) - referral fees)
    B. Yes, related to referral fees
    C. Yes, related to additional compensation arrangements

14. Malone signed up for a CFA exam but did not sit for it and signed up for the next sitting. Malone told his employer that he passed the exam. Did Malone violate any Standards of Professional Conduct?

    A. No
    *B.Yes, related to misconduct (Standard VII(B) - reference to the CFA Institute, the CFA designation, and the CFA program and Standard I(D) - misconduct)
    C. Yes, related to disclosure of conflicts

15. Which is least likely to ensure fair treatment of clients when a new investment recommendation is made?

  *A. Distribute recommendations to institutional clients before individual clients (Standard III(B) - fair dealing)
  B. Minimize the elapsed time between the decision and the dissemination of a recommendation
  C. Limit the number of people in the firm who are aware in advance that a recommendation is to be disseminated

16. CFA charterholder Chauhan is a portfolio manager. Chauhan uses the same broker exclusively for all portfolio transactions because the broker that gives Chauhan lower prices for personal sales than to Chauhan's portfolio accounts and other investors. Chauhan's employer requires monthly reports of personal stock transactions. Chauhan only files reports for months in which she has no transactions, about every fourth month. Which Standards of Professional Conduct did Chauhan least likely violate?

  A. Misconduct
  *B. Misrepresentation (Standard III(A) - loyalty, prudence, and care and Standard I(D) - misconduct)
  C. Loyalty, prudence, and care

17. According to GIPS,

  A. Terminated portfolios must be excluded in historical returns of appropriate composites
  B. Firms may not set minimum asset levels for portfolios to be included in a composite
  *C. Firms may set minimum asset levels for portfolios to be included in a composite, but the changes to a composite-specific minimum asset level are not permitted retroactively

18. Which asset classes have their own sections in the GIPS?

  A. Alternatives and real estate
  *B. Private equity and real estate
  C. Private placements and venture capital

19. What is the value of 9 years of $1,000 payments beginning in one year plus a payment of $2,000 in 10 years using a discount rate of 8% per year?

    A. $6,710
    B. $7,139
    *C.$7,173 = $1,000[(1 - 1/1.08^9) / .08] + $2,000/ (1.08^10); n = 9, i = 8, PMT = 1,000, FV = 0; PV1 = $6,247; n = 10, i = 8, PMT = 0, FV = 2,000; PV2 = $926; PV1 + PV2 = $7,173

20. What is any descriptive measure of a population characteristic?

    *A. Parameter; a parameter is a descriptive measure of a population statistic; a sample statistic is a quantity computed from or used to describe a sample; and a frequency distribution is a tabular display of data summarized into a relatively small number of intervals
    B. Sample statistic
    C. Frequency distribution

21. What are the cumulative frequencies for the return intervals for a frequency distribution with three equally spaced intervals for a range of returns for funds with returns of -20%, -10%, -6%, -5%, 0%, 6%, 12%, 14%, and 20%?

    A. 3, 2, and 4
    B. 3, 5, and 9
    *C.2, 6, and 9; for the intervals from -20% to -6.67%, -6.67% to 6.67%, and 6.67% to 20%

22. Which is closest to the sample variance for a fund with annual returns of 6%, -10%, -5%, and 29%?

    *A. 3%
    B. 15%
    C. 17%

23. What percent of a normal distribution's observations lie between plus and minus one standard deviation from the mean?

    *A. 68.3%
    B. 95.5%
    C. 99.7%

24. What means that the events cover all possible outcomes?

    A. Probability
    *B.Exhaustive
    C. Mutually exclusive

25. If a buy order at $20 has a 75% probability of being executed and a buy order on an uncorrelated different stock at $15 has a 60% probability of being executed, what is the probability that at least one of the orders will execute?

    A. 75%
    *B.90% = 75% + 60% - 75% (60%)
    C. 95%

26. If there is a 20% probability of EPS of $1.50, a 30% probability of an EPS of $9.00, and a 50% probability of an EPS of $10.00, what is the variance of the expected EPS?

    A. $2.78
    B. $7.73
    *C.$10.75 = 20% ($1.50-$8)^2 + 30% ($9-$8)^2 + 50% ($10-$8)^2

27. What is the covariance between fund A and fund B, if there is an 80% probability that fund A will return 5% and fund B will return 10%, and a 20% probability that fund A will return 15% and fund B will return -5%?

    *A. -0.24% = .8(5%-8%)(10%-7%)+.2(15-8%)(-5%-7%)
    B. -0.12%
    C. 0.12%

28. If an investment manager has a 50% probability of beating a benchmark each year, what is the probability of beating the benchmark in 4 out of 4 years?

    A. 0.03125
    *B.0.06250 = .5^4
    C. 0.25000

29. What do safety-first rules focus on?

    A. Utility function
    B. Mismatch risk
    *C.Shortfall risk

30. Which is the closest to the continuous compounding rate of return for an asset that increases from $30 to $34.50 during the holding period?

    A. 13%
    *B.14% = ln (34.5/30)
    C. 15%

31. What is the year-end book value of NYSE-listed companies an example of?

    A. Time series
    B. Sampling distribution
    *C.Cross-sectional data

32. What is accepted if the hypothesis to be tested is rejected?

    A. Test statistic
    B. Null hypothesis
    *C.Alternative hypothesis

33. Which is least likely to impact the magnitude of the elasticity of demand?

    A. The closeness of substitutes
    B. The proportion of income spent on the good
    *C.The elasticity of supply

34. What strives to achieve the greatest happiness for the greatest number?

    *A. Utilitarianism
    B. Symmetry principle
    C. The big tradeoff

35. Which best describes the demand for most farm products?

    A. Elastic
    *B.Inelastic
    C. Neither elastic nor inelastic

36. What arises when one firm produces an item that has no close substitutes and the firm is protected by a barrier to entry that prevents the entry of competitors?

    *A. Monopoly
    B. Monopolistic competition
    C. Oligopoly

37. What induces entry into a market in perfect competition?

    A. Normal profit
    B. Accounting profit
    *C.Economic profit

38. Which is least likely a characteristic of a monopoly with perfect price discrimination?

    A. Produces the same output than a perfectly competitive industry
    B. Obtains the maximum price that each consumer is willing to pay
    *C.Extracts one-half of the consumer surplus

39. What determines the real interest rate?

    *A. Capital market equilibrium
    B. Demand of physical capital
    C. Marginal revenue product

40. What is an indicator of the willingness of people of working age to take jobs, based on the labor force divided by the working-age population?

    A. Unemployment rate
    *B.Labor force participation rate
    C. Employment-to-population ratio

41. Which is most likely to change aggregate demand?

    A. Stability in expected future income, inflation, and profits
    *B.World economy and exchange rates
    C. Fluctuations in aggregate supply

42. What is least likely to trigger demand-pull inflation?

    A. Increase in exports
    B. Increase in investment stimulated by an increase in expected future profits
    *C.Increase in the interest rate

43. Which is least likely to apply to the goal of stable prices?

    *A. Expansionary fiscal policy
    B. Can conflict with other goals in the short run
    C. Maximum employment and low interest rates in the long run

44. Which is least likely to result from the Federal Reserve System buying securities in the open market?

    *A. Fed assets and liabilities decrease
    B. Selling bank exchanges securities for reserves
    C. Creates bank reserves

45. What would be best to evaluate to determine a company's profitability?

    A. Balance sheet
    *B.Income statement
    C. Cash flow statement

46. Which is an investment activity?

    A. Issuing debt
    B. Paying taxes
    *C.Buying equities of a supplier

47. Which is the most likely net result after $10,000 in products are sold with the payment due in 30 days if the products cost $8,000?

    *A. Assets increase by $2,000
    B. Assets increase by $10,000
    C. There is no change in assets

48. Which is least likely to contribute to the qualitative characteristic of reliability?

    A. Neutrality
    *B.Consistency
    C. Completeness

49. What are conflicting approaches under different financial reporting frameworks?

    A. Cash basis versus and accrual basis
    B. Transparency versus comprehensiveness
    *C.Balance sheet focus versus income statement focus

50. What is net income if revenue is $5,000; cost of goods sold equals $4,000; other operating expenses are $400; interest expense is $100; and tax expense is $100?

    *A. $400 = $5,000 - $4,000 - $400 - $100 - $100
    B. $600
    C. $1,000

51. Which inventory costing method produces the highest cost of goods sold when prices are rising?

    *A. LIFO
    B. FIFO
    C. Weighted average cost

52. Which is closest to the basic EPS for a calendar year if a company had $2 million in net income; paid $200,000 in preferred dividends; had 1,000,000 shares outstanding on January 1st; issued 800,000 shares on April 1st; repurchased 200,000 shares on July 1; and had a 2 for 1 stock split on October 1st?

    A. $0.58
    *B.$0.60 = ($2,000,000 - $200,000) /{2 [1,000,000 + (9/12)(800,000) - (6/12)(200,000)]}
    C. $0.67

53. What is net income divided by revenue?

    A. Pretax margin
    *B.Net profit margin
    C. Gross profit margin

54. What best describes long-term assets with physical substance that are used in company operations?

    *A. Tangible assets
    B. Current assets
    C. Nontangible assets

55. What is the most stringent test of liquidity?

    *A. Cash ratio
    B. Quick ratio
    C. Current ratio

56. How are dividends received classified on a cash flow statement?

    A. Operating under IFRS; financing or operating under U.S. GAAP
    B. Operating or financing under IFRS; financing under U.S. GAAP
    *C.Operating or investing under IFRS; operating under U.S. GAAP

57. Which is closest to the financing cash flow for issuing common stock if net income was $50 million; the balance sheet for the prior year showed common stock of $100 million; additional paid in capital of $100 million; retained earnings of $100 million; and total stockholder's equity of $300 million; and the balance sheet for the current year showed common stock of $105 million; additional paid in capital of $135 million; retained earnings of $125 million; and total stockholder's equity of $365 million?

   A. $25 million
   B. $30 million
   *C.$40 million = ($105 million - $100 million) + ($135 million - $100 million)

58. If a company started in 2008; and in 2008 purchased 10,000 units of inventory at $12 each; and sold 5,000 units at $15 each; then in 2009 purchased 20,000 units of inventory at $18 each; and sold 22,000 units at $20 each; which is closest to the 2009 ending inventory balance under the FIFO inventory method?

   A. $36,000
   B. $50,400
   *C.$54,000 = 3,000 ($18)

59. What impact does capitalizing expenses rather than expensing and continuing to purchase similar or increasing amounts of assets each year have on profitability?

   A. Lower profitability initially and higher profitability in subsequent years
   B. Higher profitability initially and lower profitability in subsequent years
   *C.The profitability enhancing effect of capitalization continues

60. Which estimate regarding an asset has the lowest amortization expense?

   A. Six-year useful life and no salvage value
   B. Six-year useful life and positive salvage value
   *C.Seven-year useful life and positive salvage value

61. If company A has accumulated depreciation of $4 million and annual depreciation expense of $1 million; company B has accumulated depreciation of $10 million and annual depreciation expense of $2 million; and company C has accumulated depreciation of $9 million and annual depreciation expense of $3 million; which company is least likely to require capital expenditures in the near future if all companies have the same growth rate, use the same equipment, and use the same depreciation method?

   A. Company A
   B. Company B
   *C.Company C; $9/$3 < $4/$1 < $10/$2

62. Which would most likely explain a decrease in the valuation allowance for deferred tax assets?

    A. Decreased prospects for profitability
    *B.Increased prospects for profitability
    C. Expectation of no taxable income prior to expiration of deferred tax asset

63. How are expenses incurred when issuing bonds recorded under U.S. GAAP?

    *A. Asset
    B. Liability
    C. Equity

64. What ratios measure the efficiency of a company's operations, such as collection of receivables or management of inventory?

    *A. Activity ratios
    B. Liquidity ratios
    C. Solvency ratios

65. Which is closest to ROE if the tax burden is 0.84, the interest burden is 0.88, the EBIT margin is 4.5%, asset turnover is 1.8, and leverage is 2.2?

    A. 12%
    *B.13% = 0.84(0.88)(4.5%)(1.8)(2.2)
    C. 14%

66. If ROE is 10% for both companies, what is true about company A compared to company B if company A has sales of $300 million, assets of $100 million, and liabilities of $50 million; and company B has sales of $150 million, assets of $75 million, and liabilities of $45 million?

    A. Higher profit margin
    *B.Higher total assets turnover; 300/100>150/75
    C. Higher financial leverage

67. What are the broad elements for grouping the effects of transactions and other events on financial statements?

    *A. Assets, liabilities, equity, income, and expenses
    B. Assets, liabilities, equity, statement of cash flows, and statement of changes in equity
    C. Balance sheet, income statement, statement of cash flows, and statement of changes in equity

68. How do international standards allow companies to report cash inflows from interest and dividends?

   A. Operating or financing activities
   *B. Operating or investing activities
   C. Financing or investing activities

69. Which is the cash flow realized because of a decision?

   A. Sunk cost
   B. Opportunity cost
   *C. Incremental cash flow

70. Which is least likely to be a decision rule for capital budgeting?

   A. NPV > 0
   *B. Profitability index < 1
   C. IRR > required rate of return

71. What happens to the NPV profile for a project with an initial investment of $100 and cash flows at the end of years 1 and 2 of $60; if the project is enhanced so that $20 is added to the initial investment and $20 is added to each of the cash flows at years 1 and 2?

   A. The vertical intercept shifts up and the horizontal intercept shifts left
   *B. The vertical intercept shifts up and the horizontal intercept shifts right; the new NPV when r = 0% of $60 + $20 + $60 + $20 - $100 - $20 = $40 > $60 + $60 - $20 = $20 and the new IRR 21.53% is > 13.07%; n = 2, PV = -100, PMT = 60, FV = 0; i = 13.07; n = 2, PV = -120, PMT = 80, FV = 0; i = 21.53
   C. The vertical intercept shifts down and the horizontal intercept shifts right

72. Which is closest to the cost of debt if a company sells a $1,000 face value 10-year 6% semi-annual coupon bond for $864 and the marginal tax rate is 35%?

   A. 2.6%
   *B. 5.2% = 2(4.00%)(1-35%) where PV = -$864, FV = $1,000, PMT = $30, and n = 20; i = 4.00
   C. 8.0%

73. Which is closest to the cost of equity if the risk-free rate is 5%, the equity risk premium is 4%, and beta is 1.3?

   A. 8.1%
   *B. 10.2% = 5% + 1.3(4%)
   C. 10.5%

74. What is the relationship between the asset beta and the equity beta if a company has no debt financing?

   A. Asset beta < equity beta
   *B.Asset beta = equity beta
   C. Asset beta > equity beta

75. Which is closest to the country risk premium if the bond yield for a 10-year government bond in the country is 9% compared to 5% for a similar U.S. Treasury bond, the annualized standard deviation of the equity index in the country is 25%, and the standard deviation of the country's bond market in terms of the U.S. dollar is 15%?

   A. 2.4%
   *B.6.7% = (9% - 5%)(25%/15%)
   C. 9.1%

76. What is the company's operating cycle and cash conversion cycle compared to the industry if the company's accounts receivables turnover is 5.6 times, inventory turnover is 4.2 times, and number of days of payables is 34 days; and for the industry, accounts receivables turnover is 5.7 times, inventory turnover is 4.0 times, and number of days of payables is 26 days?

   *A. The company's operating cycle and cash conversion cycle are both shorter; 365 / 5.6 + 365 / 4.2 = 152 < 365 / 5.7 + 365 / 4.0 = 155; 152 - 34 = 118 < 155 - 26 = 129
   B. The company's operating cycle is longer and cash conversion cycle is shorter
   C. The company's operating cycle and cash conversion cycle are both longer

77. DuPont analysis breaks net profit margin into

   A. Financial leverage times total asset turnover
   *B.Operating profit margin times effect of non-operating items times tax effect
   C. Operating profit margin times effect of non-operating items times tax effect times total asset turnover times financial leverage

78. Which is least likely to be supportive of shareowner protection?

   A. Code of ethics
   B. Transparency
   *C.Takeover defense

79. What type of municipal bond sales involve contractual arrangements between underwriters and issuers?

    A. Competitive bid
    *B.Negotiated sales
    C. Private placements

80. What are NASDAQ and the National Quotation Bureau (NQB) pink sheets?

    A. Regional markets
    *B.Primary listing markets
    C. Alternate trading systems

81. What is a leveraged transaction?

    A. Short sale
    B. Stop order
    *C.Buying on margin

82. For a margin account with an initial deposit of $5,000, a purchase of 300 shares at $30, and a maintenance margin of 30%, what is the margin call closest to if the stock declines to $18?

    A. $0
    *B.$220 = 30%($18)(300) - [$18(300) - (300($30) - $5,000)]
    C. $1,080

83. Which bond indexes include bonds rated Bbb or higher?

    A. High-yield bond indexes
    *B.U.S. investment-grade bond indexes
    C. Morgan Stanley Capital International (MCSI) Indexes

84. Which form of the efficient market hypothesis (EMH) has had the most mixed results from testing and is mostly supported by empirical evidence?

    A. Weak form
    B. Strong form
    *C.Semi-strong form

85. Which is least likely to be considered a problem that may prevent arbitrageurs from correcting anomalies?

    *A. It is obvious when mispricing will disappear
    B. Arbitrageurs have a limited amount of capital
    C. It is rare to find two assets with exactly the same risk

86. Forms of investment return include

    *A. Earnings, cash flows, dividends, interest payments, or capital gains
    B. Earnings, cash flows, dividends, or interest payments, but not capital gains
    C. Capital gains but not earnings, cash flows, dividends, or interest payments

87. Which is closest to the value of common stock with a current dividend of $1, a dividend growth rate of 25% for two years, a dividend growth rate of 6% from year 3 on, and a required rate of return of 10%?

    A. $34
    B. $36
    *C.$37 = $1(1.25) / 1.1 + $1(1.25)^2 / 1.1^2 + [$1[(1.25)^2](1.06) / (10% - 6%)] / 1.1^2

88. Which component of a country's risk premium varies based on leverage within a country?

    *A. Financial risk
    B. Liquidity risk
    C. Exchange rate risk

89. What best describes steel and machinery companies?

    *A. Cyclical companies
    B. Defensive companies
    C. Speculative companies

90. If the market price is $20, the EPS over the previous 12 months is $2, and the forecast EPS over the next 12 months is $3, which is closest to the trailing P/E?

    A. 7
    B. 9
    *C.10 = $20 / $2

91. What is a swap with a single payment most likely similar to?

    A. Option
    B. Futures contract
    *C.Forward contract

92. For derivative contracts, the notional principal is best described as

    A. A stock index
    *B.The amount of the underlying asset
    C. A measure of payments made under the contract

93. For a $10 million FRA with a contract rate of 5% on 180-day LIBOR, if 180-day LIBOR is 4% at settlement, the short will

    A. Pay $49,020
    *B.Receive $49,020; where -$49,020 = $10,000,000{[(4% - 5%)(180/360)] / [1+4%(180/360)]}
    C. Receive $49,260

94. Which is least accurate regarding futures contracts?

    A. Treasury bill futures have an underlying asset of $1 million in 90-day T-bills
    B. Eurodollar futures have an underlying asset is $1 million of a 90-day Eurodollar time deposit
    *C.Treasury bond futures have an underlying asset of a $10 million Treasury bond with a minimum 5-year maturity

95. Which way to terminate a swap is most common, could involve a swaption, and exposes the company to potential default risk if entered into with a third party?

    A. Selling the swap
    B. Agreeing to terminate
    *C.Entering into an offsetting swap

96. What is the breakeven point of a covered call option, where the exercise price is X and the price of the underlying security is S?

    *A. S_0 - option cost
    B. S_0 + option cost
    C. S_0 - Max $(0, X - S_t)$ + option cost

97. What is an advantage to the issuer and disadvantage to the bondholder?

    A. Sinking fund
    B. Put provision
    *C.Call provision

98. Which is a collateralized borrowing arrangement used by investors with a commitment to buy the security back?

    A. Sinking fund
    B. Make-whole premium
    *C.Repurchase agreement

99. Which feature decreases interest rate risk?

    *A. High yield
    B. Low coupon
    C. Long maturity

100. Which is closest to the duration of a bond if the current price is 102, and the price changes by 2.5 if the yield changes by 0.50%?

    A. 2.5
    *B.4.9 = 2.5 / [(102)(.0050)]
    C. 5.0

101. Which has the greatest credit risk?

    A. 10-year Treasury security
    B. 30-year Treasury security
    *C.AAA 10-year corporate bond

102. Under what system does a government issue additional bonds of a previously outstanding bond issue via an auction?

    *A. Tap system
    B. Ad hoc auction system
    C. Regular auction system

103. What are bonds secured by receipts from projects such as utilities, bridges, or toll roads?

    A. Insured bonds
    *B.Revenue bonds
    C. Tax-backed debt

104. What is the yield on bond X divided by the yield of an on-the-run Treasury?

    *A. Yield ratio
    B. Yield spread
    C. Relative yield spread

105. What bond features are most likely to make estimating cash flows a challenge?

    A. Zero-coupon and sinking funds
    B. High coupon and sinking funds
    *C.Put and call options, resets, and conversion options

106. Which is the arbitrage opportunity if the market value of a Treasury bond maturing in 2 years with a face value of $1,000 and a 5% annual coupon is selling for $1,035, if the Treasury spot rate is 3.0% for year 1, and 3.5% for year 2?

    *A. Sell the bond and buy the pieces for a profit of $6.28; where $1,035 - $50 / 1.03 + $1,050 / $1.035^2 = $6.28
    B. Buy the bond and sell the pieces for a profit of $6.28
    C. Buy the bond and sell the pieces for a profit of $9.42

107. An investor buys a CD with 8 years to maturity at a price of $94.17, a par value of $100, interest of 4% payable every six months, and a bond-equivalent yield of 8%. Which is closest to the percentage of the dollar return that must be generated from reinvestment income in order to generate a yield of 8%?

    *A. 25% = $20.38 / $82.21 = {[$94.17 $(1.04)^{16}$ - $94.17] - ($56 + $5.83)} / [$94.17 $(1.04)^{16}$ - 94.17]
    B. 50%
    C. 75%

108. Which is a characteristic of an option free bond for large increases in yield?

    *A. The price decreases at a decreasing rate
    B. The price increases at a decreasing rate
    C. The price increases at an increasing rate

109. What statement about duration and the pricing curve is least accurate?

    A. Duration is the tangent line to the actual pricing curve for a given interest rate
    *B.The actual pricing curve for an option-free bond is concave
    C. Actual prices will always be at or above the tangent line for bonds with positive convexity

110. What approximates bond price changes not explained by duration?

    A. Kurtosis
    B. Skewness
    *C.Convexity

111. Which types of risk are most likely to affect all ETFs?

    *A. Market risk, trading risk, and tracking error risk
    B. Derivatives risk, sector risk, and tracking error risk
    C. Country and currency risk, trading risk, and sector risk

112. Which real estate valuation approach values property is least likely to be accurate for longer lease terms that delay the pass-through of inflation, and performs all calculations before tax?

    *A. Income approach
    B. Sales comparison approach
    C. Discounted cash flow approach

113. A real estate investment project has a first-year NOI of $170,000 that is expected to grow by 4% per year. The purchase price is $1.5 million which is financed 20% by equity and 80% by a mortgage loan at 9% pre-tax interest and level annual payments of $120,000. Which is closest to the second-year after-tax cash flow if depreciation is $37,500 per year , the marginal tax rate is 30%, and the second year mortgage interest is $106,920?

    A. $42,650
    *B.$47,086 = ($170,000(1.04) - $37,500 - $106,920)(1 - 30%) + $37,500 - ($120,000
      - $106,920)
    C. $51,683

114. Which statement is least accurate regarding hedge funds?

    *A. Hedge funds have fixed fees
    B. Hedge funds search for absolute returns
    C. Hedge funds have a legal structure that avoids some government regulations

115. Which portfolio is most appropriate for a very short-term investor with low risk tolerance?

    *A. 100% cash
    B. 20% bonds, 80% stocks
    C. 30% cash, 50% bonds, 20% stocks

116. Across all funds, an average of what percent of the variation in fund returns is explained by the asset allocation decision?

 A. 20%
 B. 30%
 *C.40%

117. What is the correlation coefficient closest to if the variance of security A is 4%, the variance of security B is 2.25%, and the covariance is 1.5%?

 A. 0.4
 *B.0.5 = 1.5% / [((4%)^.5) ((2.25%)^.5)]
 C. 0.6

118. Which is closest to the standard deviation of a portfolio with a 50% weight in each of two securities, one with an expected return of 10% and a standard deviation of 7%, and the other with an expected return of 20% and a standard deviation of 10%, if the correlation coefficient is -0.5?

 *A. 4.4% = [(50%^2)(7%^2) + (50%^2)(10%^2) + 2(50%)(50%)(-0.5)(7%)(10%)]^.5
 B. 6.1%
 C. 7.4%

119. What is the shape of the set of portfolio possibilities from combining the risk-free rate with any risky asset on the efficient frontier?

 A. Convex
 B. Concave
 *C.Straight line

120. What could most likely make additional diversification costs exceed its benefits after a portfolio reaches 90% of complete diversification?

 A. Taxes
 *B.Transaction costs
 C. Different borrowing and lending rates

1. A. B. C.	41. A. B. C.	81. A. B. C.
2. A. B. C.	42. A. B. C.	82. A. B. C.
3. A. B. C.	43. A. B. C.	83. A. B. C.
4. A. B. C.	44. A. B. C.	84. A. B. C.
5. A. B. C.	45. A. B. C.	85. A. B. C.
6. A. B. C.	46. A. B. C.	86. A. B. C.
7. A. B. C.	47. A. B. C.	87. A. B. C.
8. A. B. C.	48. A. B. C.	88. A. B. C.
9. A. B. C.	49. A. B. C.	89. A. B. C.
10. A. B. C.	50. A. B. C.	90. A. B. C.
11. A. B. C.	51. A. B. C.	91. A. B. C.
12. A. B. C.	52. A. B. C.	92. A. B. C.
13. A. B. C.	53. A. B. C.	93. A. B. C.
14. A. B. C.	54. A. B. C.	94. A. B. C.
15. A. B. C.	55. A. B. C.	95. A. B. C.
16. A. B. C.	56. A. B. C.	96. A. B. C.
17. A. B. C.	57. A. B. C.	97. A. B. C.
18. A. B. C.	58. A. B. C.	98. A. B. C.
19. A. B. C.	59. A. B. C.	99. A. B. C.
20. A. B. C.	60. A. B. C.	100. A. B. C.
21. A. B. C.	61. A. B. C.	101. A. B. C.
22. A. B. C.	62. A. B. C.	102. A. B. C.
23. A. B. C.	63. A. B. C.	103. A. B. C.
24. A. B. C.	64. A. B. C.	104. A. B. C.
25. A. B. C.	65. A. B. C.	105. A. B. C.
26. A. B. C.	66. A. B. C.	106. A. B. C.
27. A. B. C.	67. A. B. C.	107. A. B. C.
28. A. B. C.	68. A. B. C.	108. A. B. C.
29. A. B. C.	69. A. B. C.	109. A. B. C.
30. A. B. C.	70. A. B. C.	110. A. B. C.
31. A. B. C.	71. A. B. C.	111. A. B. C.
32. A. B. C.	72. A. B. C.	112. A. B. C.
33. A. B. C.	73. A. B. C.	113. A. B. C.
34. A. B. C.	74. A. B. C.	114. A. B. C.
35. A. B. C.	75. A. B. C.	115. A. B. C.
36. A. B. C.	76. A. B. C.	116. A. B. C.
37. A. B. C.	77. A. B. C.	117. A. B. C.
38. A. B. C.	78. A. B. C.	118. A. B. C.
39. A. B. C.	79. A. B. C.	119. A. B. C.
40. A. B. C.	80. A. B. C.	120. A. B. C.

Made in the USA
Lexington, KY
17 May 2010